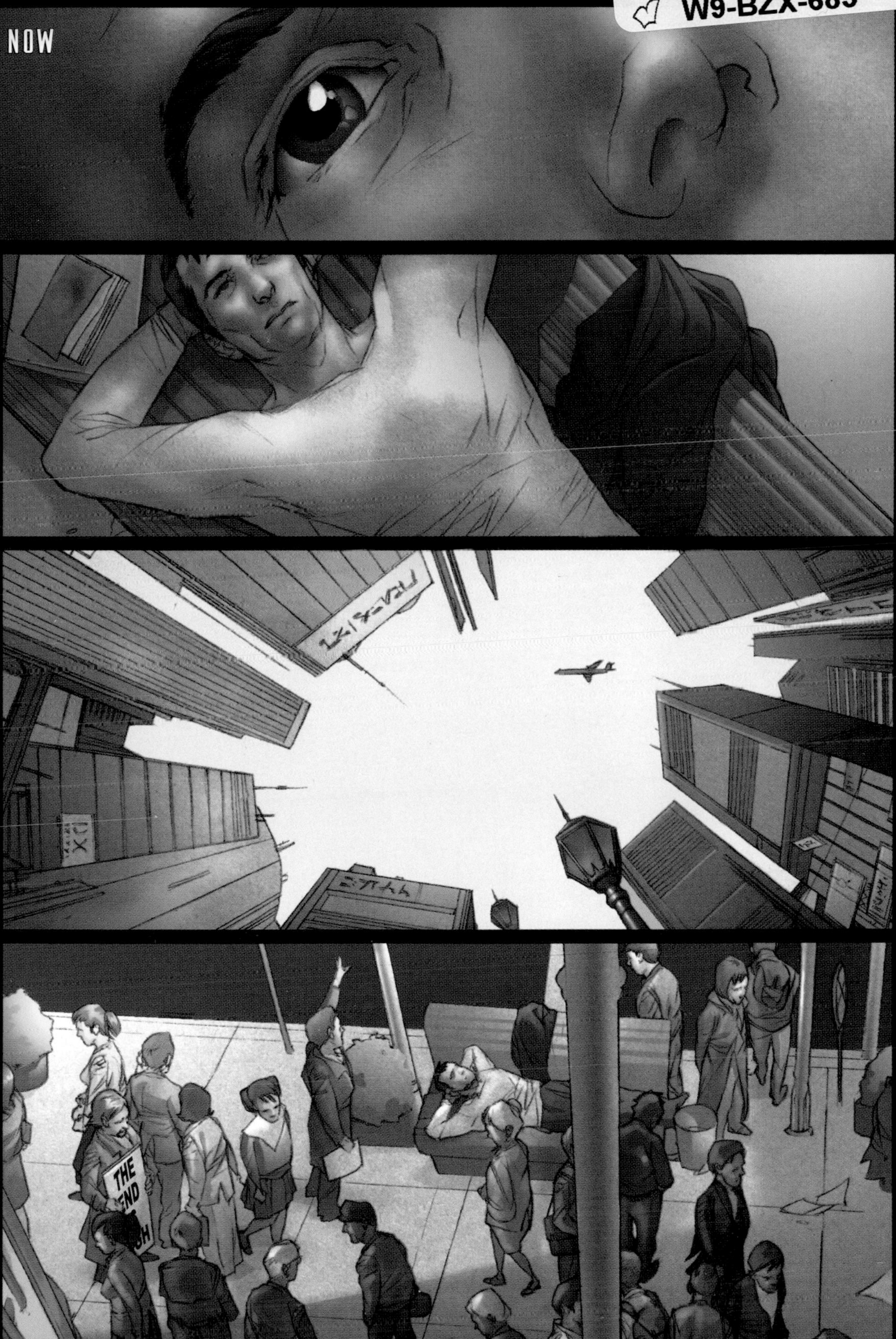
NOW
THE

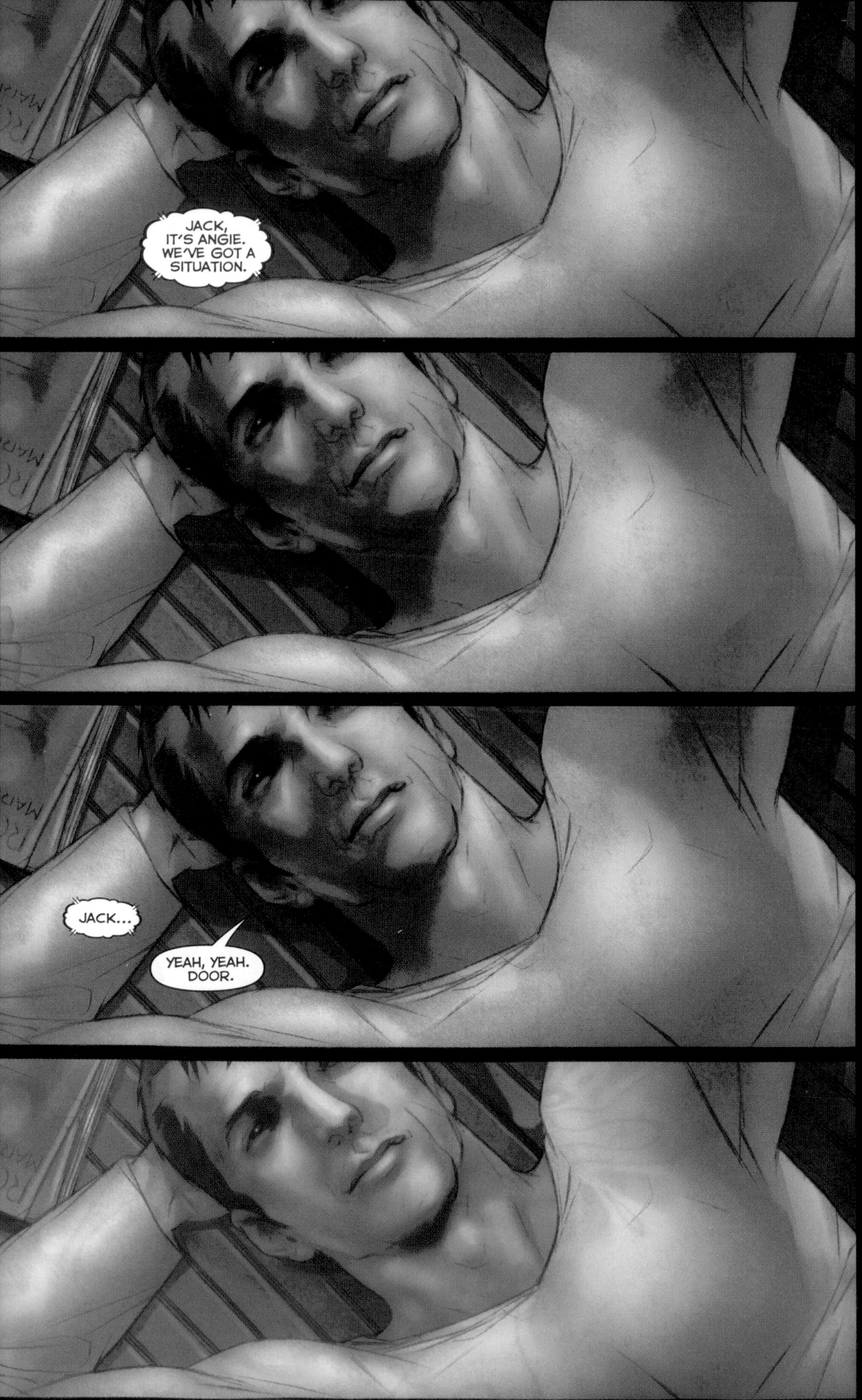
JACK, IT'S ANGIE. WE'VE GOT A SITUATION.
JACK...
YEAH, YEAH. DOOR.

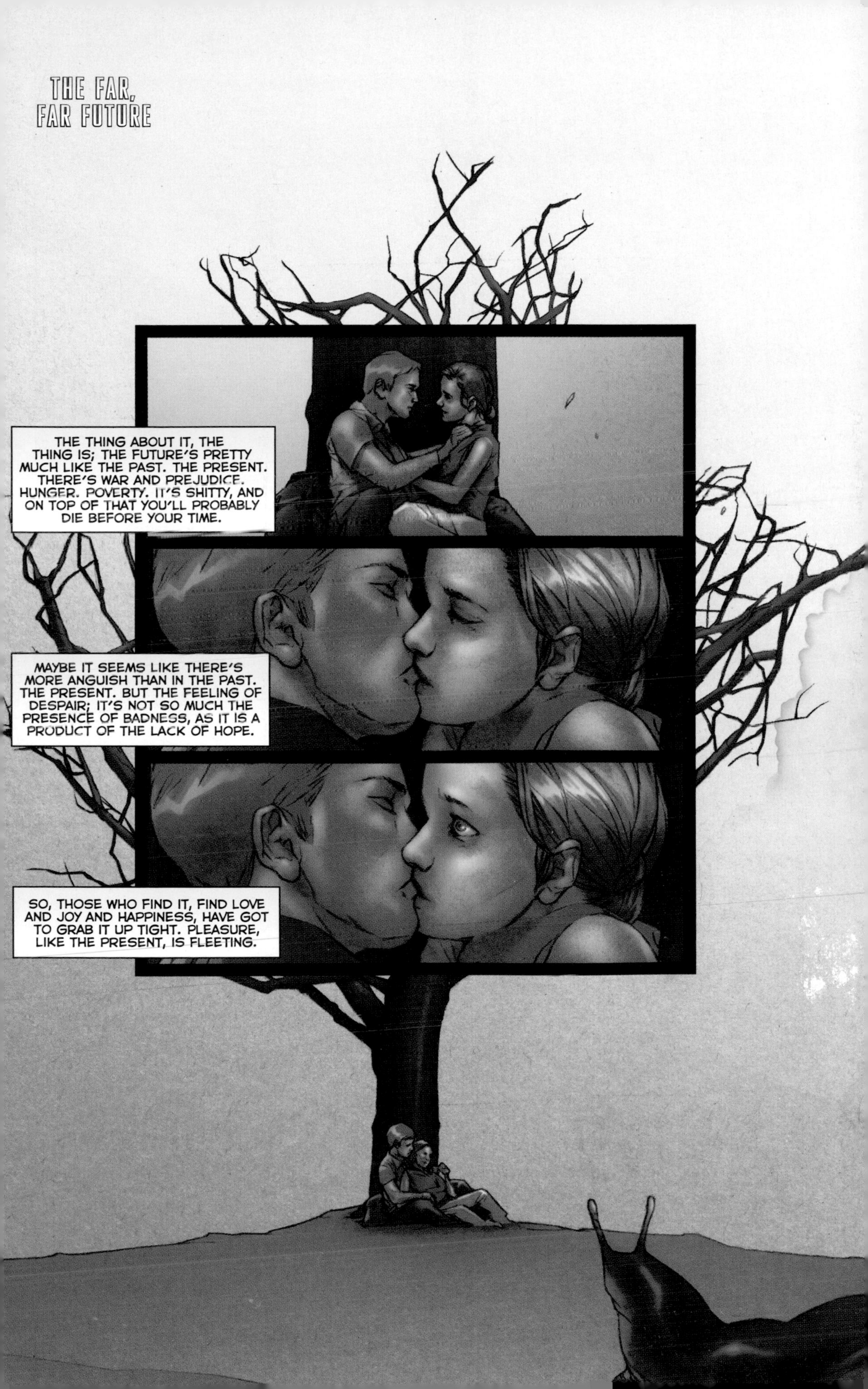
THE FAR, FAR FUTURE
THE THING ABOUT IT, THE THING IS; THE FUTURE'S PRETTY MUCH LIKE THE PAST. THE PRESENT. THERE'S WAR AND PREJUDICE. HUNGER. POVERTY. IT'S SHITTY, AND ON TOP OF THAT YOU'LL PROBABLY DIE BEFORE YOUR TIME.
MAYBE IT SEEMS LIKE THERE'S MORE ANGUISH THAN IN THE PAST. THE PRESENT. BUT THE FEELING OF DESPAIR; IT'S NOT SO MUCH THE PRESENCE OF BADNESS, AS IT IS A PRODUCT OF THE LACK OF HOPE.
SO, THOSE WHO FIND IT, FIND LOVE AND JOY AND HAPPINESS, HAVE GOT TO GRAB IT UP TIGHT. PLEASURE, LIKE THE PRESENT, IS FLEETING.

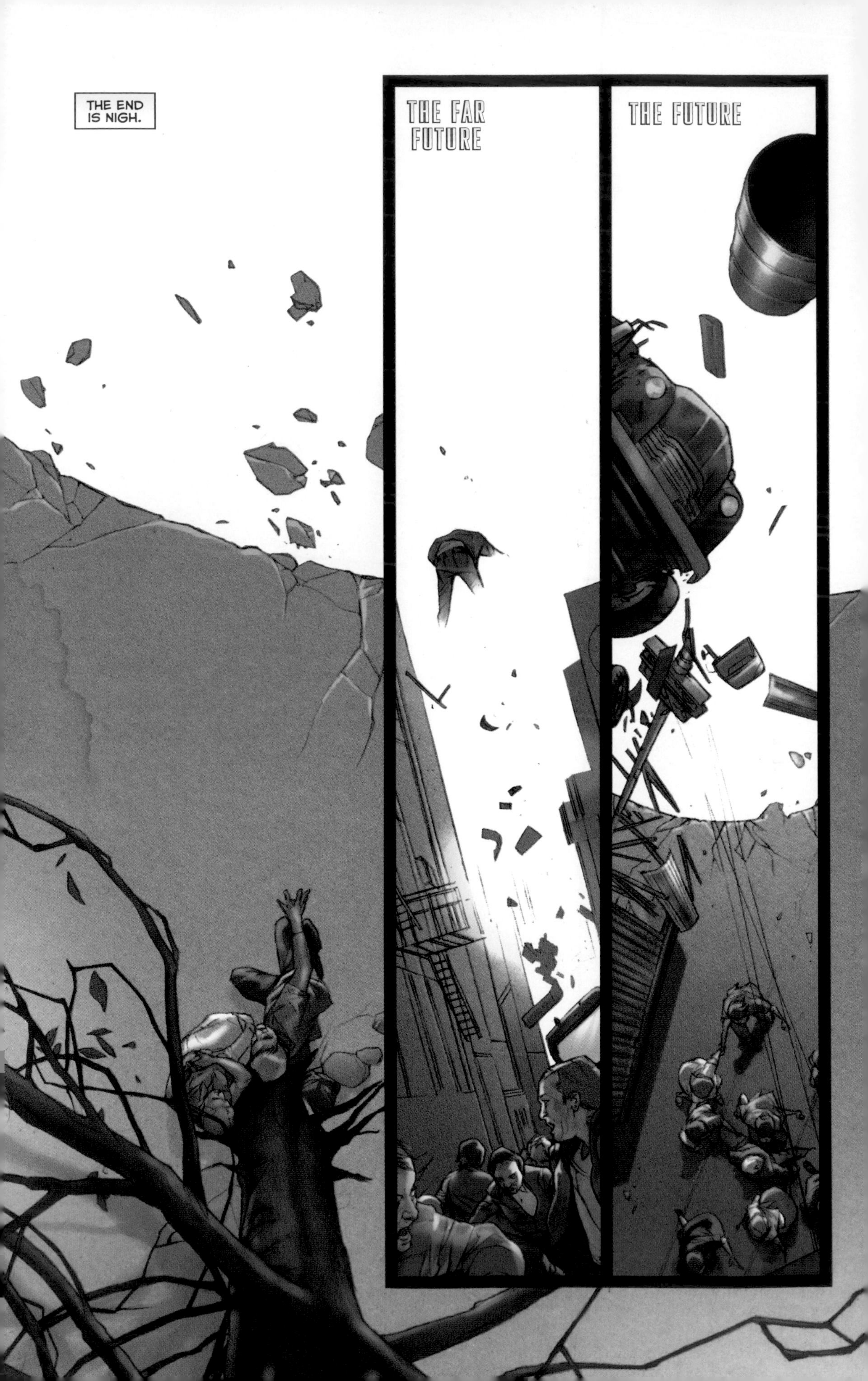
THE END IS NIGH.
THE FAR FUTURE
THE FUTURE

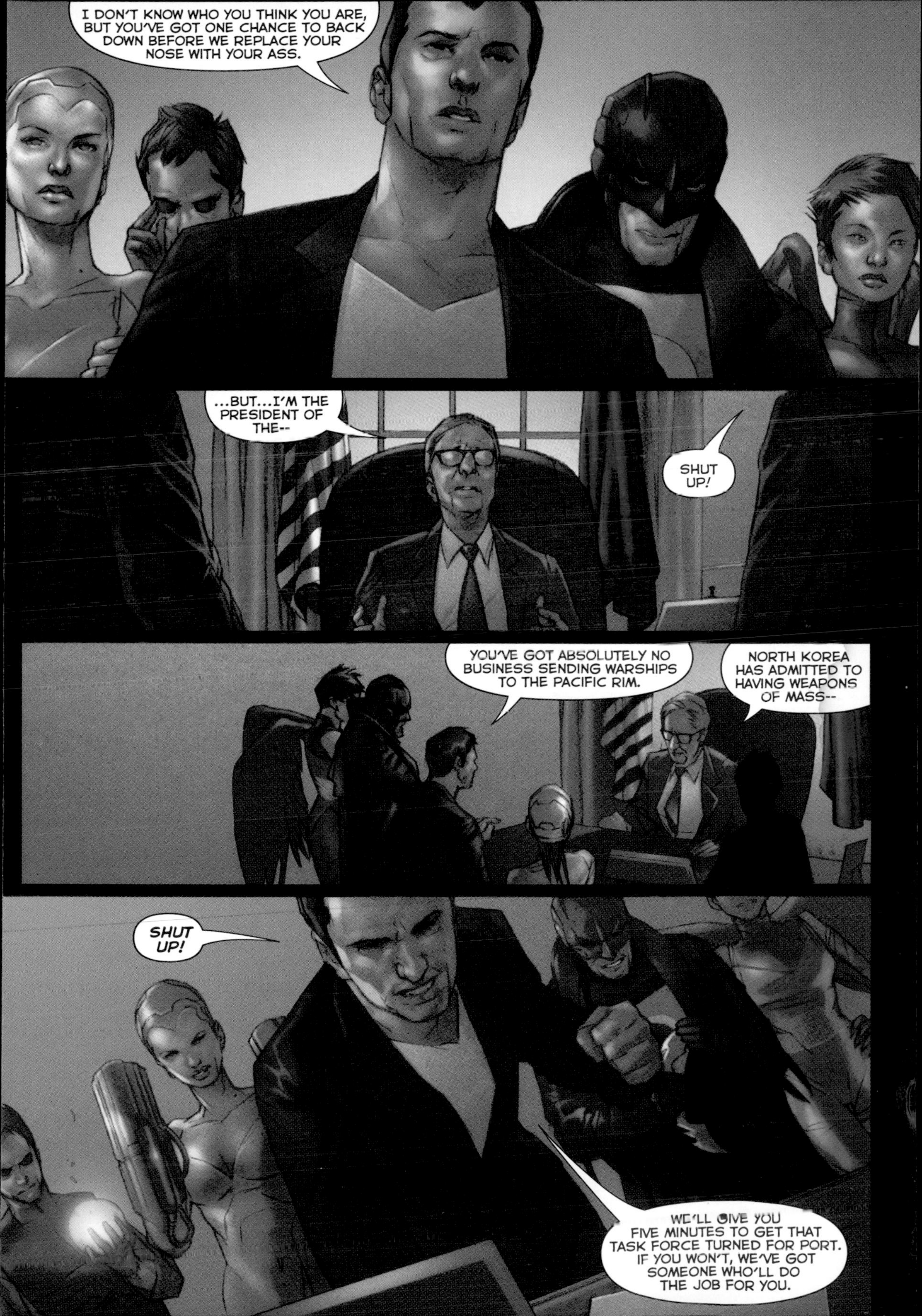
I DON'T KNOW WHO YOU THINK YOU ARE, BUT YOU'VE GOT ONE CHANCE TO BACK DOWN BEFORE WE REPLACE YOUR NOSE WITH YOUR ASS.
...BUT...I'M THE PRESIDENT OF THE--
SHUT UP!
YOU'VE GOT ABSOLUTELY NO BUSINESS SENDING WARSHIPS TO THE PACIFIC RIM.
NORTH KOREA HAS ADMITTED TO HAVING WEAPONS OF MASS--
SHUT UP!
WE'LL GIVE YOU FIVE MINUTES TO GET THAT TASK FORCE TURNED FOR PORT. IF YOU WON'T, WE'VE GOT SOMEONE WHO'LL DO THE JOB FOR YOU.

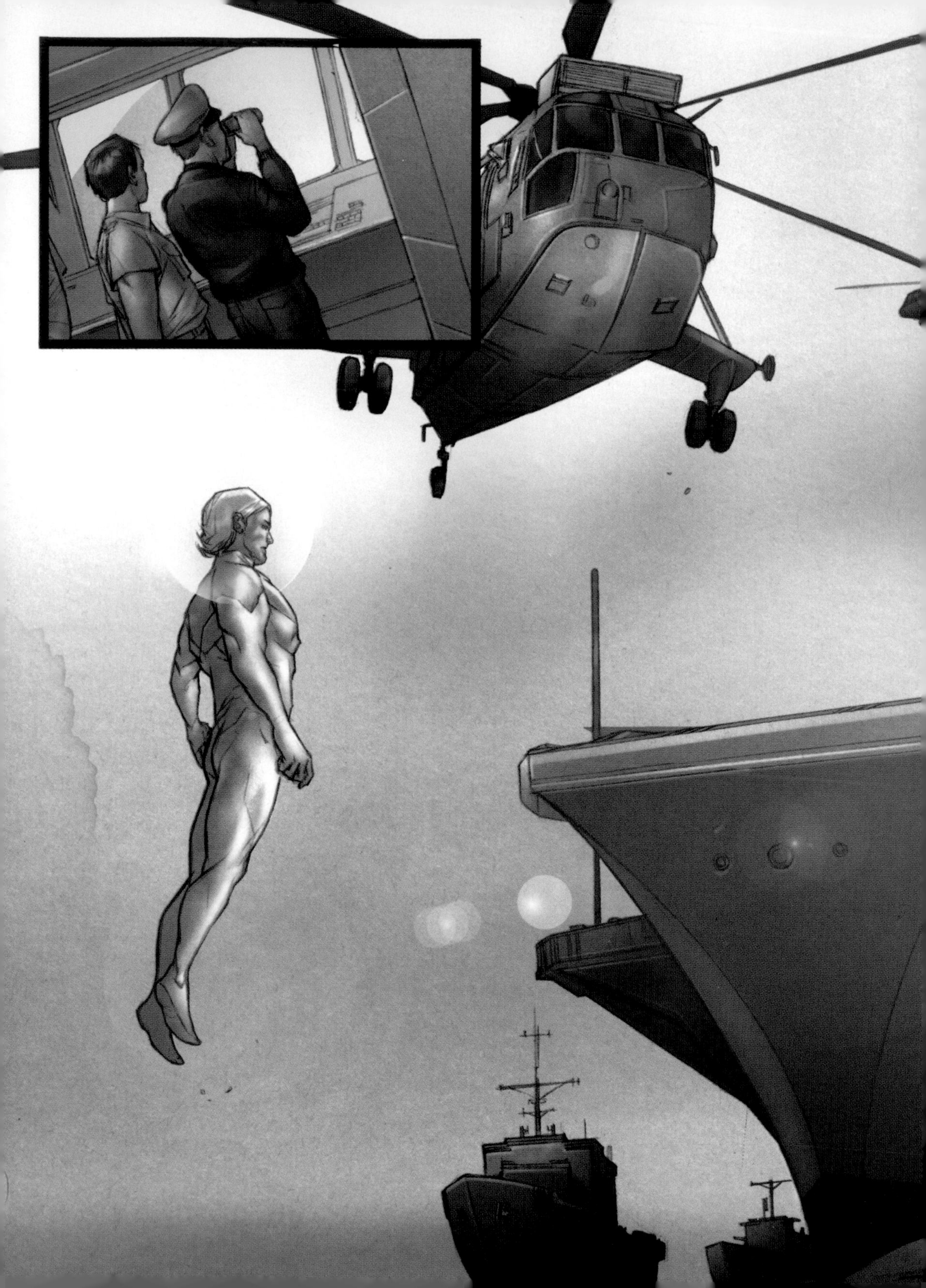

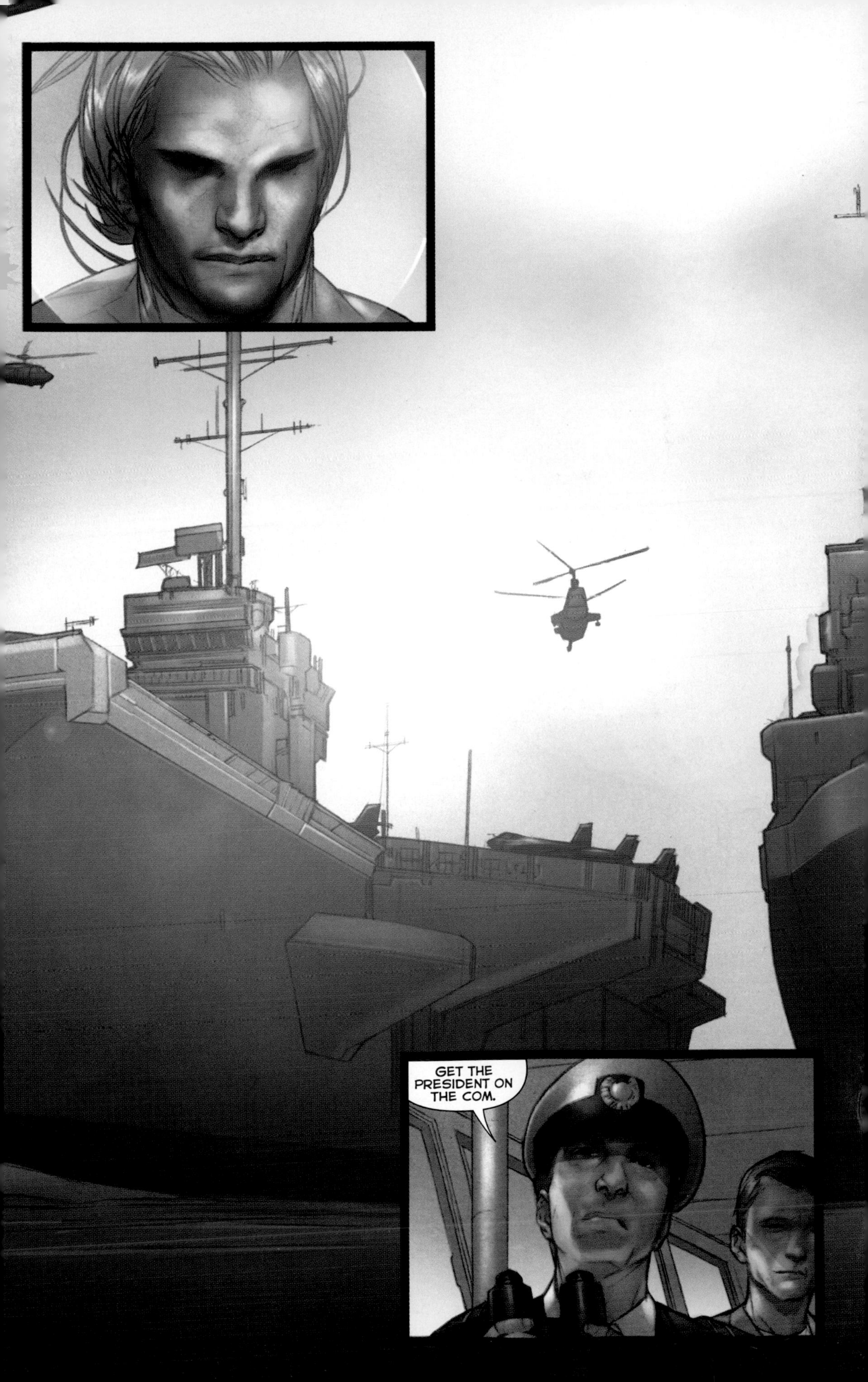
GET THE PRESIDENT ON THE COM.

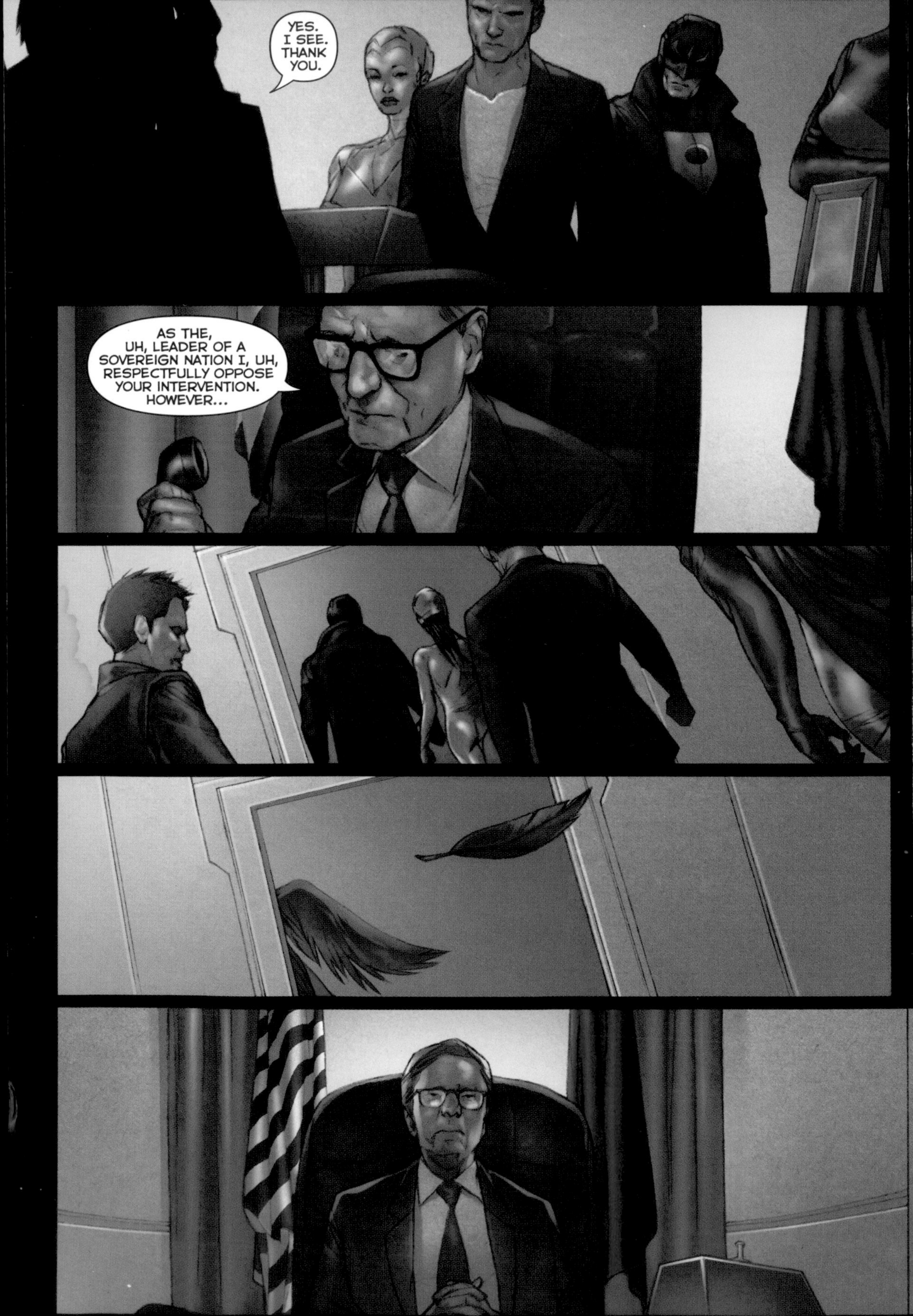
YES. I SEE. THANK YOU.
AS THE, UH, LEADER OF A SOVEREIGN NATION I, UH, RESPECTFULLY OPPOSE YOUR INTERVENTION. HOWEVER...

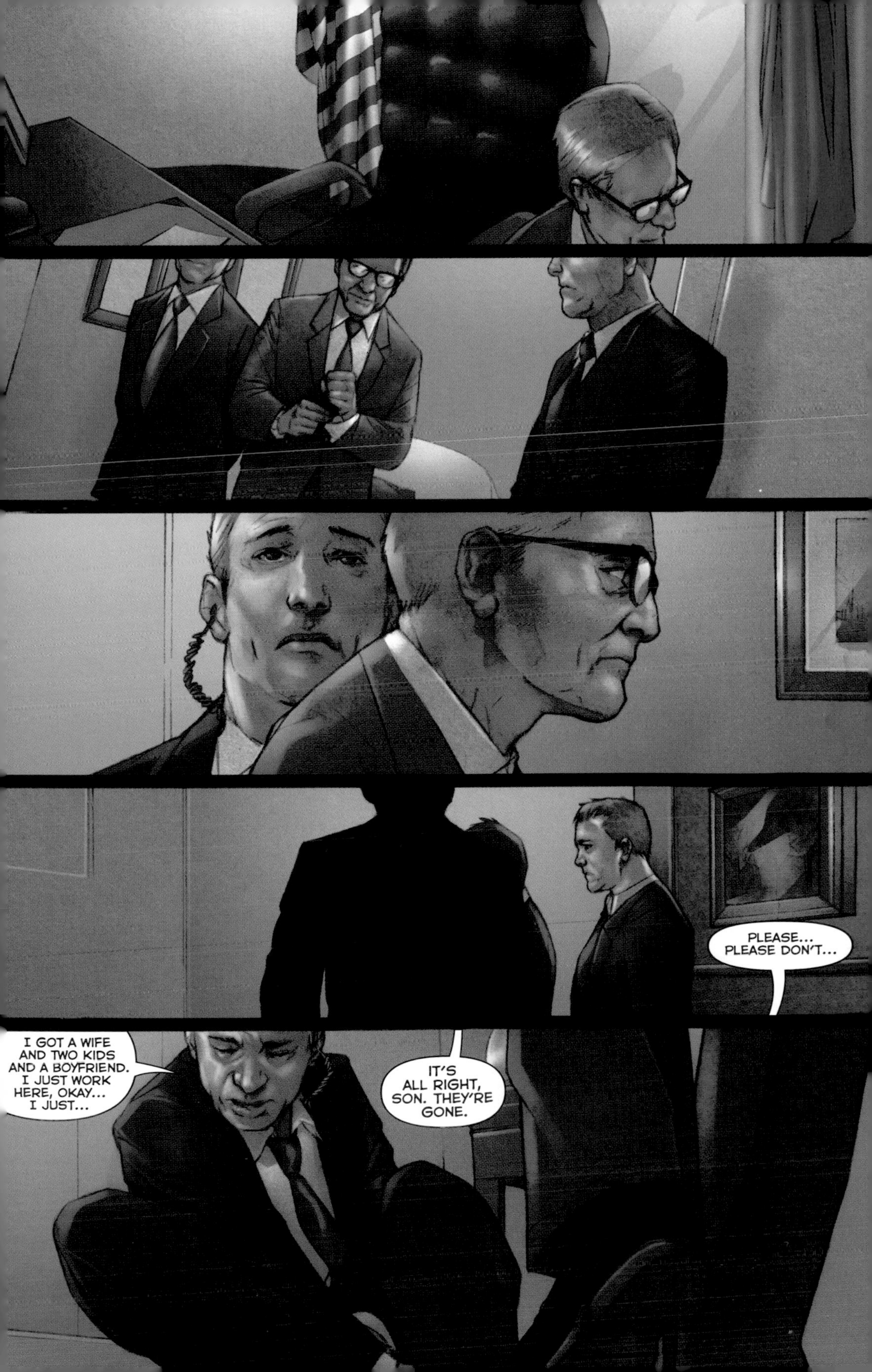
PLEASE... PLEASE DON'T...
I GOT A WIFE AND TWO KIDS AND A BOYFRIEND. I JUST WORK HERE, OKAY... I JUST...
IT'S ALL RIGHT, SON. THEY'RE GONE.

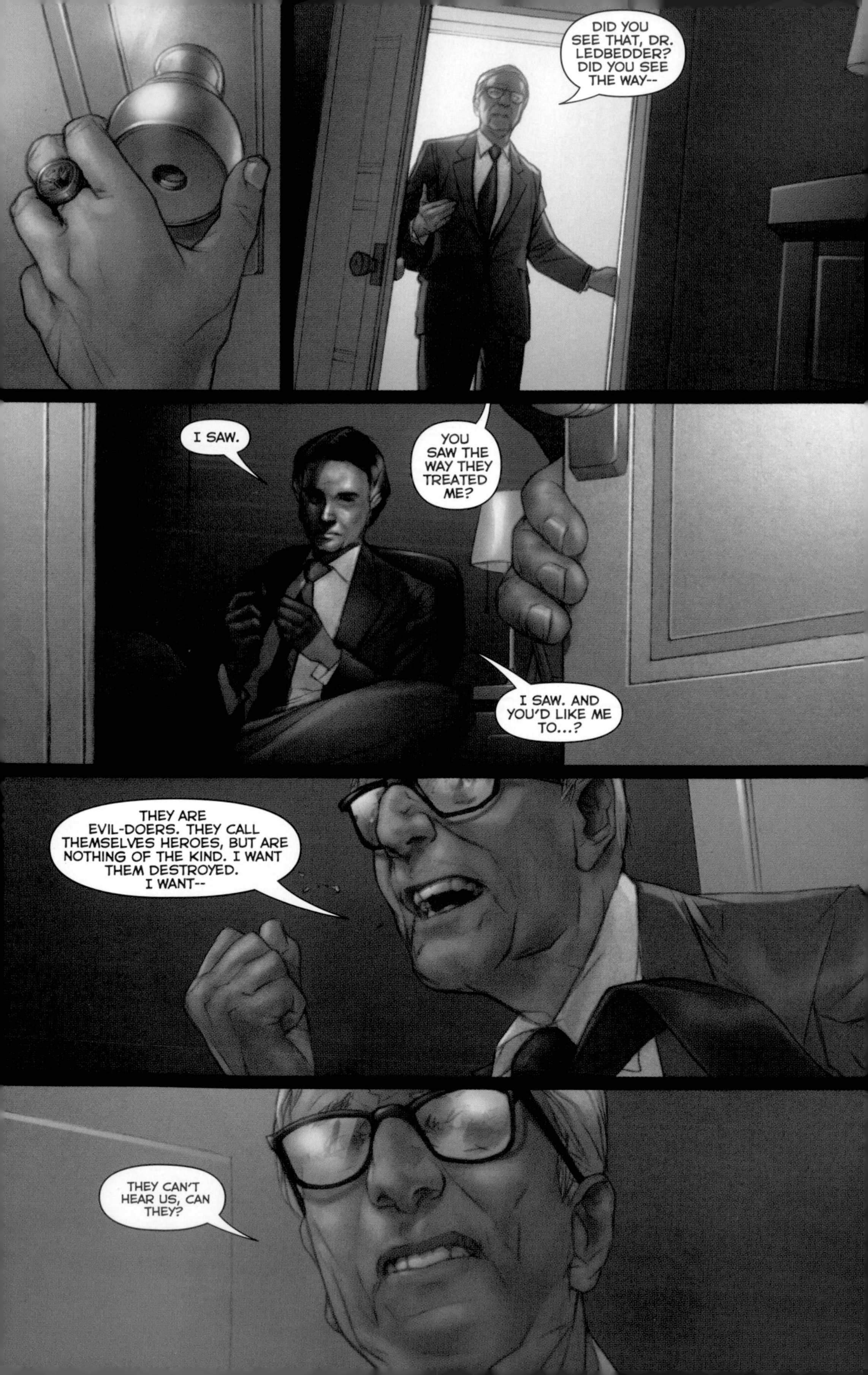
DID YOU SEE THAT, DR. LEDBEDDER? DID YOU SEE THE WAY--
I SAW.
YOU SAW THE WAY THEY TREATED ME?
I SAW. AND YOU'D LIKE ME TO...?
THEY ARE EVIL-DOERS. THEY CALL THEMSELVES HEROES, BUT ARE NOTHING OF THE KIND. I WANT THEM DESTROYED. I WANT--
THEY CAN'T HEAR US, CAN THEY?

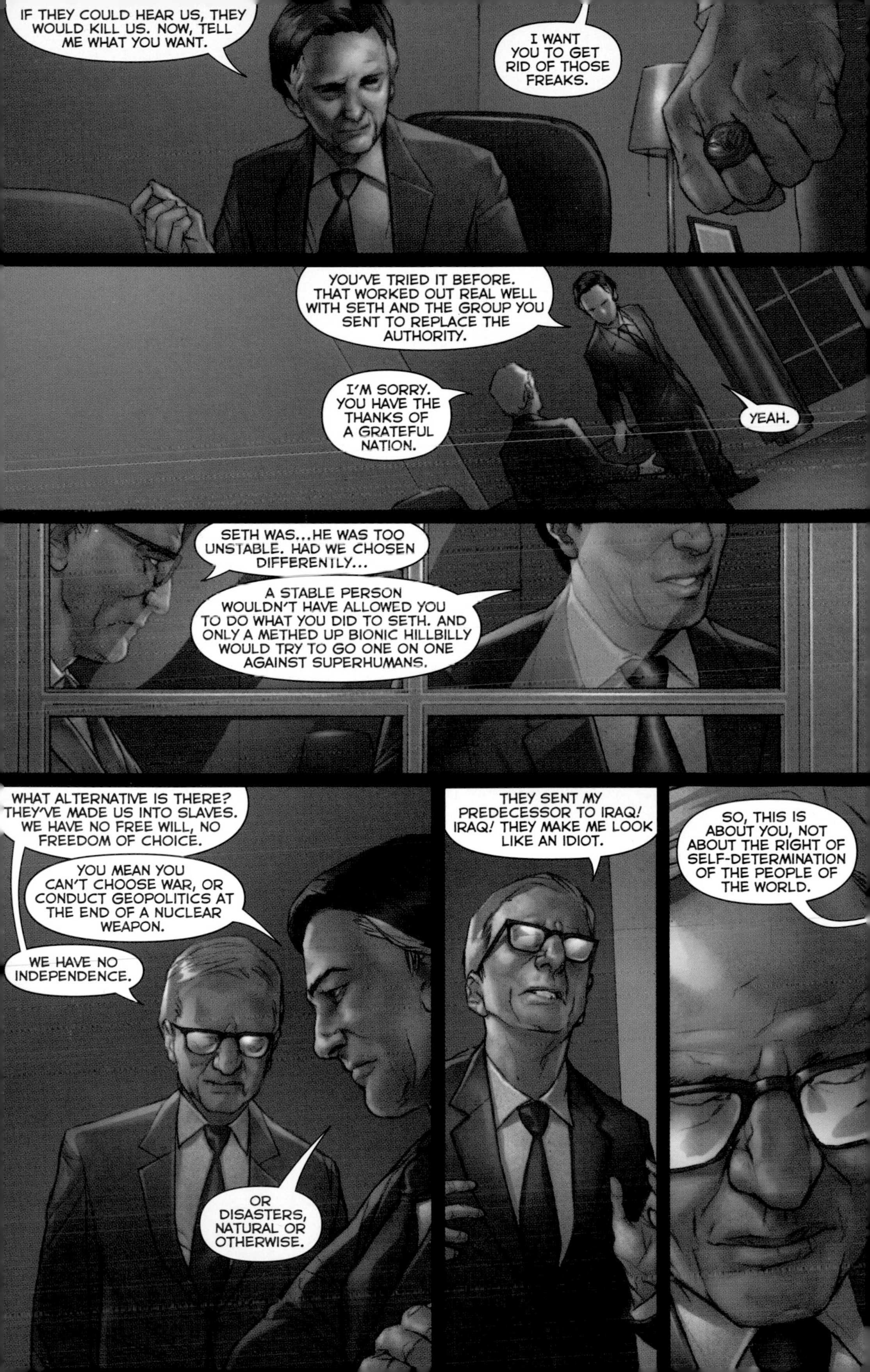
IF THEY COULD HEAR US, THEY WOULD KILL US. NOW, TELL ME WHAT YOU WANT.
I WANT YOU TO GET RID OF THOSE FREAKS.
YOU'VE TRIED IT BEFORE. THAT WORKED OUT REAL WELL WITH SETH AND THE GROUP YOU SENT TO REPLACE THE AUTHORITY.
I'M SORRY. YOU HAVE THE THANKS OF A GRATEFUL NATION.
YEAH.
SETH WAS...HE WAS TOO UNSTABLE. HAD WE CHOSEN DIFFERENTLY...
A STABLE PERSON WOULDN'T HAVE ALLOWED YOU TO DO WHAT YOU DID TO SETH. AND ONLY A METHED UP BIONIC HILLBILLY WOULD TRY TO GO ONE ON ONE AGAINST SUPERHUMANS.
WHAT ALTERNATIVE IS THERE? THEY'VE MADE US INTO SLAVES. WE HAVE NO FREE WILL, NO FREEDOM OF CHOICE.
YOU MEAN YOU CAN'T CHOOSE WAR, OR CONDUCT GEOPOLITICS AT THE END OF A NUCLEAR WEAPON.
WE HAVE NO INDEPENDENCE.
OR DISASTERS, NATURAL OR OTHERWISE.
THEY SENT MY PREDECESSOR TO IRAQ! IRAQ! THEY MAKE ME LOOK LIKE AN IDIOT.
SO, THIS IS ABOUT YOU, NOT ABOUT THE RIGHT OF SELF-DETERMINATION OF THE PEOPLE OF THE WORLD.

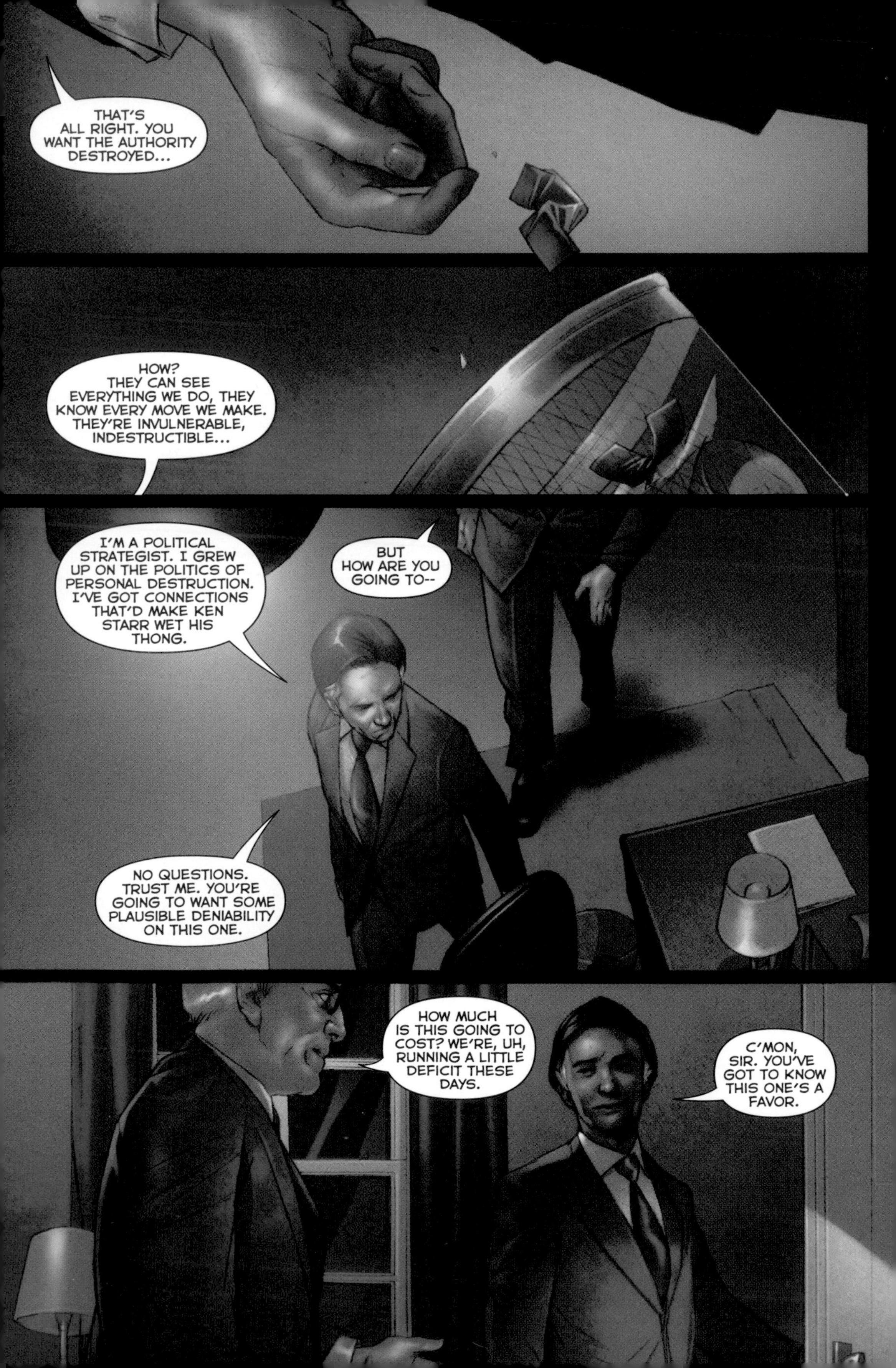
THAT'S ALL RIGHT. YOU WANT THE AUTHORITY DESTROYED...
HOW? THEY CAN SEE EVERYTHING WE DO, THEY KNOW EVERY MOVE WE MAKE. THEY'RE INVULNERABLE, INDESTRUCTIBLE...
I'M A POLITICAL STRATEGIST. I GREW UP ON THE POLITICS OF PERSONAL DESTRUCTION. I'VE GOT CONNECTIONS THAT'D MAKE KEN STARR WET HIS THONG.
BUT HOW ARE YOU GOING TO--
NO QUESTIONS. TRUST ME. YOU'RE GOING TO WANT SOME PLAUSIBLE DENIABILITY ON THIS ONE.
HOW MUCH IS THIS GOING TO COST? WE'RE, UH, RUNNING A LITTLE DEFICIT THESE DAYS.
C'MON, SIR. YOU'VE GOT TO KNOW THIS ONE'S A FAVOR.

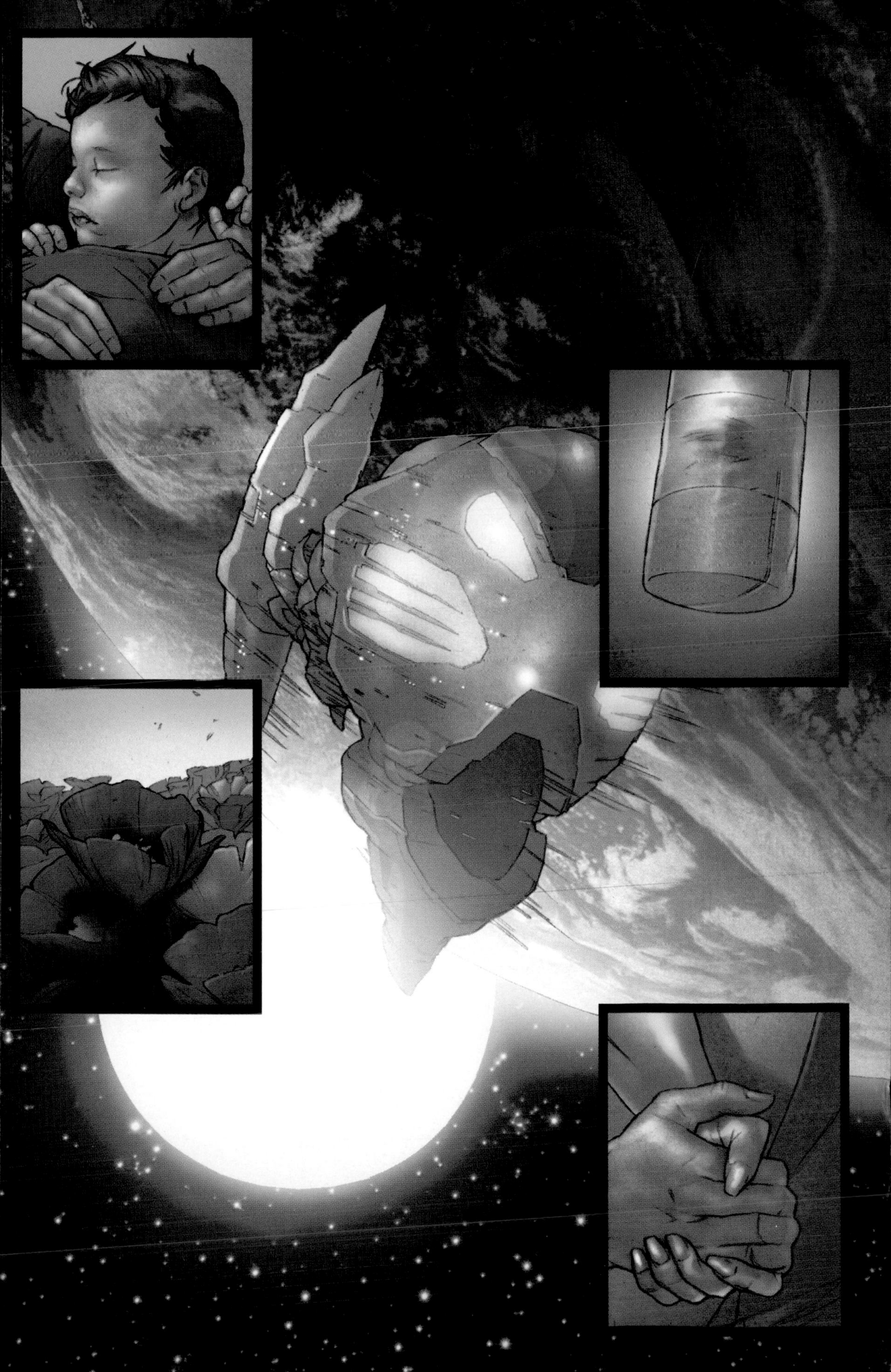

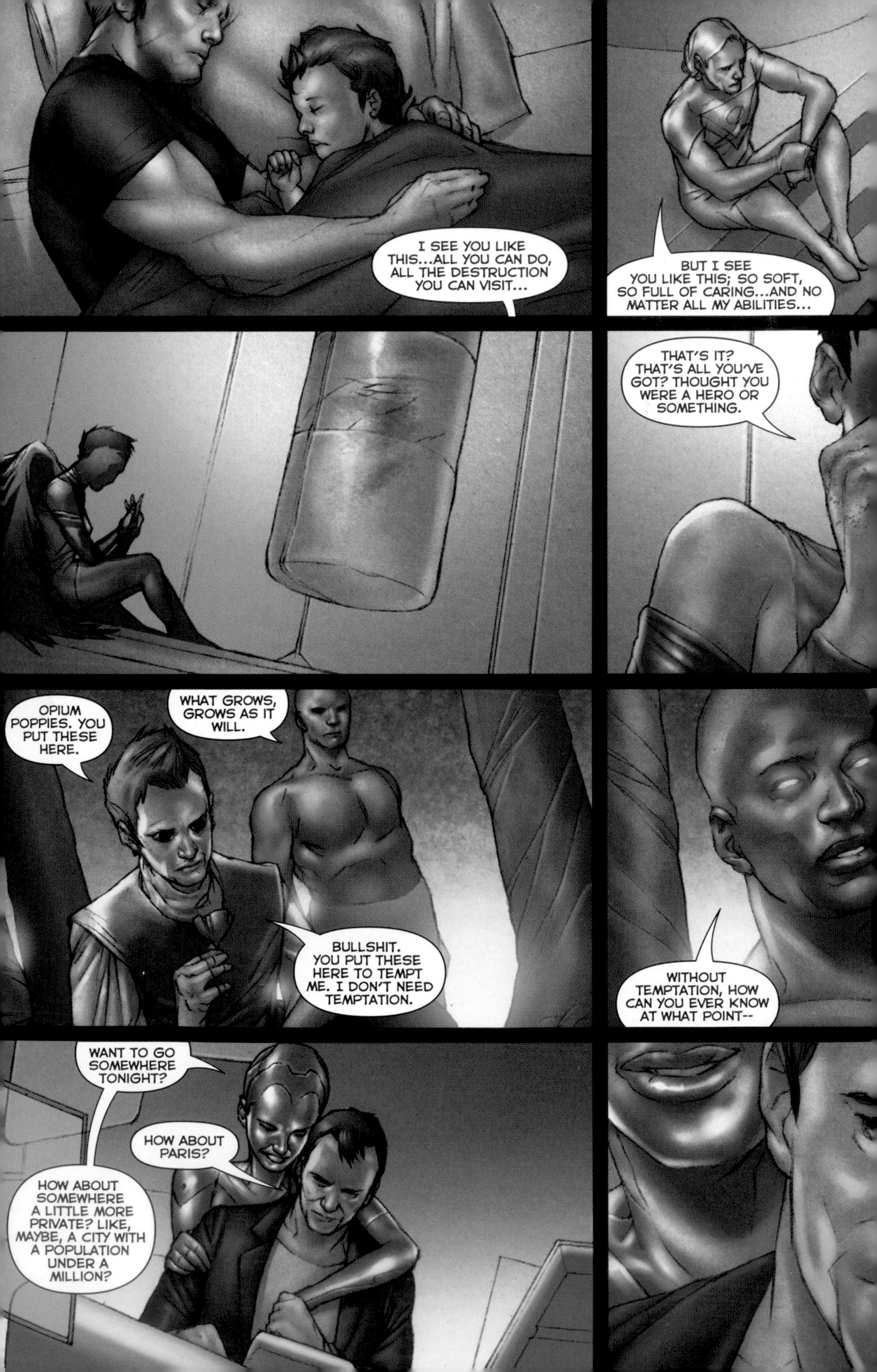
I SEE YOU LIKE THIS...ALL YOU CAN DO, ALL THE DESTRUCTION YOU CAN VISIT...
BUT I SEE YOU LIKE THIS; SO SOFT, SO FULL OF CARING...AND NO MATTER ALL MY ABILITIES...
THAT'S IT? THAT'S ALL YOU'VE GOT? THOUGHT YOU WERE A HERO OR SOMETHING.
OPIUM POPPIES. YOU PUT THESE HERE.
WHAT GROWS, GROWS AS IT WILL.
BULLSHIT. YOU PUT THESE HERE TO TEMPT ME. I DON'T NEED TEMPTATION.
WITHOUT TEMPTATION, HOW CAN YOU EVER KNOW AT WHAT POINT--
WANT TO GO SOMEWHERE TONIGHT?
HOW ABOUT PARIS?
HOW ABOUT SOMEWHERE A LITTLE MORE PRIVATE? LIKE, MAYBE, A CITY WITH A POPULATION UNDER A MILLION?

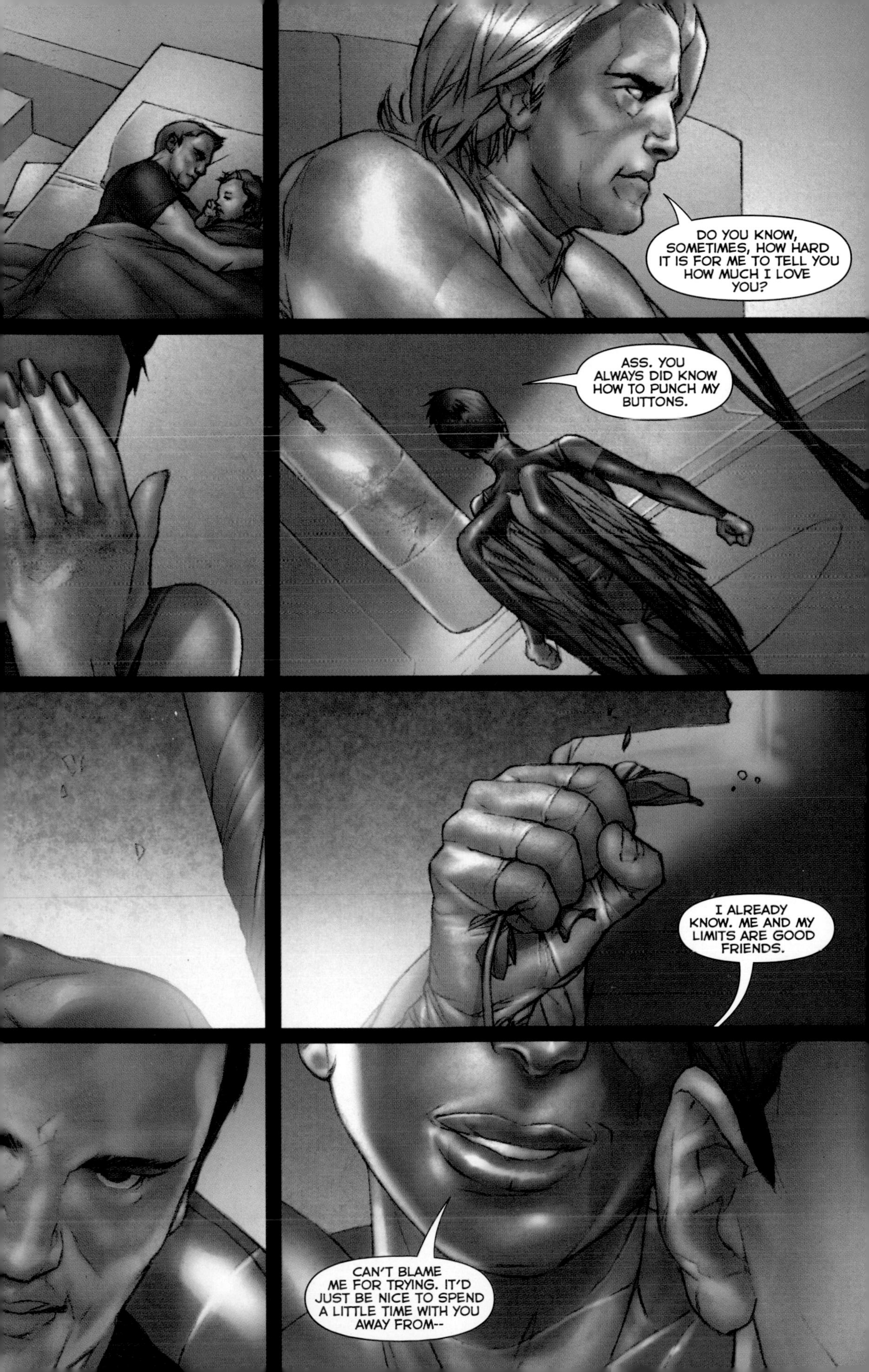
DO YOU KNOW, SOMETIMES, HOW HARD IT IS FOR ME TO TELL YOU HOW MUCH I LOVE YOU?
ASS. YOU ALWAYS DID KNOW HOW TO PUNCH MY BUTTONS.
I ALREADY KNOW. ME AND MY LIMITS ARE GOOD FRIENDS.
CAN'T BLAME ME FOR TRYING. IT'D JUST BE NICE TO SPEND A LITTLE TIME WITH YOU AWAY FROM--

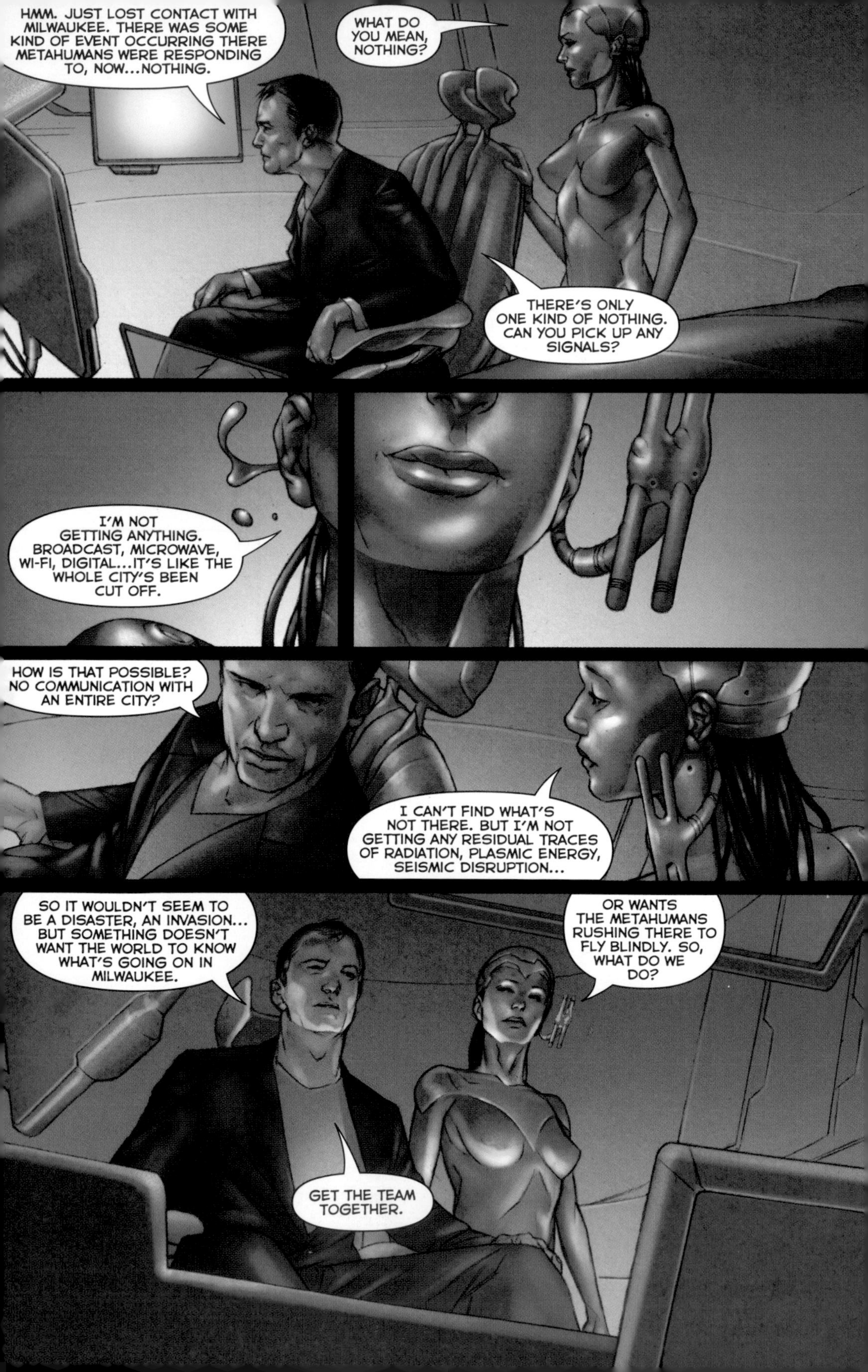
HMM. JUST LOST CONTACT WITH MILWAUKEE. THERE WAS SOME KIND OF EVENT OCCURRING THERE METAHUMANS WERE RESPONDING TO, NOW...NOTHING.
WHAT DO YOU MEAN, NOTHING?
THERE'S ONLY ONE KIND OF NOTHING. CAN YOU PICK UP ANY SIGNALS?
I'M NOT GETTING ANYTHING. BROADCAST, MICROWAVE, WI-FI, DIGITAL...IT'S LIKE THE WHOLE CITY'S BEEN CUT OFF.
HOW IS THAT POSSIBLE? NO COMMUNICATION WITH AN ENTIRE CITY?
I CAN'T FIND WHAT'S NOT THERE. BUT I'M NOT GETTING ANY RESIDUAL TRACES OF RADIATION, PLASMIC ENERGY, SEISMIC DISRUPTION...
SO IT WOULDN'T SEEM TO BE A DISASTER, AN INVASION... BUT SOMETHING DOESN'T WANT THE WORLD TO KNOW WHAT'S GOING ON IN MILWAUKEE.
OR WANTS THE METAHUMANS RUSHING THERE TO FLY BLINDLY. SO, WHAT DO WE DO?
GET THE TEAM TOGETHER.

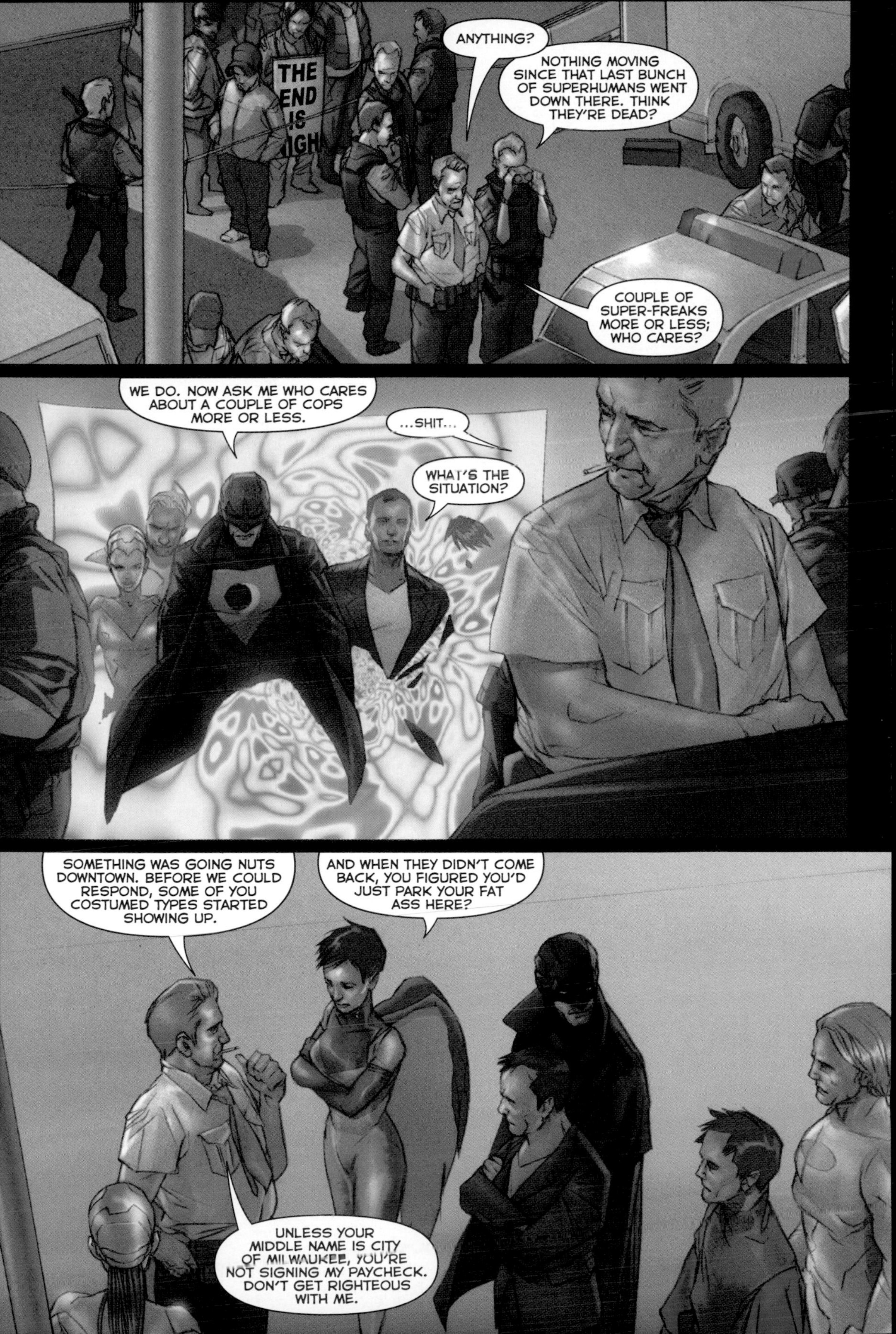
THE END IS NIGH
ANYTHING?
NOTHING MOVING SINCE THAT LAST BUNCH OF SUPERHUMANS WENT DOWN THERE. THINK THEY'RE DEAD?
COUPLE OF SUPER-FREAKS MORE OR LESS; WHO CARES?
WE DO. NOW ASK ME WHO CARES ABOUT A COUPLE OF COPS MORE OR LESS.
...SHIT...
WHAT'S THE SITUATION?
SOMETHING WAS GOING NUTS DOWNTOWN. BEFORE WE COULD RESPOND, SOME OF YOU COSTUMED TYPES STARTED SHOWING UP.
AND WHEN THEY DIDN'T COME BACK, YOU FIGURED YOU'D JUST PARK YOUR FAT ASS HERE?
UNLESS YOUR MIDDLE NAME IS CITY OF MILWAUKEE, YOU'RE NOT SIGNING MY PAYCHECK. DON'T GET RIGHTEOUS WITH ME.

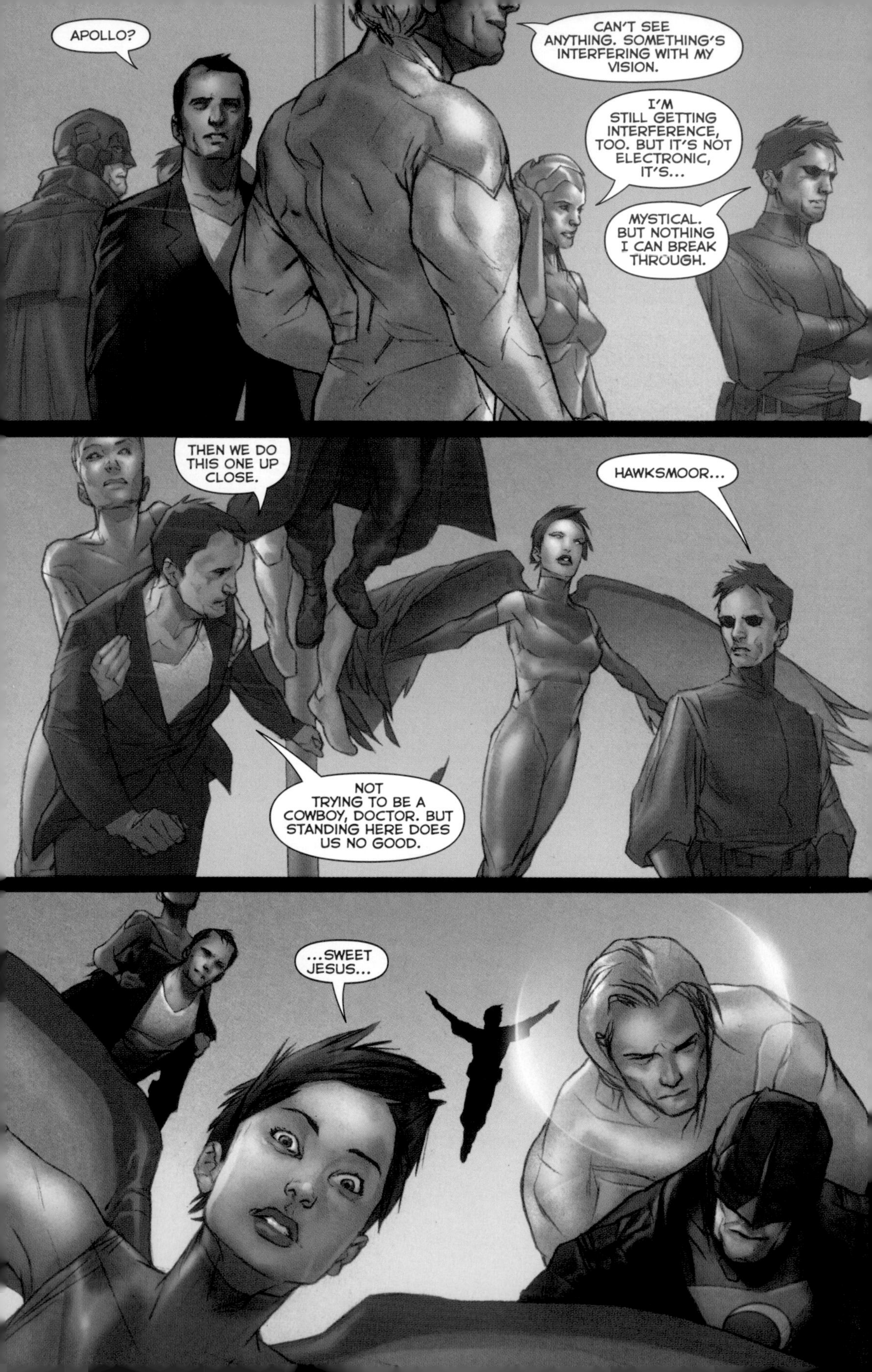
APOLLO?
CAN'T SEE ANYTHING. SOMETHING'S INTERFERING WITH MY VISION.
I'M STILL GETTING INTERFERENCE, TOO. BUT IT'S NOT ELECTRONIC, IT'S...
MYSTICAL. BUT NOTHING I CAN BREAK THROUGH.
THEN WE DO THIS ONE UP CLOSE.
HAWKSMOOR...
NOT TRYING TO BE A COWBOY, DOCTOR. BUT STANDING HERE DOES US NO GOOD.
...SWEET JESUS...

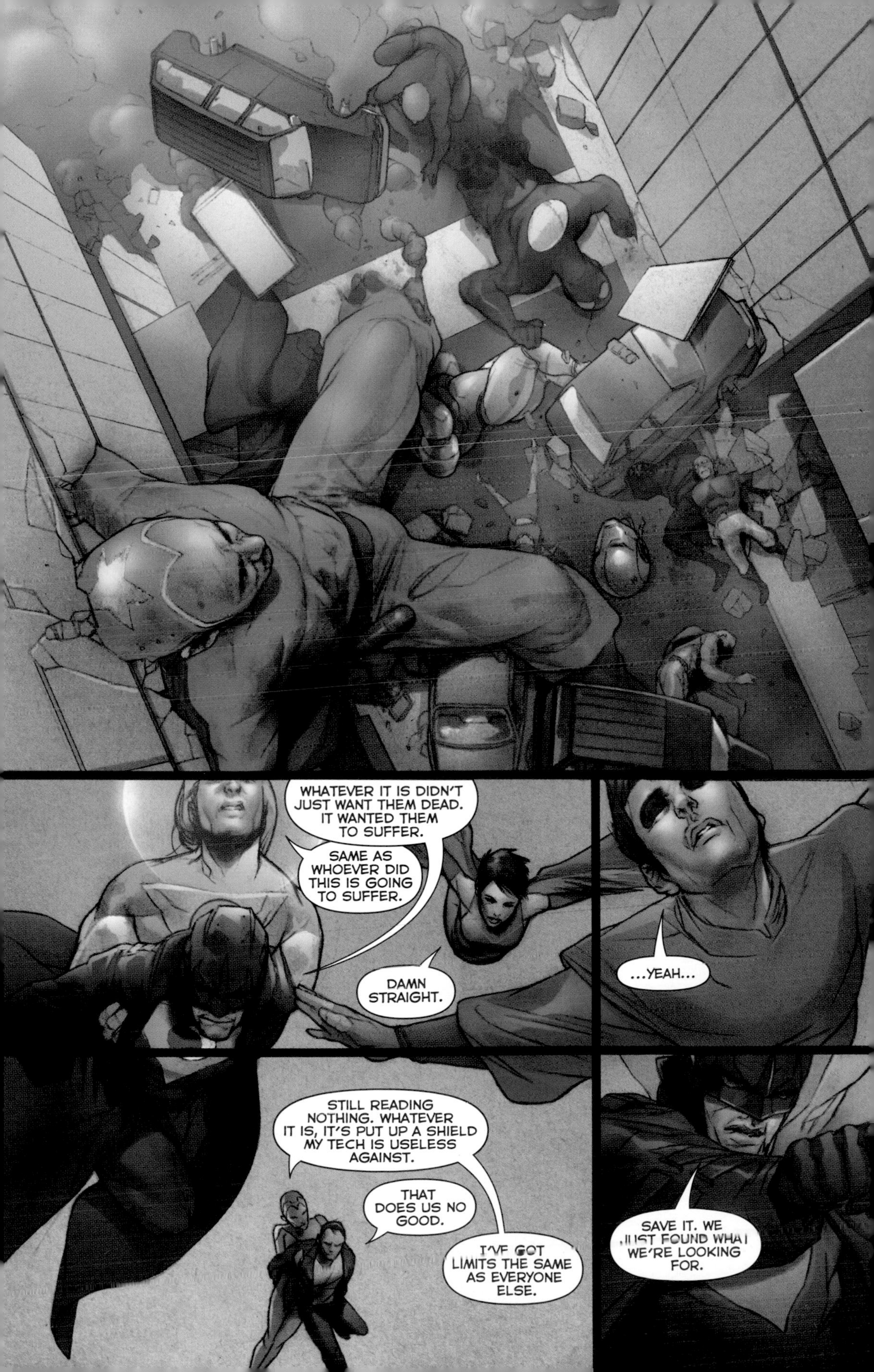
WHATEVER IT IS DIDN'T JUST WANT THEM DEAD. IT WANTED THEM TO SUFFER.
SAME AS WHOEVER DID THIS IS GOING TO SUFFER.
DAMN STRAIGHT.
...YEAH...
STILL READING NOTHING. WHATEVER IT IS, IT'S PUT UP A SHIELD MY TECH IS USELESS AGAINST.
THAT DOES US NO GOOD.
I'VE GOT LIMITS THE SAME AS EVERYONE ELSE.
SAVE IT. WE JUST FOUND WHAT WE'RE LOOKING FOR.

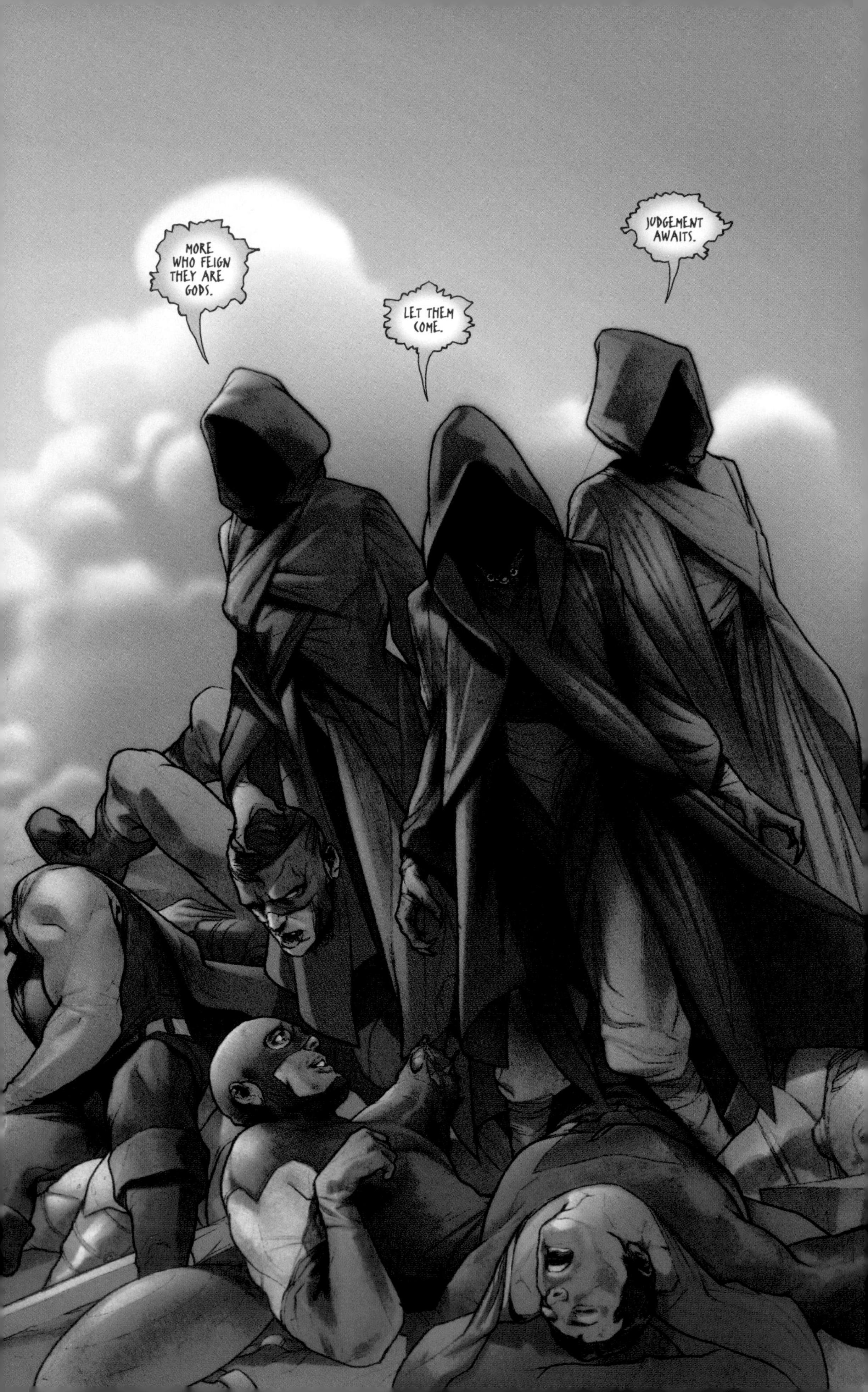
MORE WHO FEIGN THEY ARE GODS.
LET THEM COME.
JUDGEMENT AWAITS.

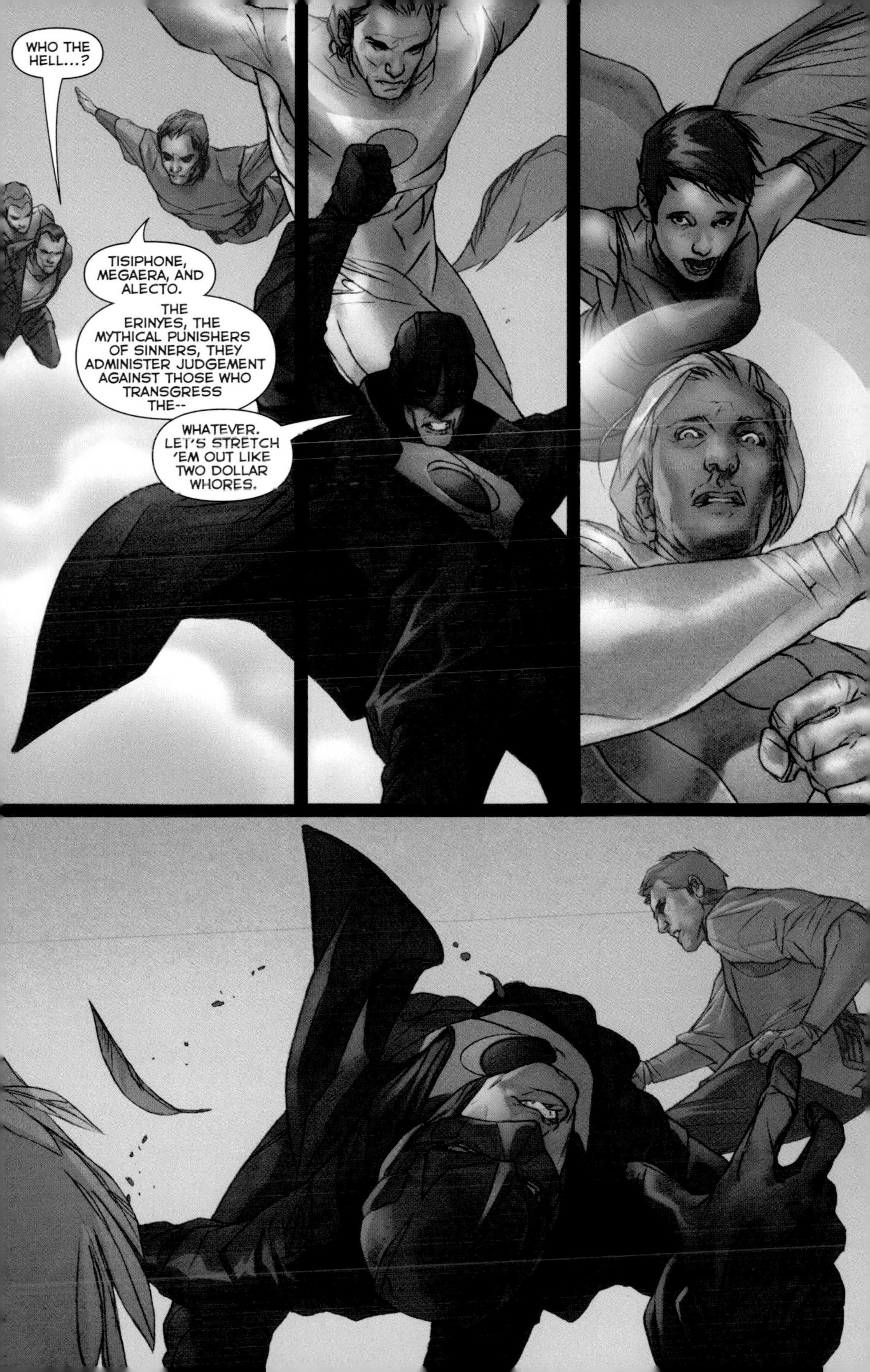
WHO THE HELL...?
TISIPHONE, MEGAERA, AND ALECTO.
THE ERINYES, THE MYTHICAL PUNISHERS OF SINNERS, THEY ADMINISTER JUDGEMENT AGAINST THOSE WHO TRANSGRESS THE--
WHATEVER. LET'S STRETCH 'EM OUT LIKE TWO DOLLAR WHORES.

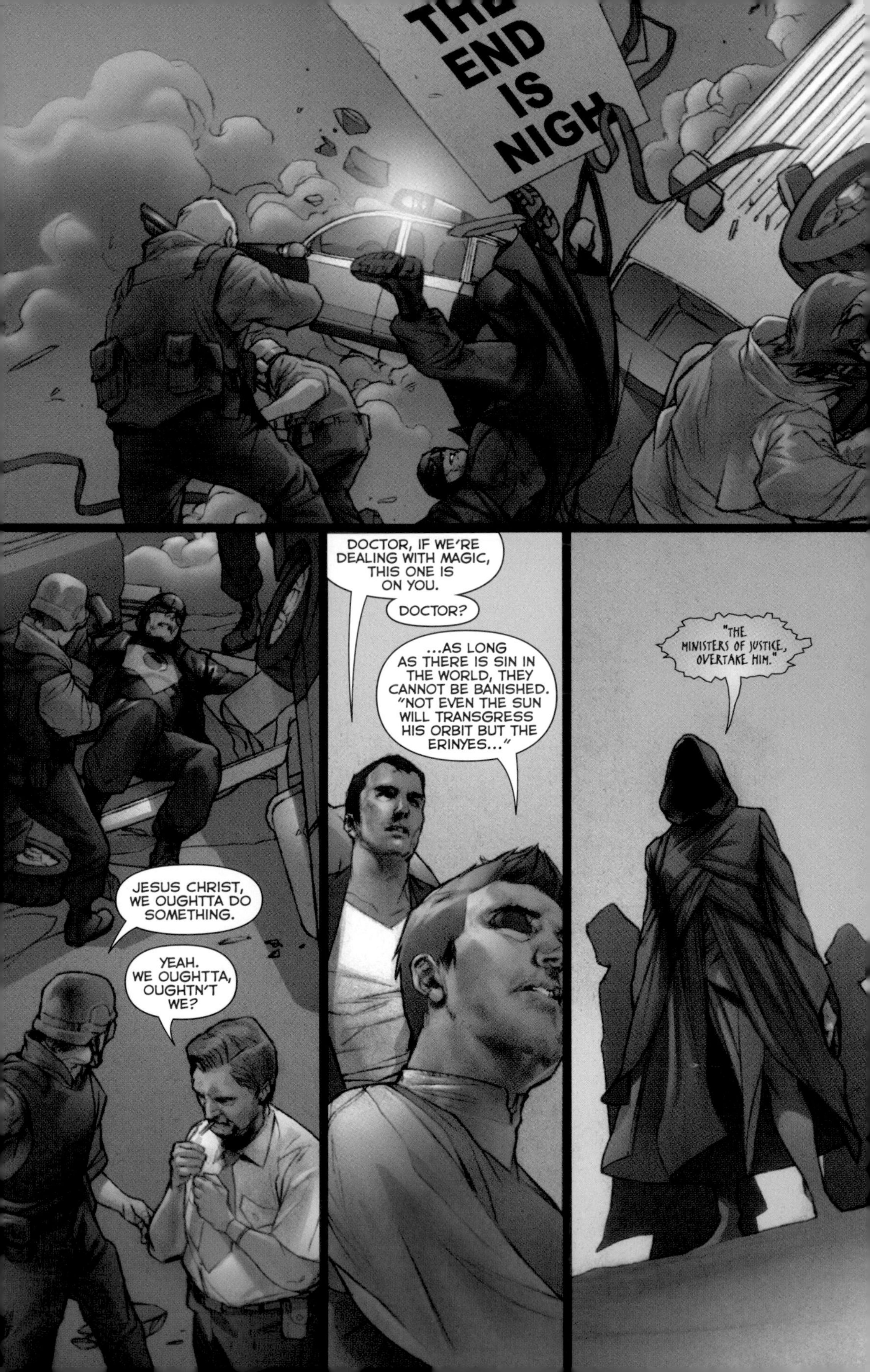
THE END IS NIGH
JESUS CHRIST, WE OUGHTTA DO SOMETHING.
YEAH. WE OUGHTTA, OUGHTN'T WE?
DOCTOR, IF WE'RE DEALING WITH MAGIC, THIS ONE IS ON YOU.
DOCTOR?
...AS LONG AS THERE IS SIN IN THE WORLD, THEY CANNOT BE BANISHED. "NOT EVEN THE SUN WILL TRANSGRESS HIS ORBIT BUT THE ERINYES..."
"THE MINISTERS OF JUSTICE, OVERTAKE HIM."

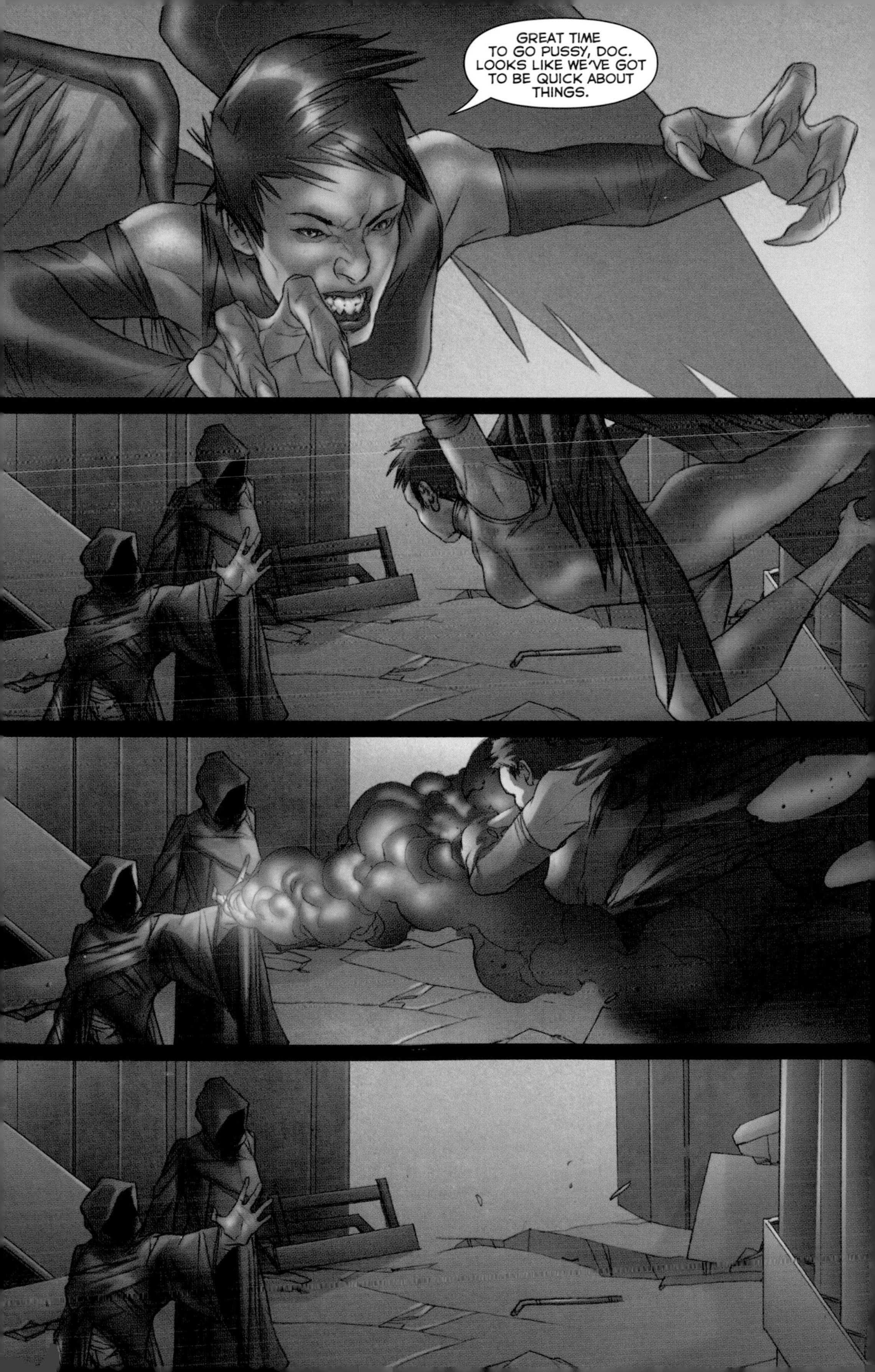
GREAT TIME TO GO PUSSY, DOC. LOOKS LIKE WE'VE GOT TO BE QUICK ABOUT THINGS.

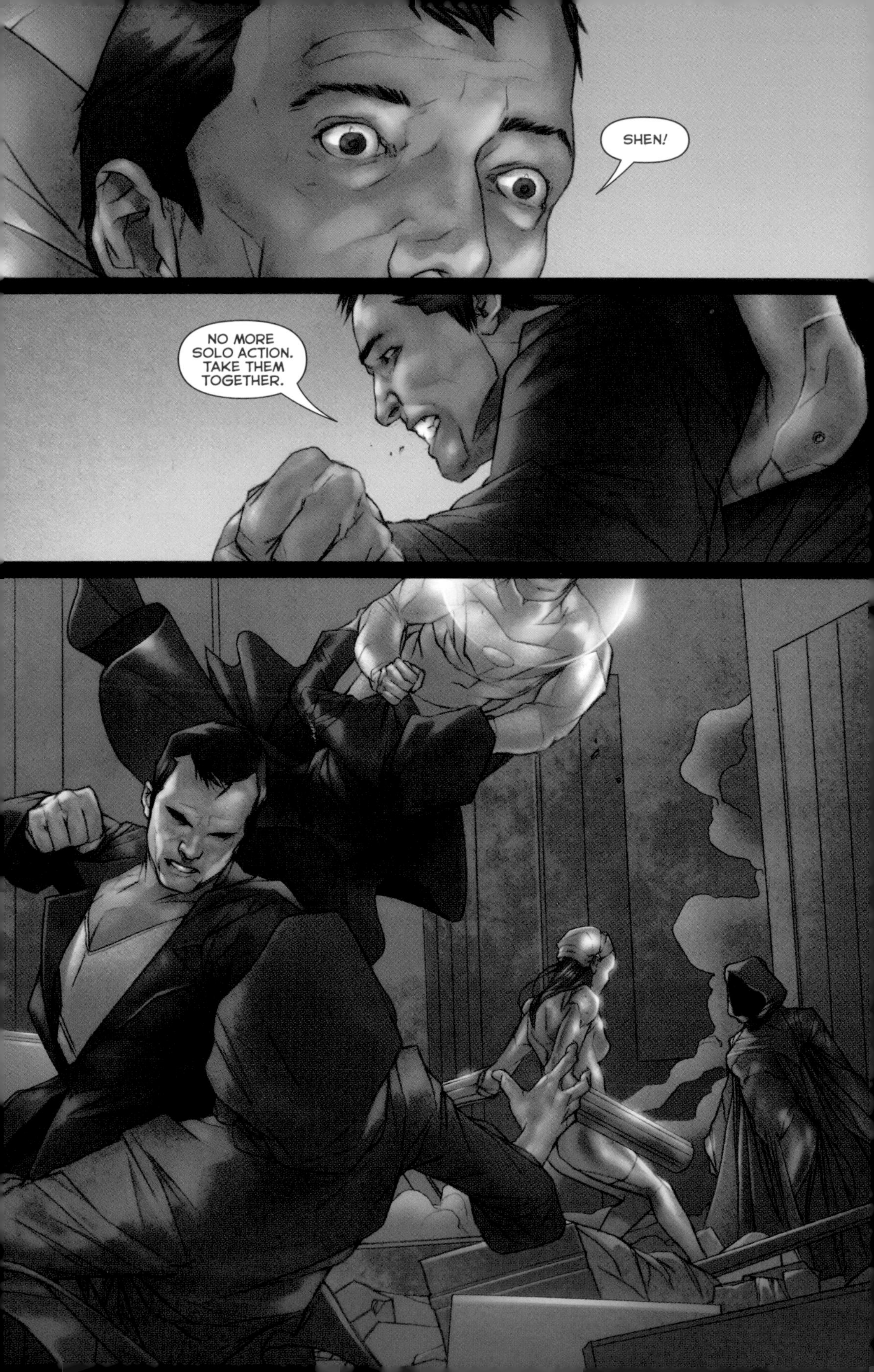
SHEN!
NO MORE SOLO ACTION. TAKE THEM TOGETHER.

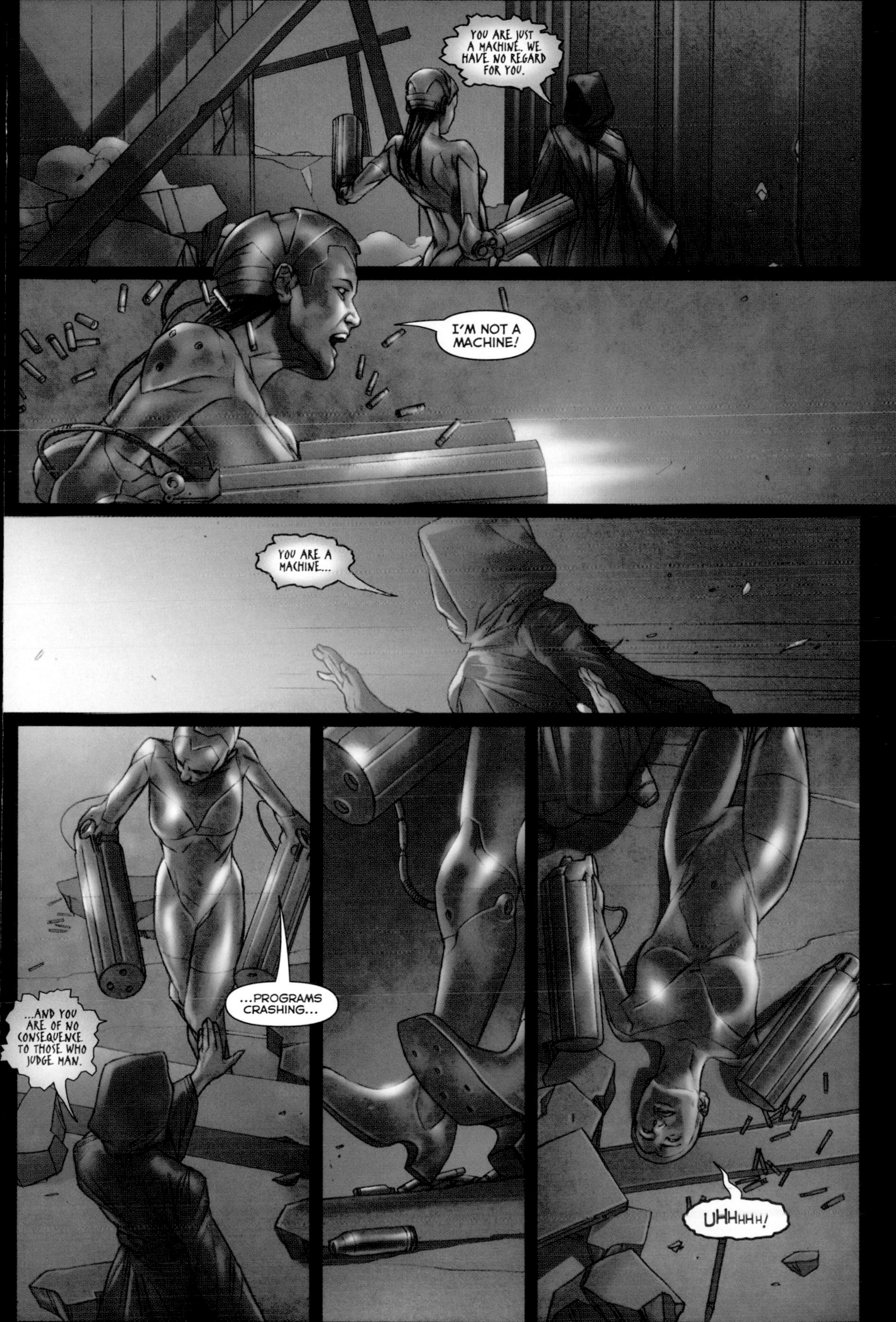
YOU ARE JUST A MACHINE. WE HAVE NO REGARD FOR YOU.
I'M NOT A MACHINE!
YOU ARE A MACHINE...
...AND YOU ARE OF NO CONSEQUENCE TO THOSE WHO JUDGE MAN.
...PROGRAMS CRASHING...
UHHHHH!

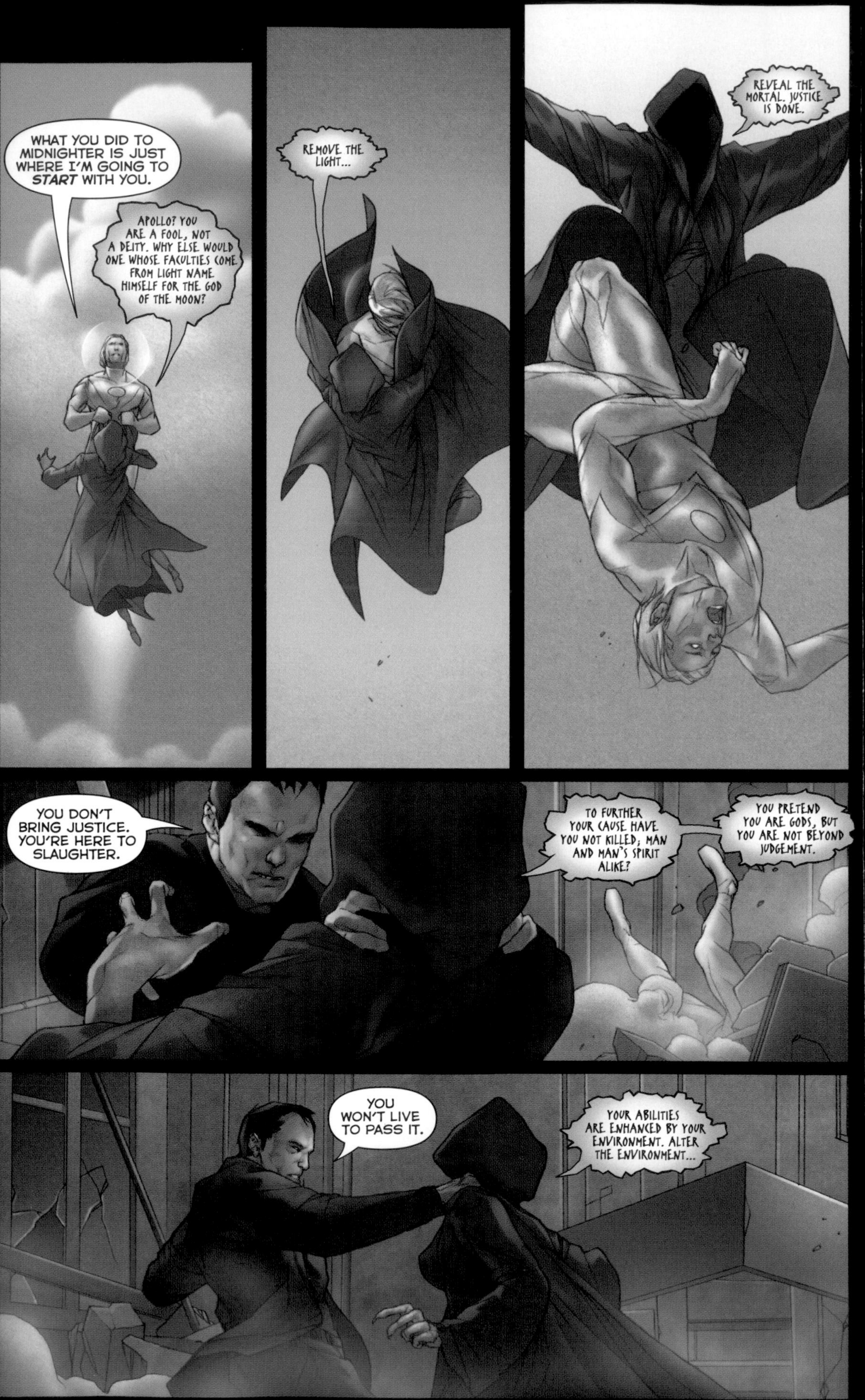
WHAT YOU DID TO MIDNIGHTER IS JUST WHERE I'M GOING TO *START* WITH YOU.
APOLLO? YOU ARE A FOOL, NOT A DEITY. WHY ELSE WOULD ONE WHOSE FACULTIES COME FROM LIGHT NAME HIMSELF FOR THE GOD OF THE MOON?
REMOVE THE LIGHT...
REVEAL THE MORTAL. JUSTICE IS DONE.
YOU DON'T BRING JUSTICE. YOU'RE HERE TO SLAUGHTER.
TO FURTHER YOUR CAUSE HAVE YOU NOT KILLED; MAN AND MAN'S SPIRIT ALIKE?
YOU PRETEND YOU ARE GODS, BUT YOU ARE NOT BEYOND JUDGEMENT.
YOU WON'T LIVE TO PASS IT.
YOUR ABILITIES ARE ENHANCED BY YOUR ENVIRONMENT. ALTER THE ENVIRONMENT...

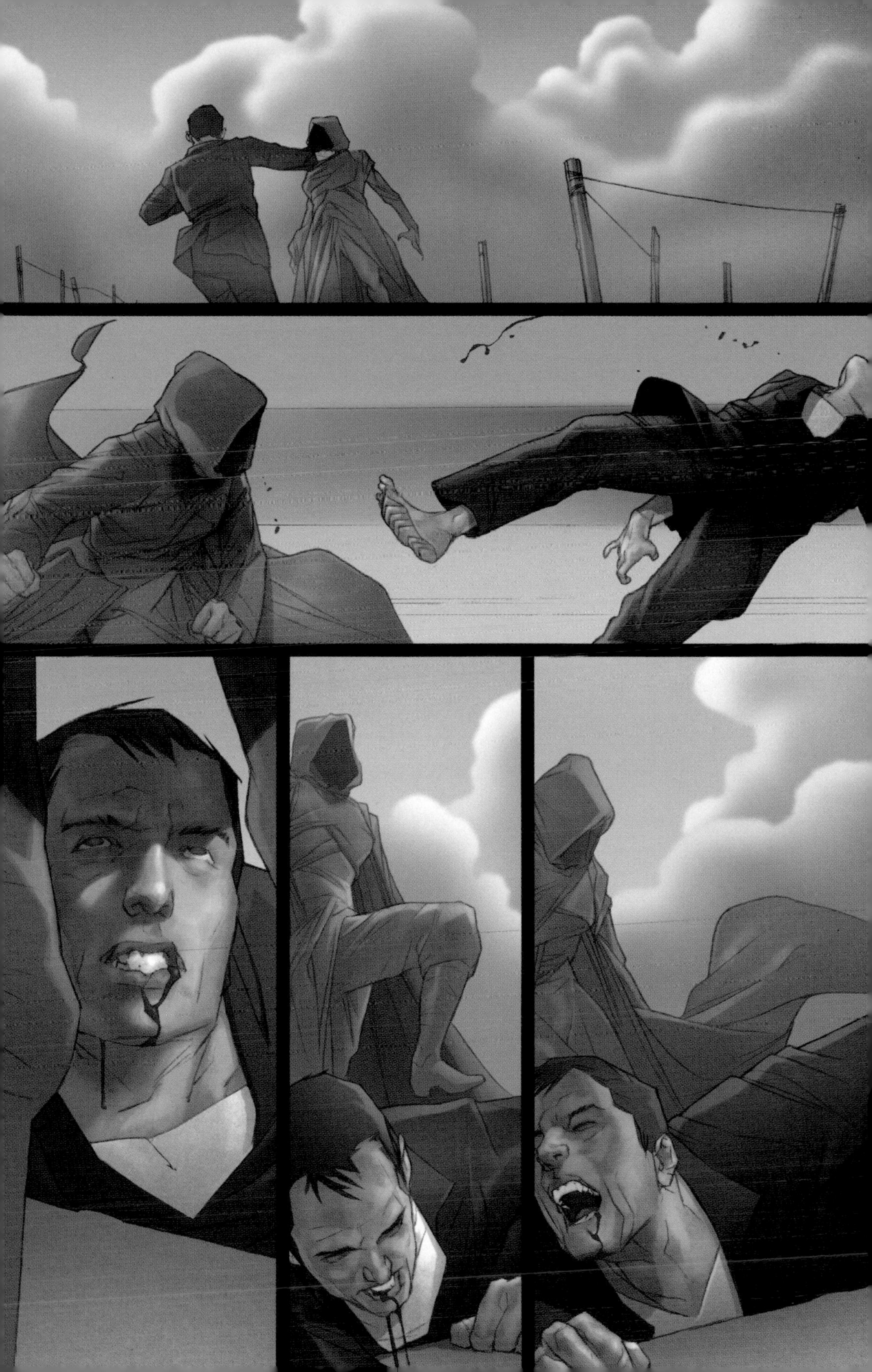

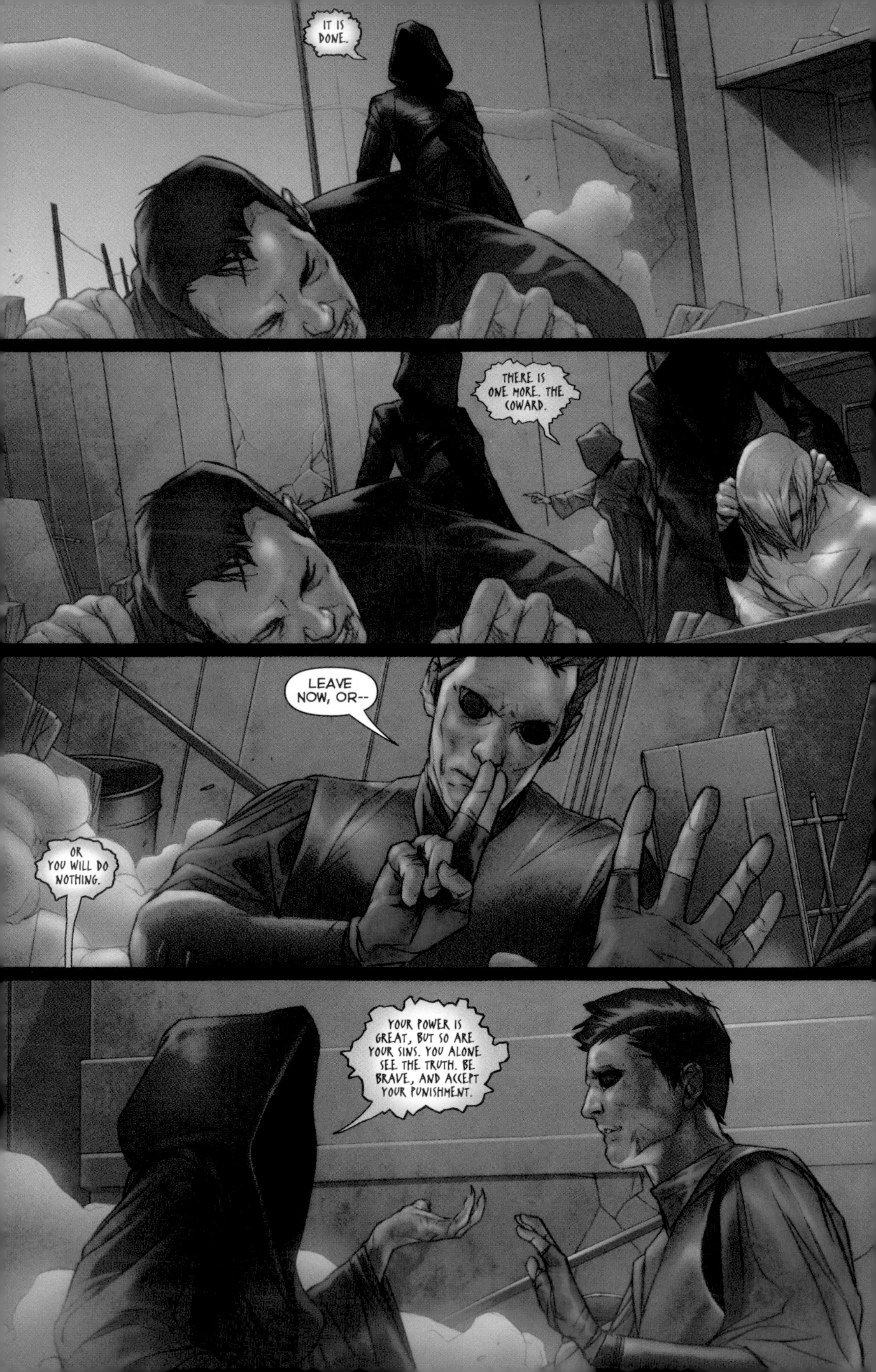
IT IS DONE.
THERE IS ONE MORE. THE COWARD.
LEAVE NOW, OR--
OR YOU WILL DO NOTHING.
YOUR POWER IS GREAT, BUT SO ARE YOUR SINS. YOU ALONE SEE THE TRUTH. BE BRAVE, AND ACCEPT YOUR PUNISHMENT.

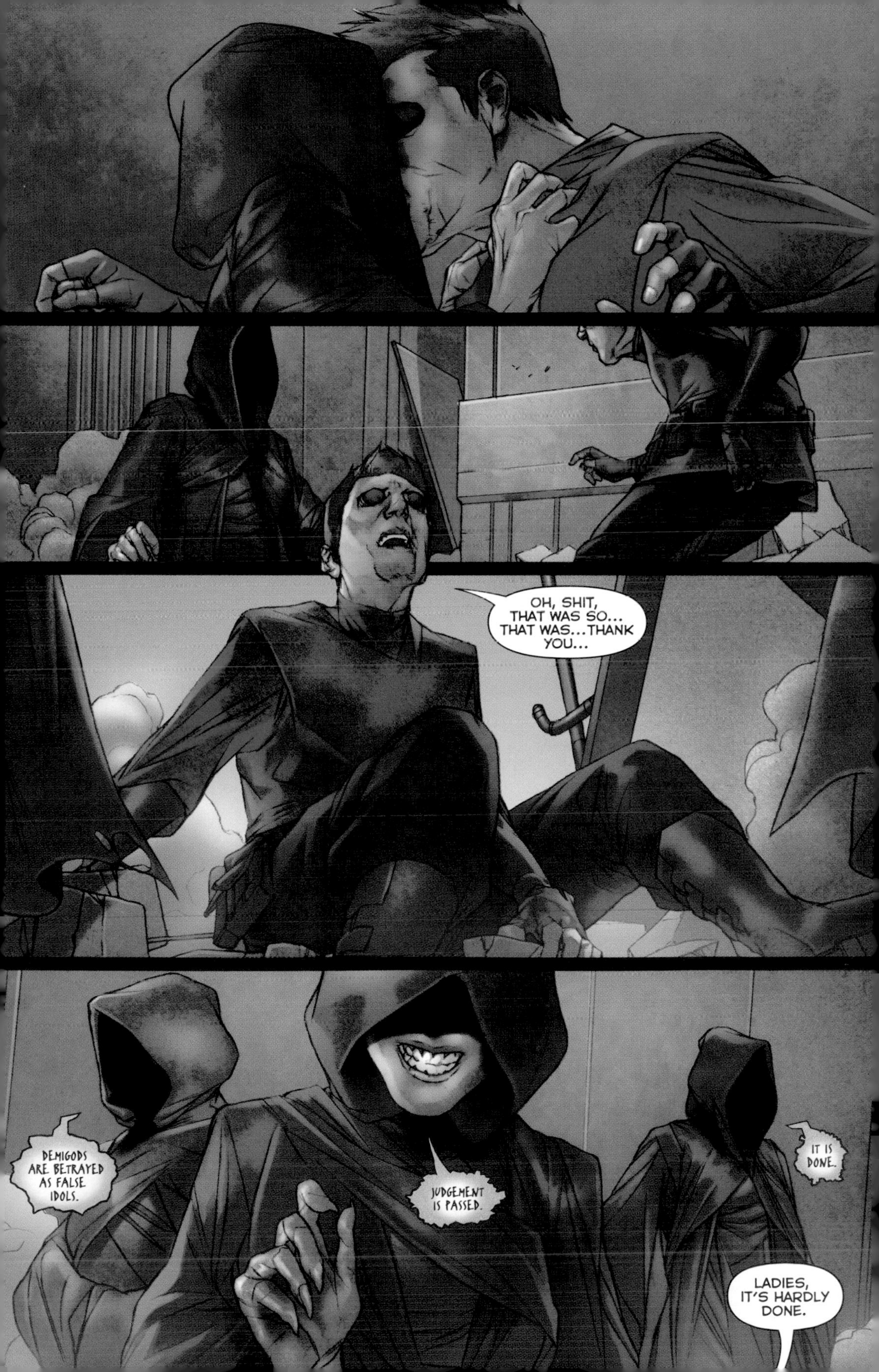
OH, SHIT, THAT WAS SO... THAT WAS...THANK YOU...
DEMIGODS ARE BETRAYED AS FALSE IDOLS.
JUDGEMENT IS PASSED.
IT IS DONE.
LADIES, IT'S HARDLY DONE.

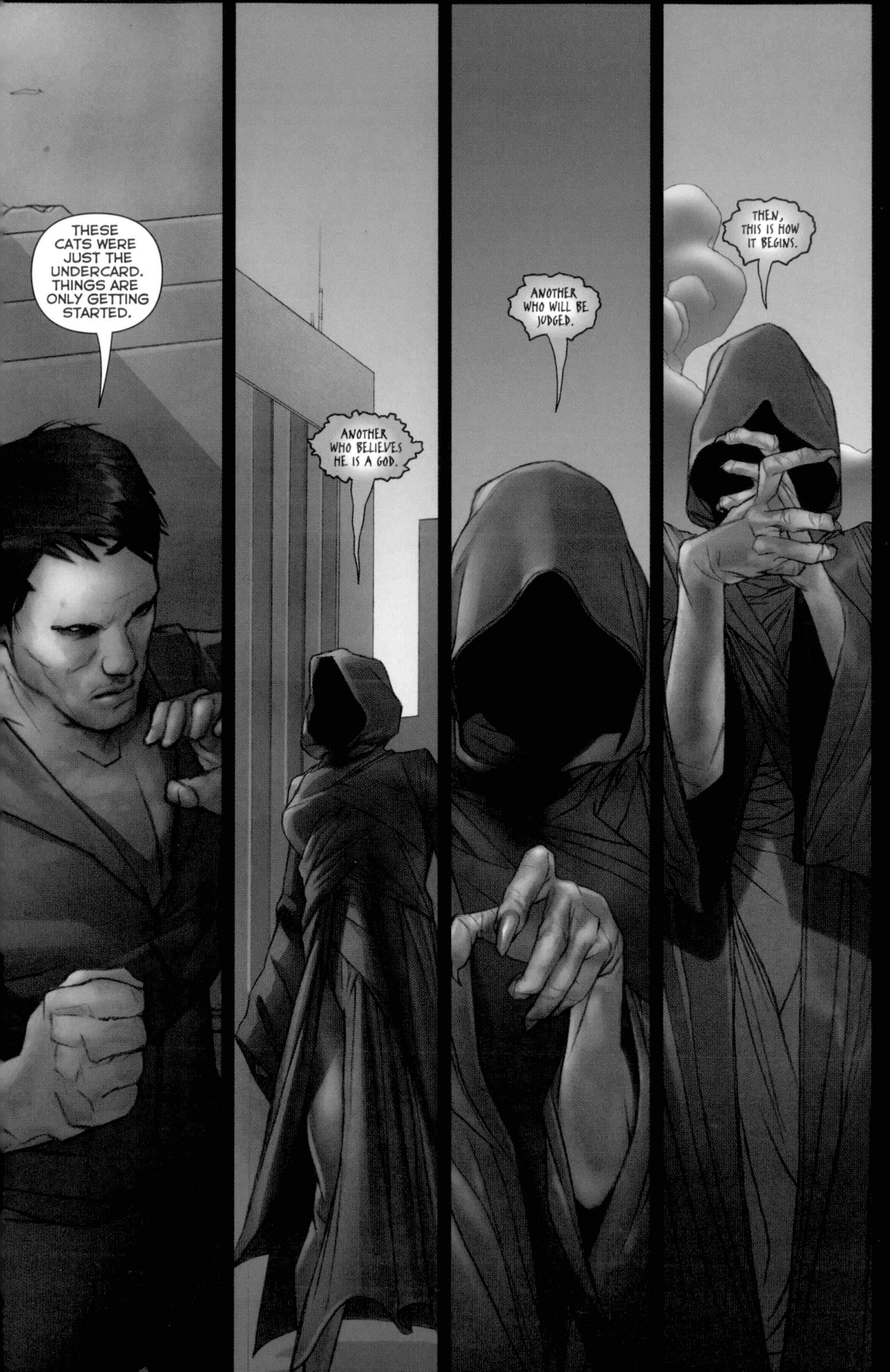
THESE CATS WERE JUST THE UNDERCARD. THINGS ARE ONLY GETTING STARTED.
ANOTHER WHO BELIEVES HE IS A GOD.
ANOTHER WHO WILL BE JUDGED.
THEN, THIS IS HOW IT BEGINS.

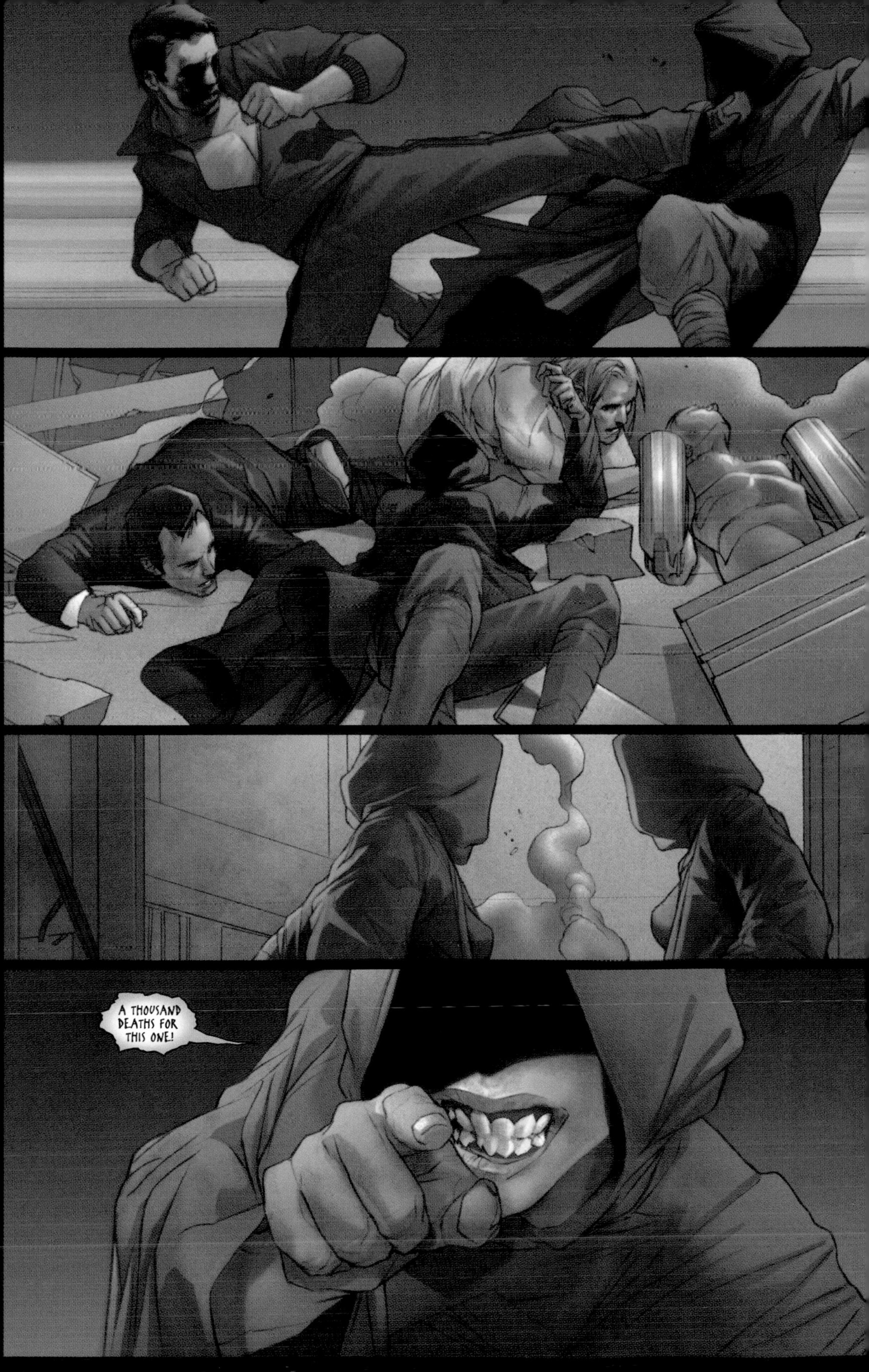
A THOUSAND DEATHS FOR THIS ONE!

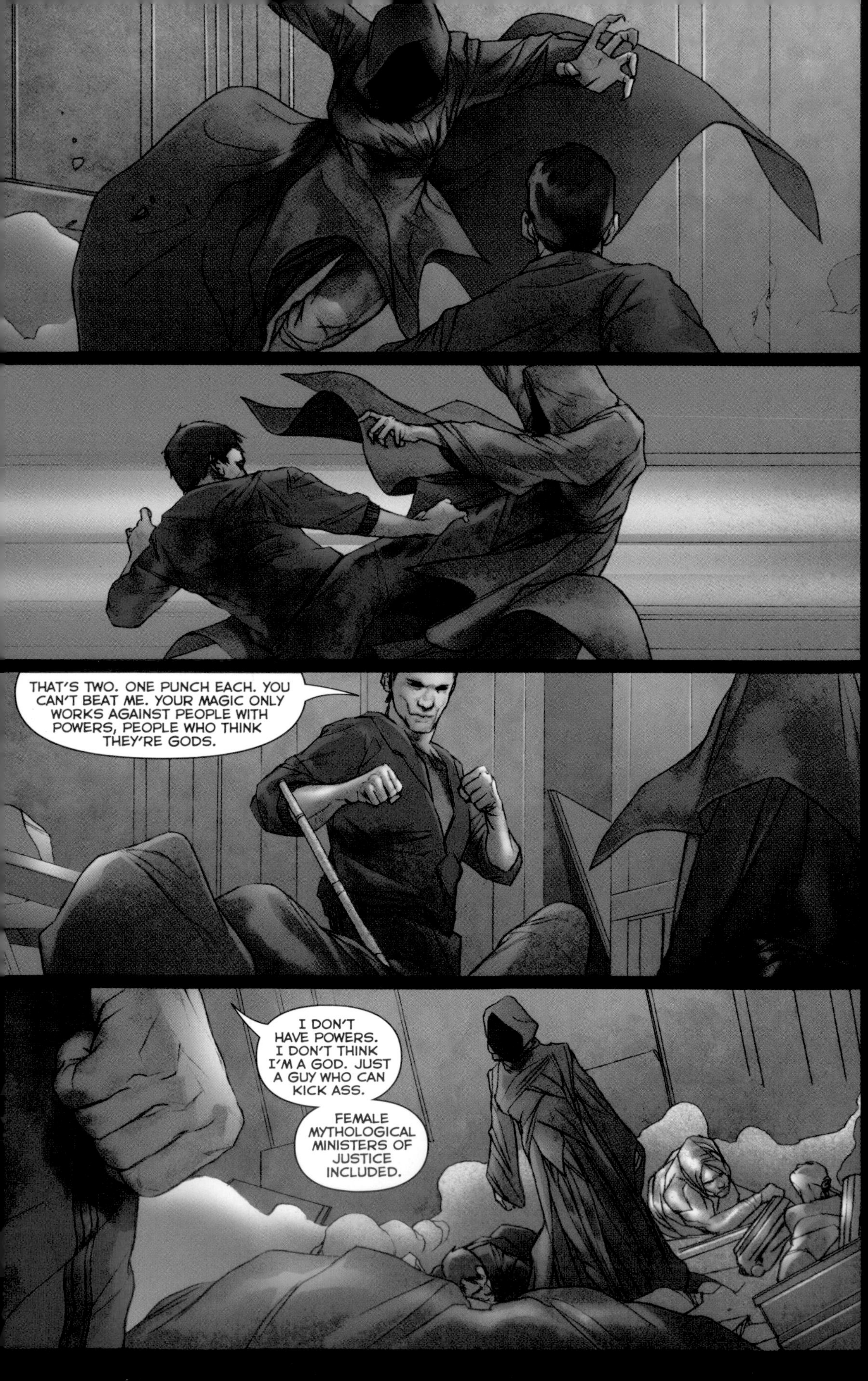
THAT'S TWO. ONE PUNCH EACH. YOU CAN'T BEAT ME. YOUR MAGIC ONLY WORKS AGAINST PEOPLE WITH POWERS, PEOPLE WHO THINK THEY'RE GODS.
I DON'T HAVE POWERS. I DON'T THINK I'M A GOD. JUST A GUY WHO CAN KICK ASS.
FEMALE MYTHOLOGICAL MINISTERS OF JUSTICE INCLUDED.

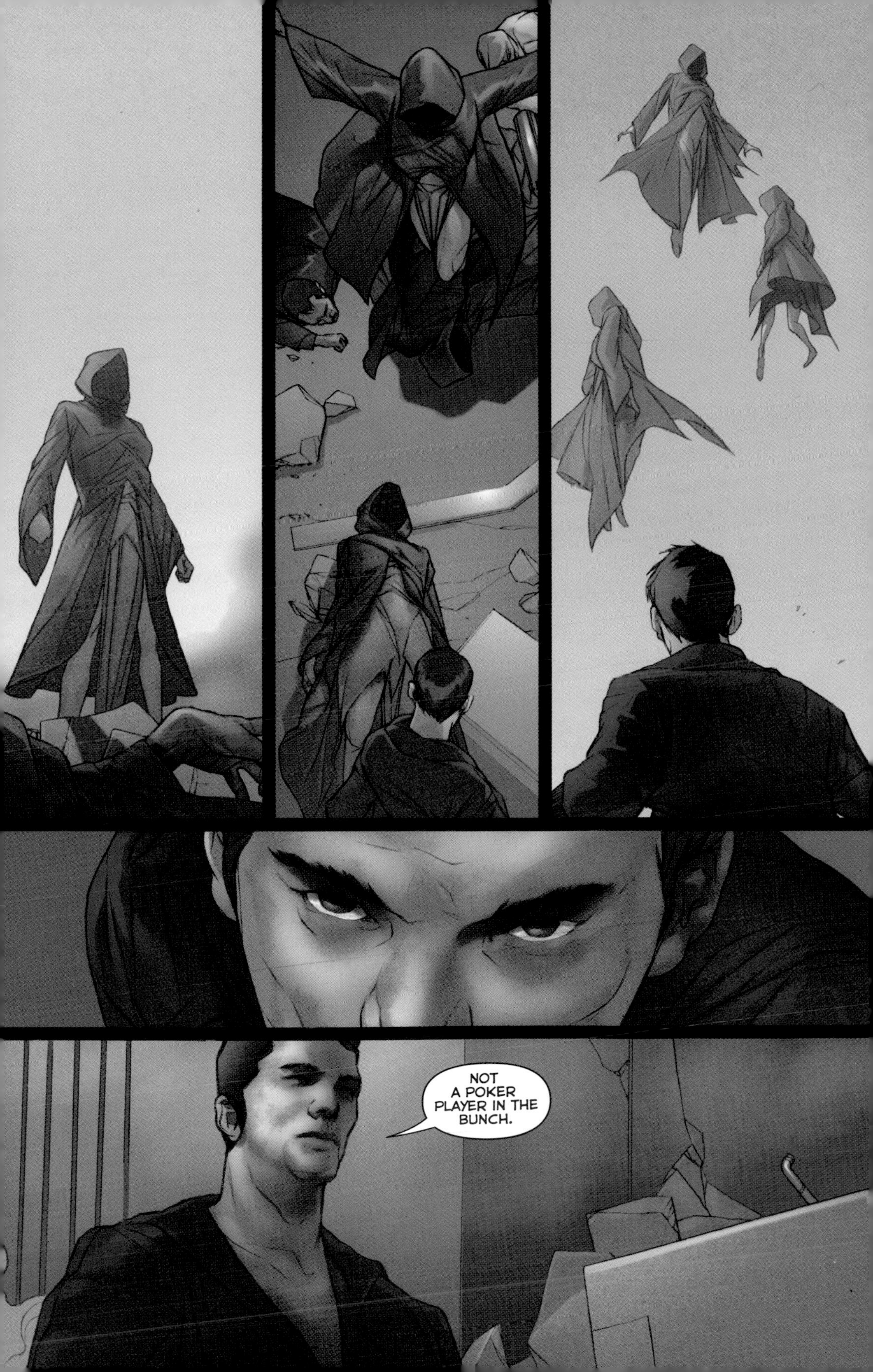
NOT A POKER PLAYER IN THE BUNCH.

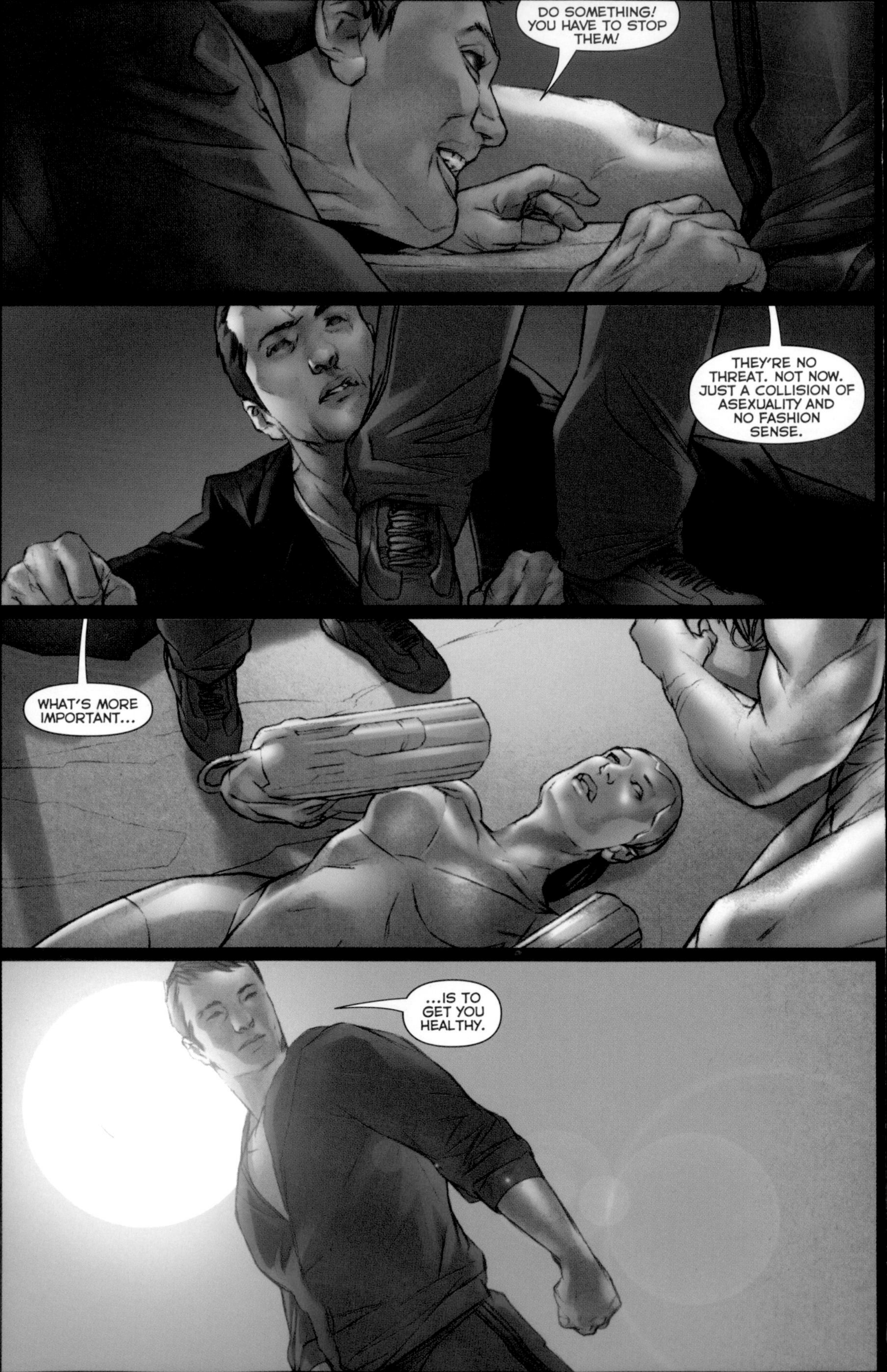
DO SOMETHING! YOU HAVE TO STOP THEM!
THEY'RE NO THREAT. NOT NOW. JUST A COLLISION OF ASEXUALITY AND NO FASHION SENSE.
WHAT'S MORE IMPORTANT...
...IS TO GET YOU HEALTHY.

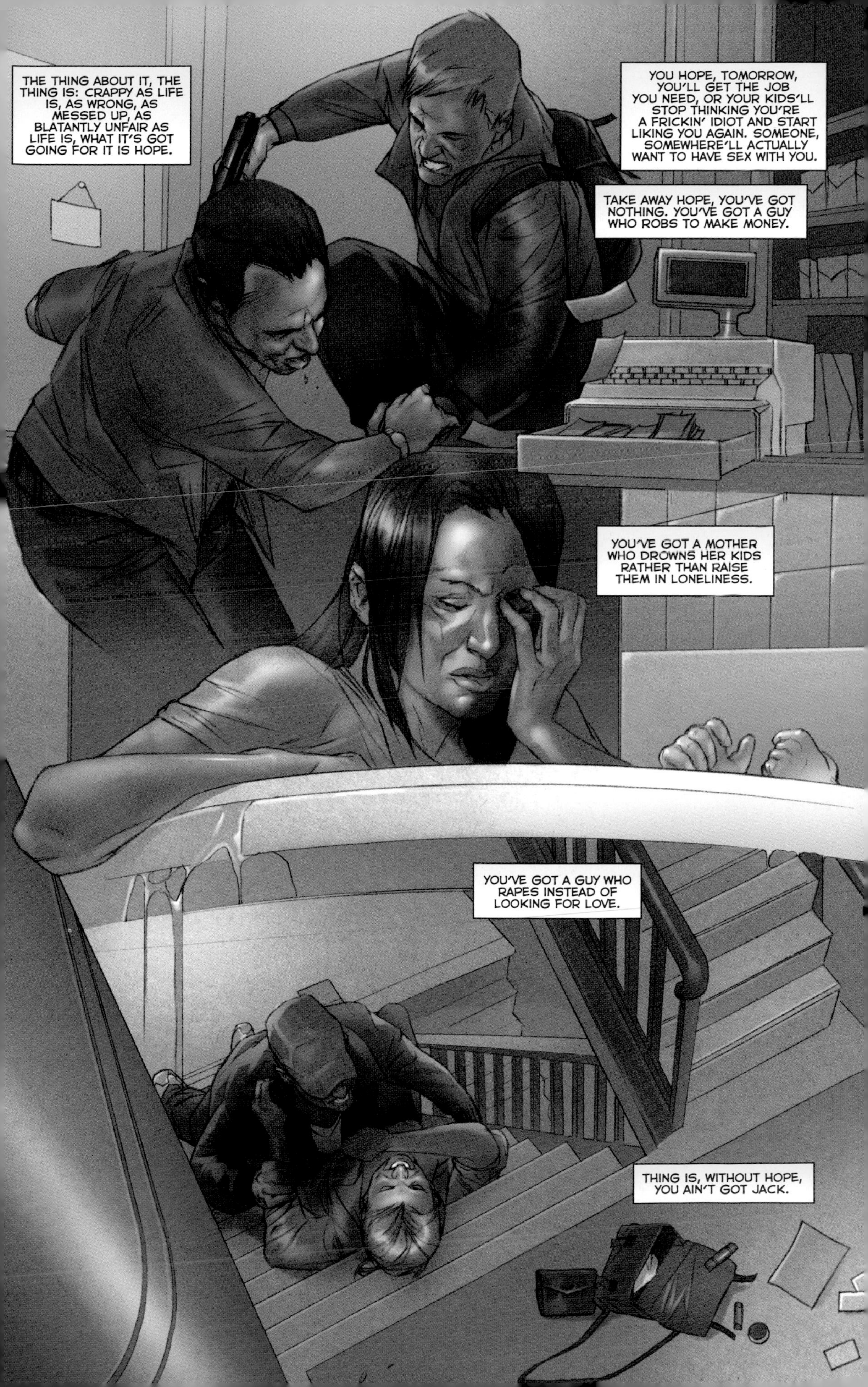
THE THING ABOUT IT, THE THING IS: CRAPPY AS LIFE IS, AS WRONG, AS MESSED UP, AS BLATANTLY UNFAIR AS LIFE IS, WHAT IT'S GOT GOING FOR IT IS HOPE.
YOU HOPE, TOMORROW, YOU'LL GET THE JOB YOU NEED, OR YOUR KIDS'LL STOP THINKING YOU'RE A FRICKIN' IDIOT AND START LIKING YOU AGAIN. SOMEONE, SOMEWHERE'LL ACTUALLY WANT TO HAVE SEX WITH YOU.
TAKE AWAY HOPE, YOU'VE GOT NOTHING. YOU'VE GOT A GUY WHO ROBS TO MAKE MONEY.
YOU'VE GOT A MOTHER WHO DROWNS HER KIDS RATHER THAN RAISE THEM IN LONELINESS.
YOU'VE GOT A GUY WHO RAPES INSTEAD OF LOOKING FOR LOVE.
THING IS, WITHOUT HOPE, YOU AIN'T GOT JACK.

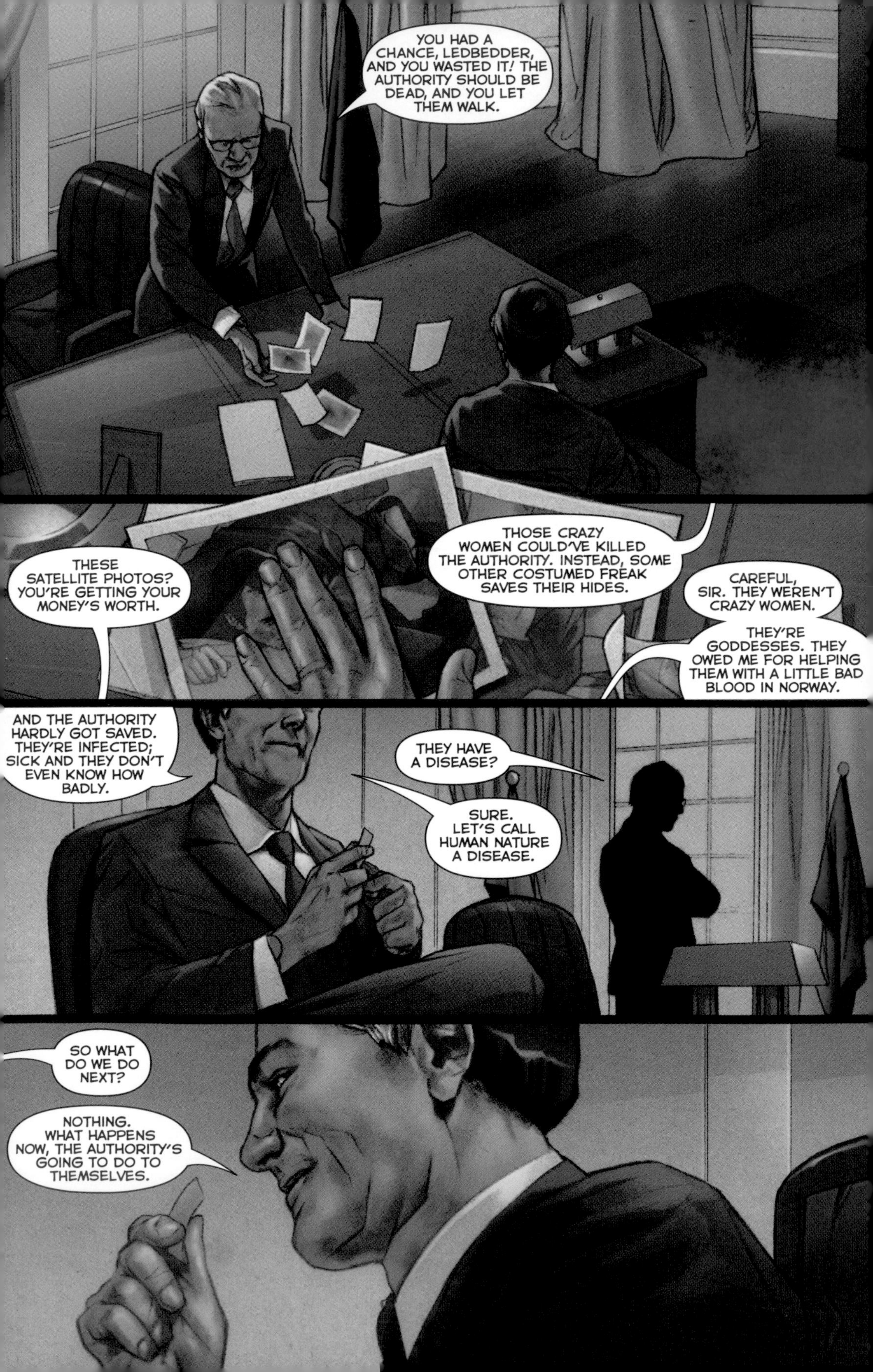
YOU HAD A CHANCE, LEDBEDDER, AND YOU WASTED IT! THE AUTHORITY SHOULD BE DEAD, AND YOU LET THEM WALK.
THESE SATELLITE PHOTOS? YOU'RE GETTING YOUR MONEY'S WORTH.
THOSE CRAZY WOMEN COULD'VE KILLED THE AUTHORITY. INSTEAD, SOME OTHER COSTUMED FREAK SAVES THEIR HIDES.
CAREFUL, SIR. THEY WEREN'T CRAZY WOMEN.
THEY'RE GODDESSES. THEY OWED ME FOR HELPING THEM WITH A LITTLE BAD BLOOD IN NORWAY.
AND THE AUTHORITY HARDLY GOT SAVED. THEY'RE INFECTED; SICK AND THEY DON'T EVEN KNOW HOW BADLY.
THEY HAVE A DISEASE?
SURE. LET'S CALL HUMAN NATURE A DISEASE.
SO WHAT DO WE DO NEXT?
NOTHING. WHAT HAPPENS NOW, THE AUTHORITY'S GOING TO DO TO THEMSELVES.

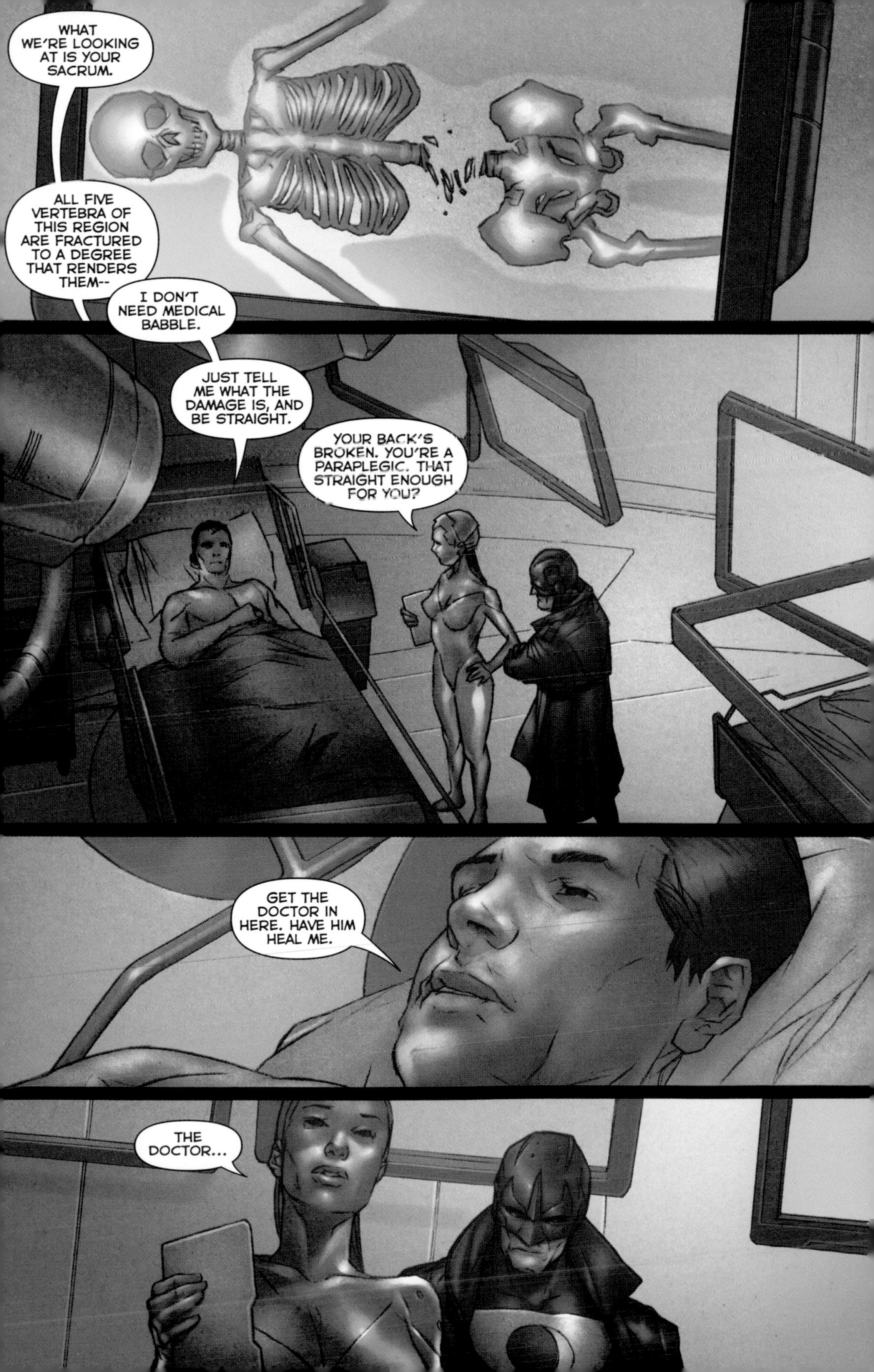
WHAT WE'RE LOOKING AT IS YOUR SACRUM.
ALL FIVE VERTEBRA OF THIS REGION ARE FRACTURED TO A DEGREE THAT RENDERS THEM--
I DON'T NEED MEDICAL BABBLE.
JUST TELL ME WHAT THE DAMAGE IS, AND BE STRAIGHT.
YOUR BACK'S BROKEN. YOU'RE A PARAPLEGIC. THAT STRAIGHT ENOUGH FOR YOU?
GET THE DOCTOR IN HERE. HAVE HIM HEAL ME.
THE DOCTOR...

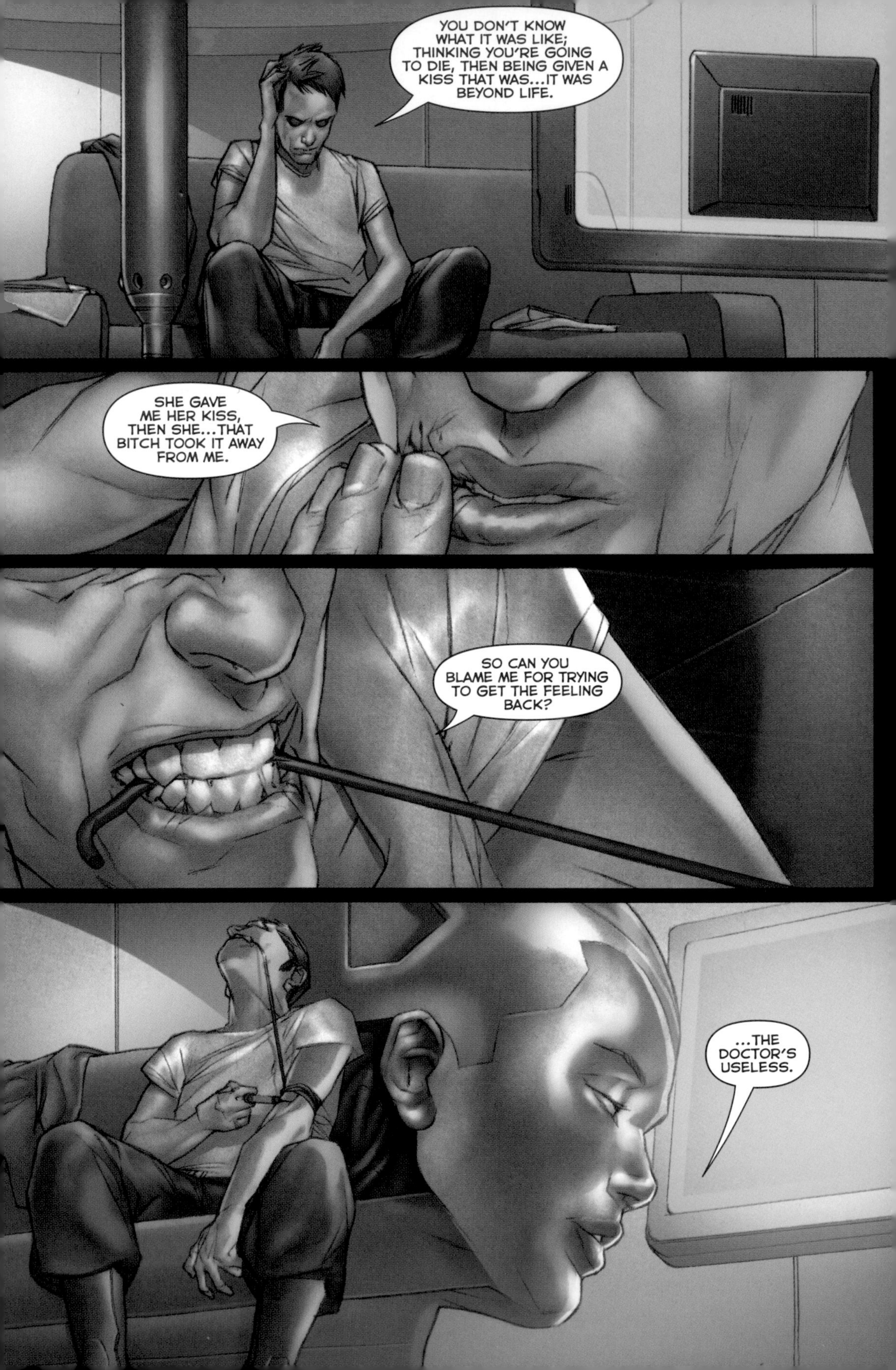
YOU DON'T KNOW WHAT IT WAS LIKE; THINKING YOU'RE GOING TO DIE, THEN BEING GIVEN A KISS THAT WAS...IT WAS BEYOND LIFE.
SHE GAVE ME HER KISS, THEN SHE...THAT BITCH TOOK IT AWAY FROM ME.
SO CAN YOU BLAME ME FOR TRYING TO GET THE FEELING BACK?
...THE DOCTOR'S USELESS.

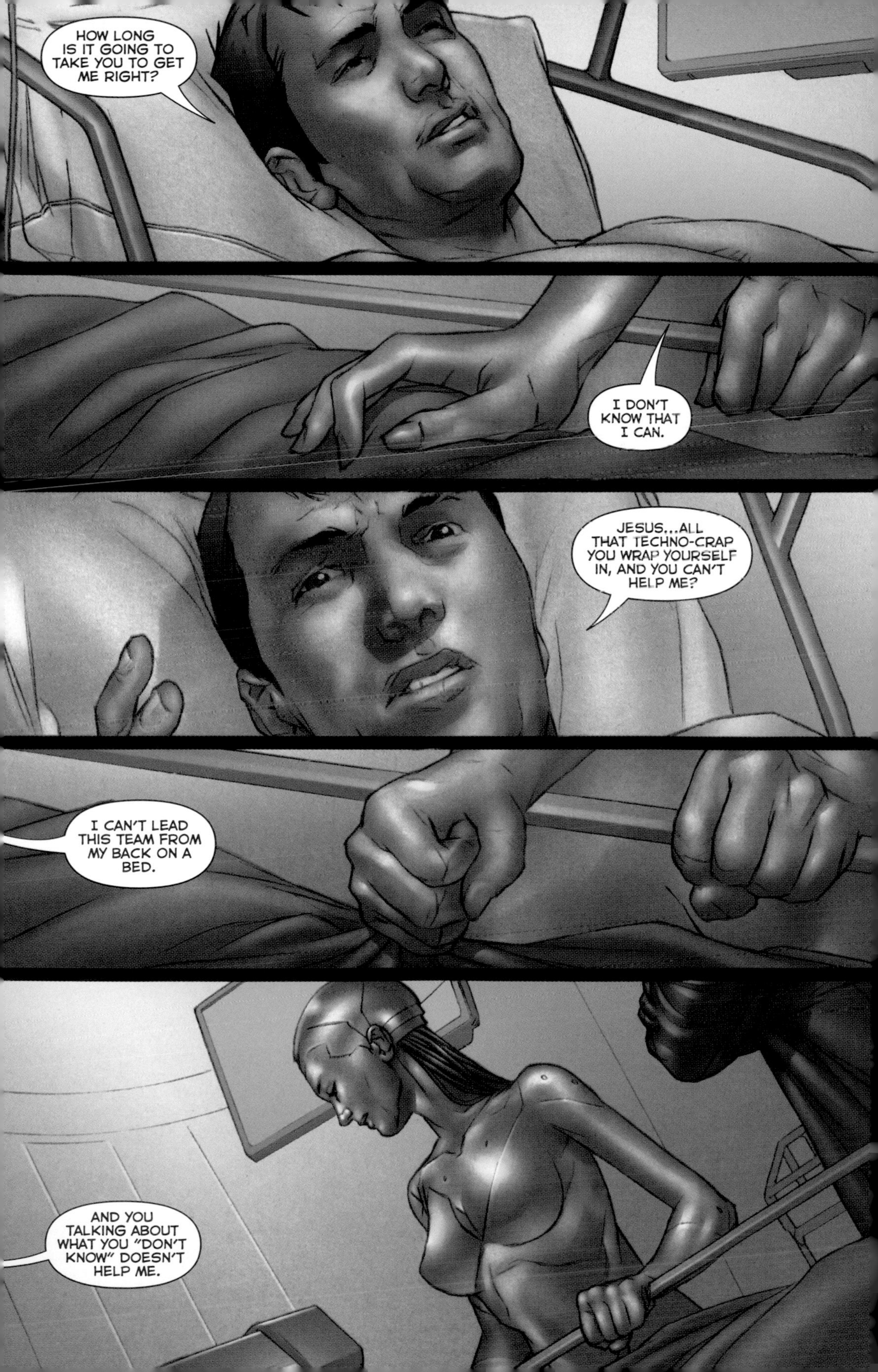

HOW LONG IS IT GOING TO TAKE YOU TO GET ME RIGHT?
I DON'T KNOW THAT I CAN.
JESUS...ALL THAT TECHNO-CRAP YOU WRAP YOURSELF IN, AND YOU CAN'T HELP ME?
I CAN'T LEAD THIS TEAM FROM MY BACK ON A BED.
AND YOU TALKING ABOUT WHAT YOU "DON'T KNOW" DOESN'T HELP ME.

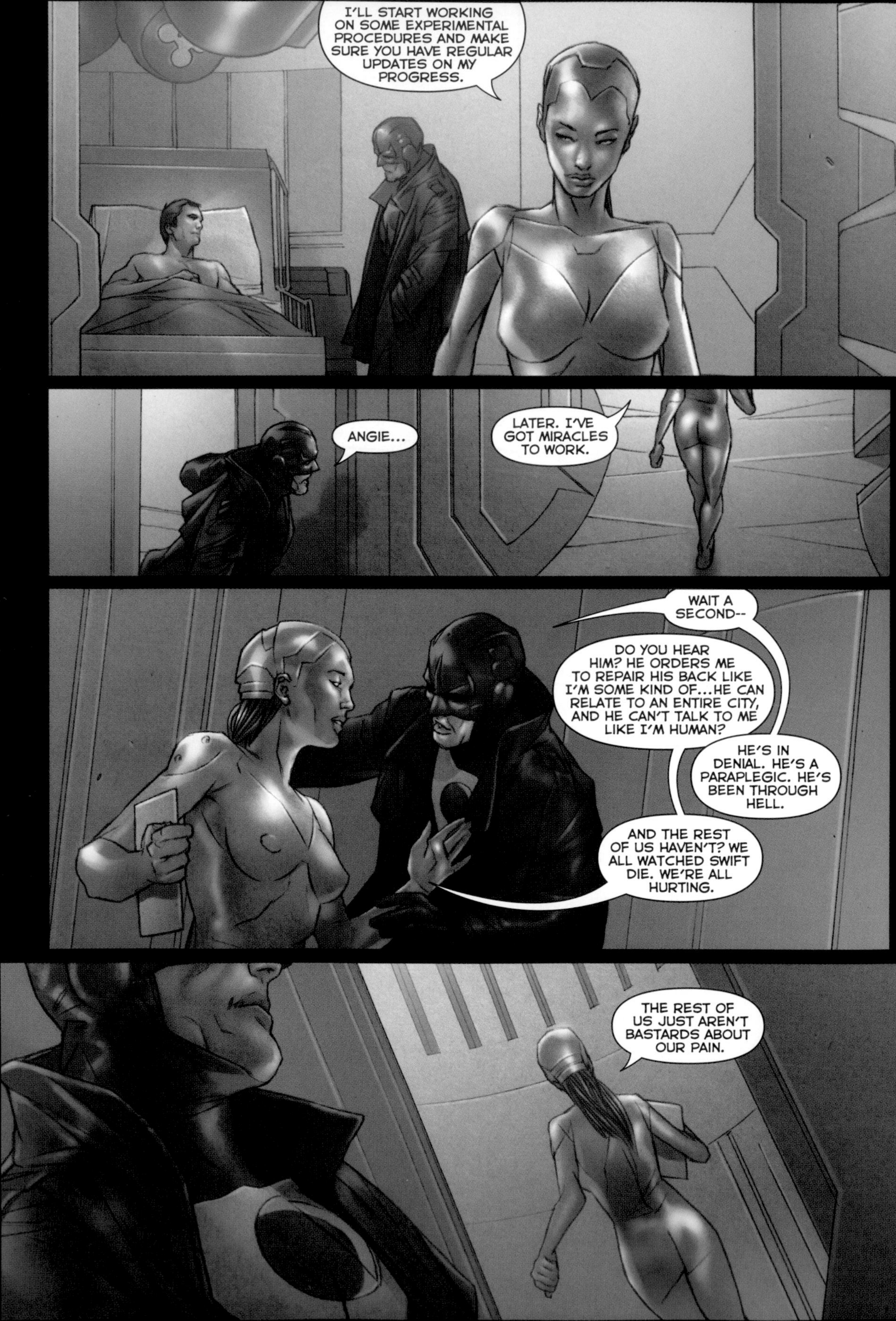
I'LL START WORKING ON SOME EXPERIMENTAL PROCEDURES AND MAKE SURE YOU HAVE REGULAR UPDATES ON MY PROGRESS.
ANGIE...
LATER. I'VE GOT MIRACLES TO WORK.
WAIT A SECOND--
DO YOU HEAR HIM? HE ORDERS ME TO REPAIR HIS BACK LIKE I'M SOME KIND OF...HE CAN RELATE TO AN ENTIRE CITY, AND HE CAN'T TALK TO ME LIKE I'M HUMAN?
HE'S IN DENIAL. HE'S A PARAPLEGIC. HE'S BEEN THROUGH HELL.
AND THE REST OF US HAVEN'T? WE ALL WATCHED SWIFT DIE. WE'RE ALL HURTING.
THE REST OF US JUST AREN'T BASTARDS ABOUT OUR PAIN.

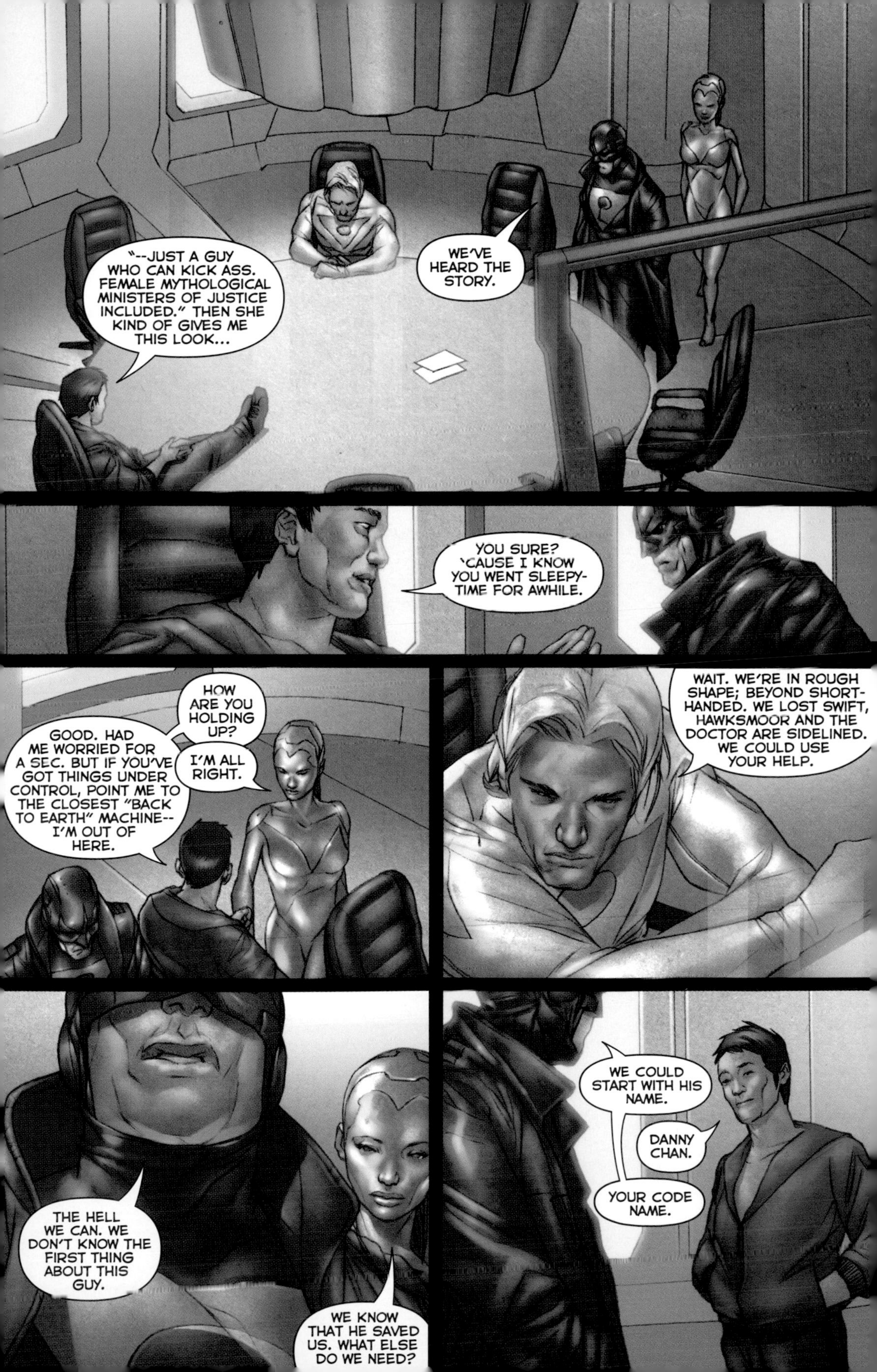
"--JUST A GUY WHO CAN KICK ASS. FEMALE MYTHOLOGICAL MINISTERS OF JUSTICE INCLUDED." THEN SHE KIND OF GIVES ME THIS LOOK...
WE'VE HEARD THE STORY.
YOU SURE? 'CAUSE I KNOW YOU WENT SLEEPY-TIME FOR AWHILE.
HOW ARE YOU HOLDING UP?
I'M ALL RIGHT.
GOOD. HAD ME WORRIED FOR A SEC. BUT IF YOU'VE GOT THINGS UNDER CONTROL, POINT ME TO THE CLOSEST "BACK TO EARTH" MACHINE-- I'M OUT OF HERE.
WAIT. WE'RE IN ROUGH SHAPE; BEYOND SHORT-HANDED. WE LOST SWIFT, HAWKSMOOR AND THE DOCTOR ARE SIDELINED. WE COULD USE YOUR HELP.
THE HELL WE CAN. WE DON'T KNOW THE FIRST THING ABOUT THIS GUY.
WE KNOW THAT HE SAVED US. WHAT ELSE DO WE NEED?
WE COULD START WITH HIS NAME.
DANNY CHAN.
YOUR CODE NAME.

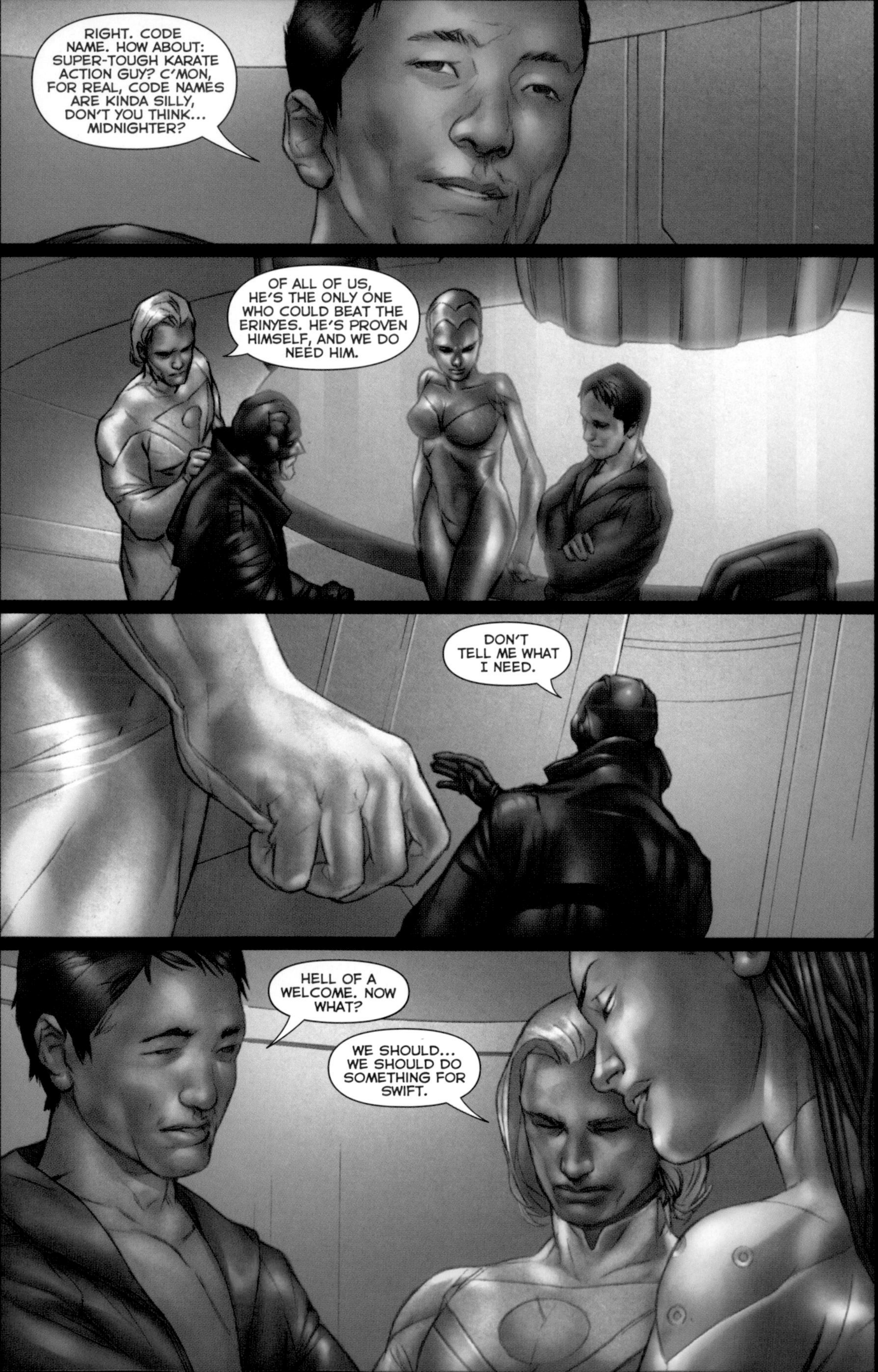
RIGHT. CODE NAME. HOW ABOUT: SUPER-TOUGH KARATE ACTION GUY? C'MON, FOR REAL, CODE NAMES ARE KINDA SILLY, DON'T YOU THINK... MIDNIGHTER?
OF ALL OF US, HE'S THE ONLY ONE WHO COULD BEAT THE ERINYES. HE'S PROVEN HIMSELF, AND WE DO NEED HIM.
DON'T TELL ME WHAT I NEED.
HELL OF A WELCOME. NOW WHAT?
WE SHOULD... WE SHOULD DO SOMETHING FOR SWIFT.

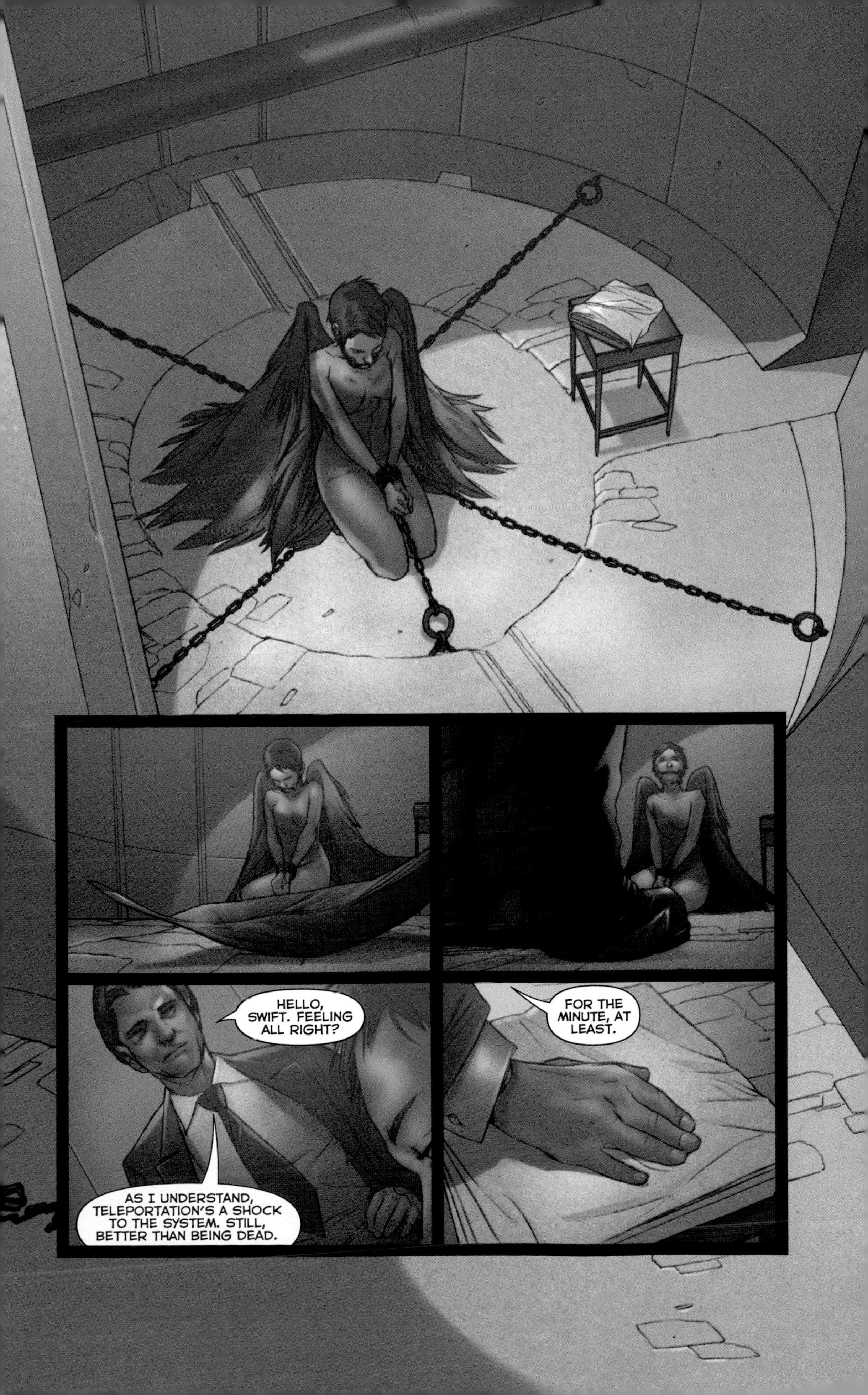
HELLO, SWIFT. FEELING ALL RIGHT?
AS I UNDERSTAND, TELEPORTATION'S A SHOCK TO THE SYSTEM. STILL, BETTER THAN BEING DEAD.
FOR THE MINUTE, AT LEAST.

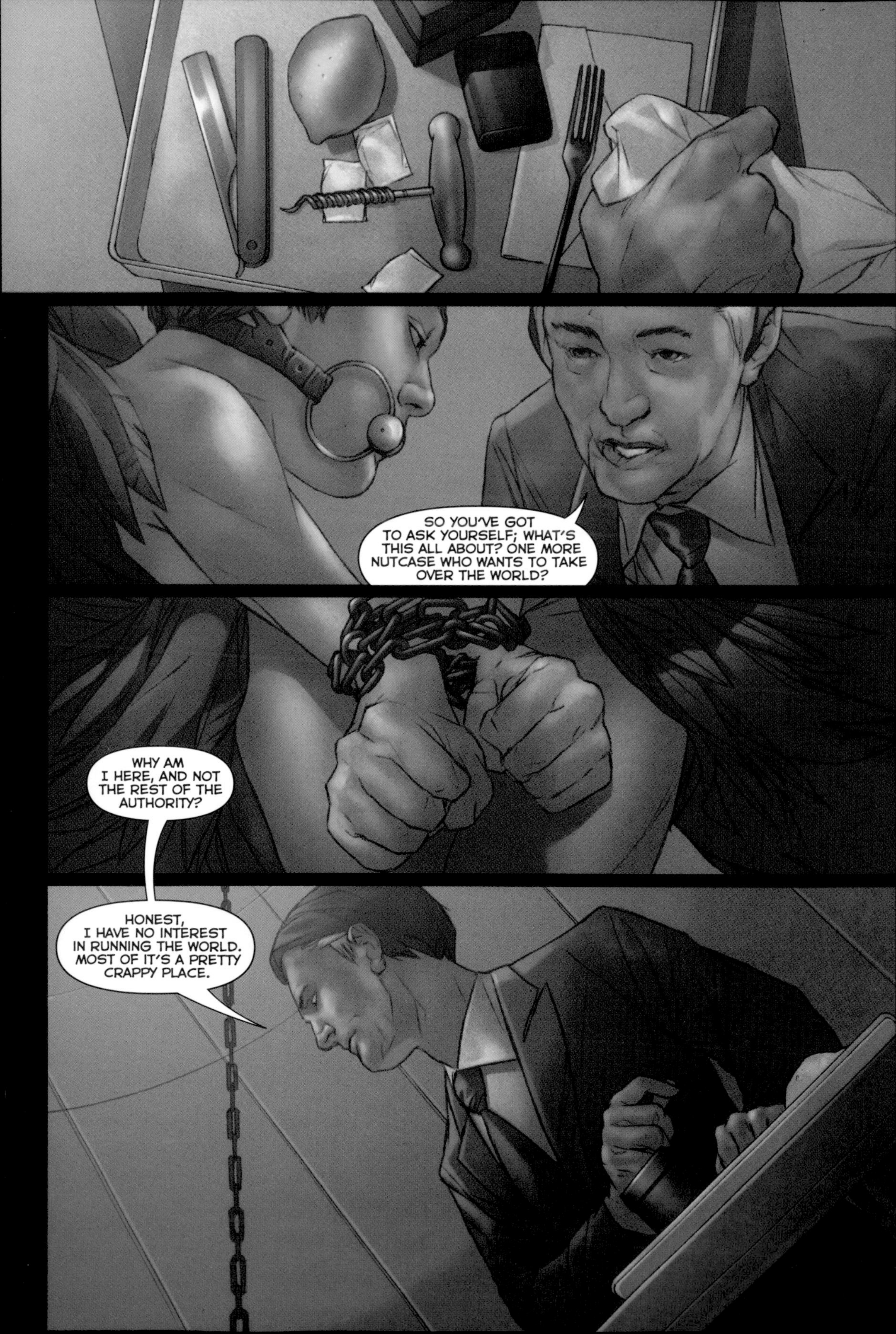
SO YOU'VE GOT TO ASK YOURSELF; WHAT'S THIS ALL ABOUT? ONE MORE NUTCASE WHO WANTS TO TAKE OVER THE WORLD?
WHY AM I HERE, AND NOT THE REST OF THE AUTHORITY?
HONEST, I HAVE NO INTEREST IN RUNNING THE WORLD. MOST OF IT'S A PRETTY CRAPPY PLACE.

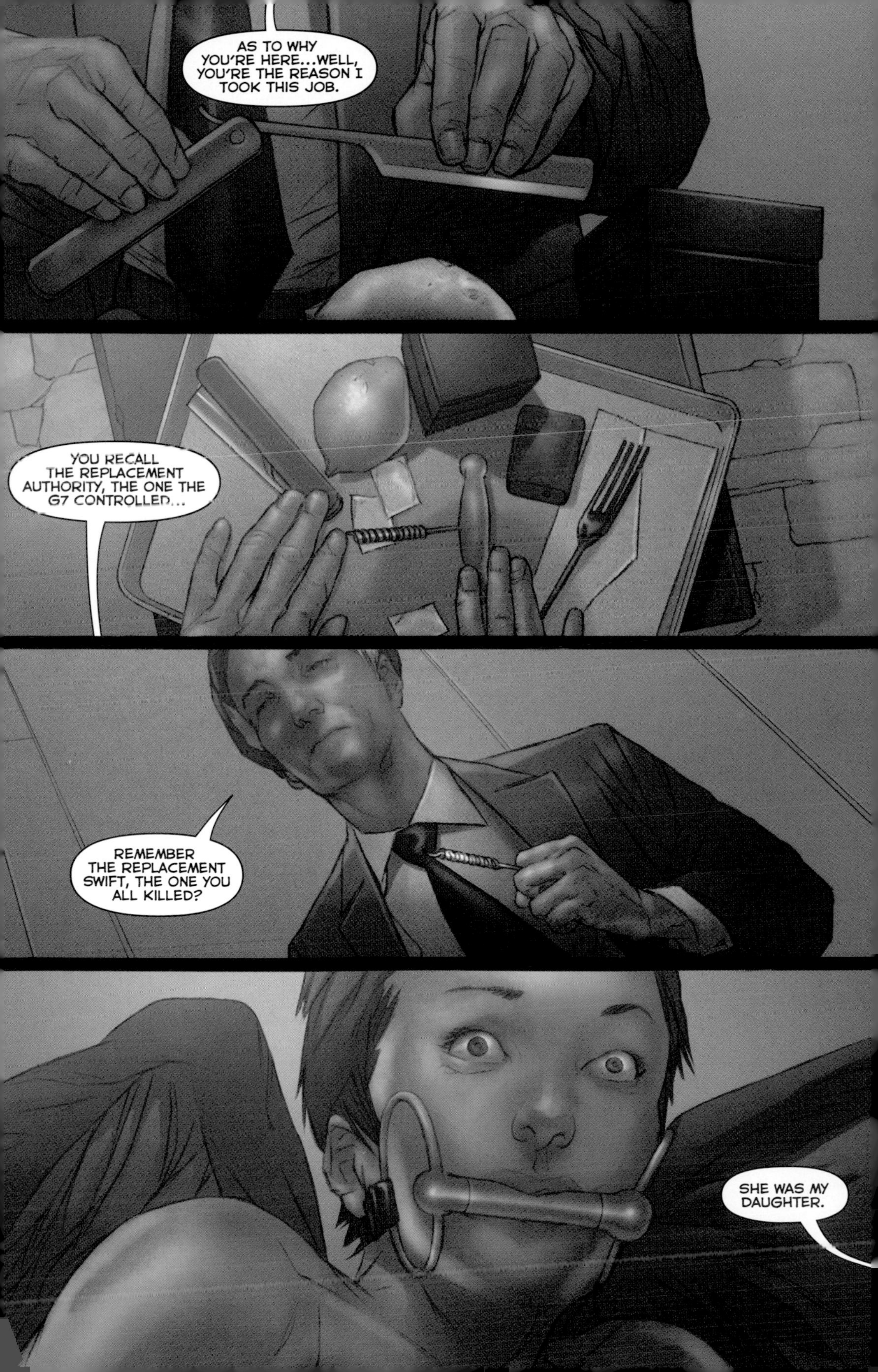
AS TO WHY YOU'RE HERE...WELL, YOU'RE THE REASON I TOOK THIS JOB.
YOU RECALL THE REPLACEMENT AUTHORITY, THE ONE THE G7 CONTROLLED...
REMEMBER THE REPLACEMENT SWIFT, THE ONE YOU ALL KILLED?
SHE WAS MY DAUGHTER.

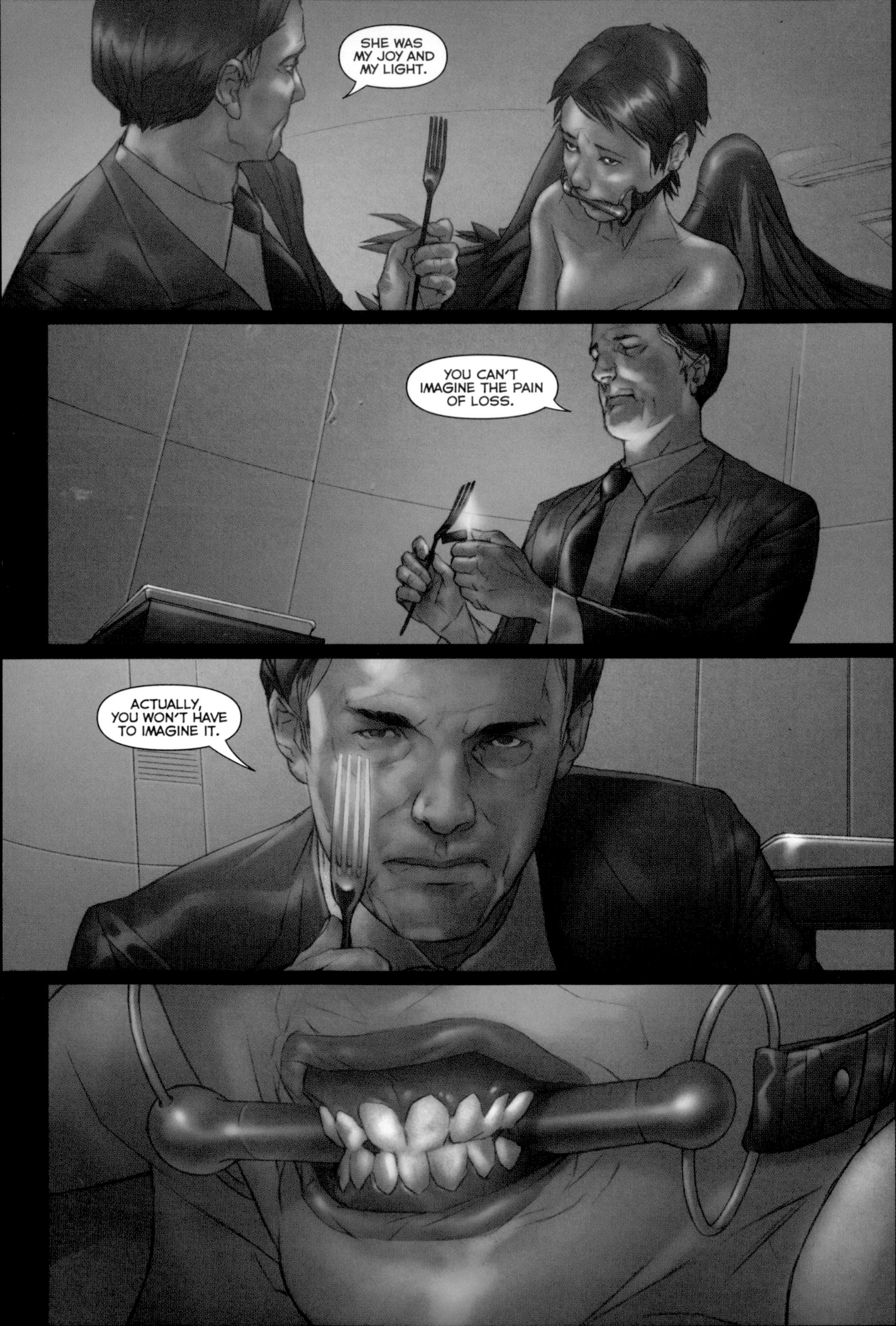
SHE WAS MY JOY AND MY LIGHT.
YOU CAN'T IMAGINE THE PAIN OF LOSS.
ACTUALLY, YOU WON'T HAVE TO IMAGINE IT.

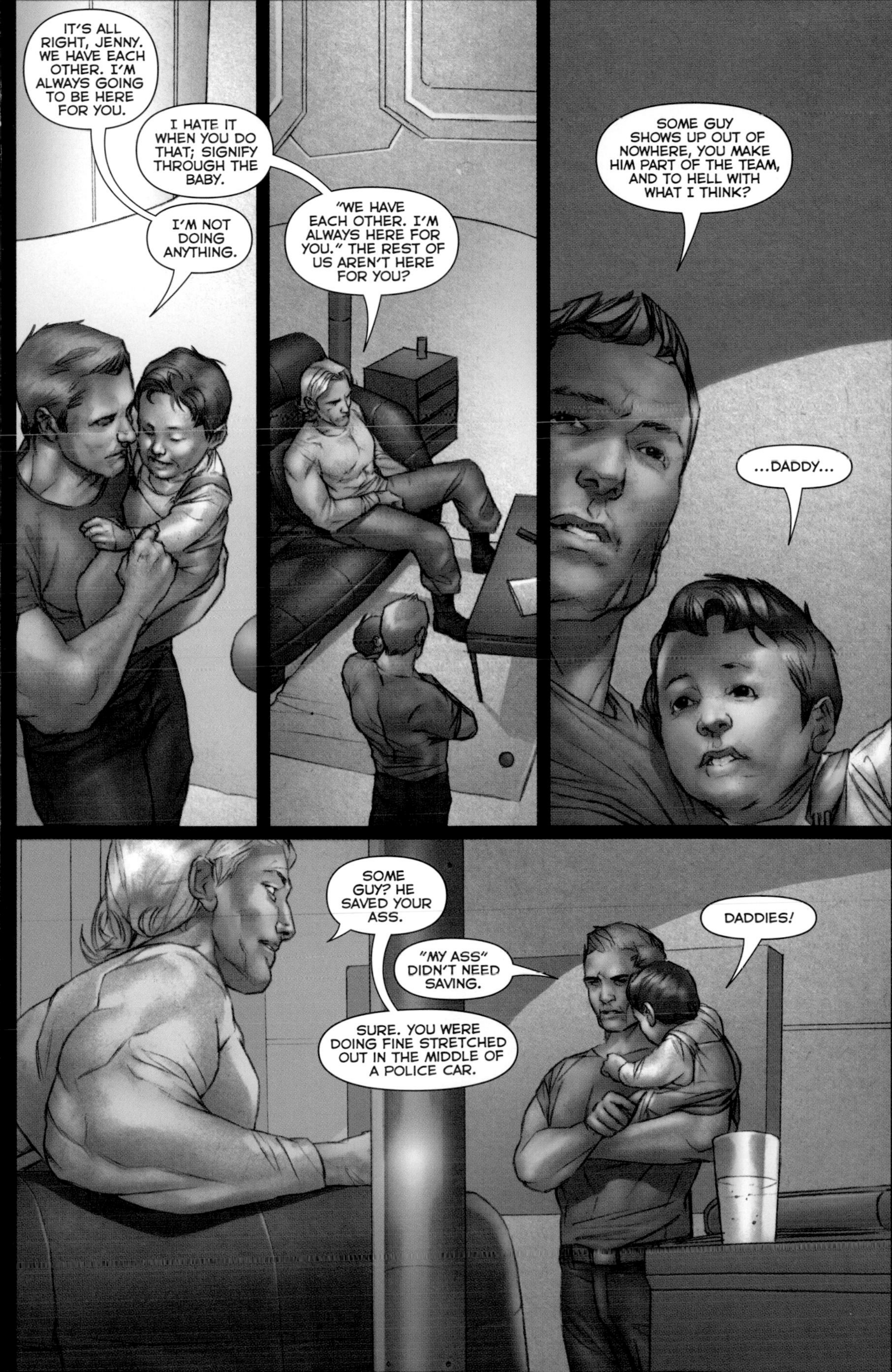
IT'S ALL RIGHT, JENNY. WE HAVE EACH OTHER. I'M ALWAYS GOING TO BE HERE FOR YOU.
I HATE IT WHEN YOU DO THAT; SIGNIFY THROUGH THE BABY.
I'M NOT DOING ANYTHING.
"WE HAVE EACH OTHER. I'M ALWAYS HERE FOR YOU." THE REST OF US AREN'T HERE FOR YOU?
SOME GUY SHOWS UP OUT OF NOWHERE, YOU MAKE HIM PART OF THE TEAM, AND TO HELL WITH WHAT I THINK?
...DADDY...
SOME GUY? HE SAVED YOUR ASS.
"MY ASS" DIDN'T NEED SAVING.
SURE. YOU WERE DOING FINE STRETCHED OUT IN THE MIDDLE OF A POLICE CAR.
DADDIES!

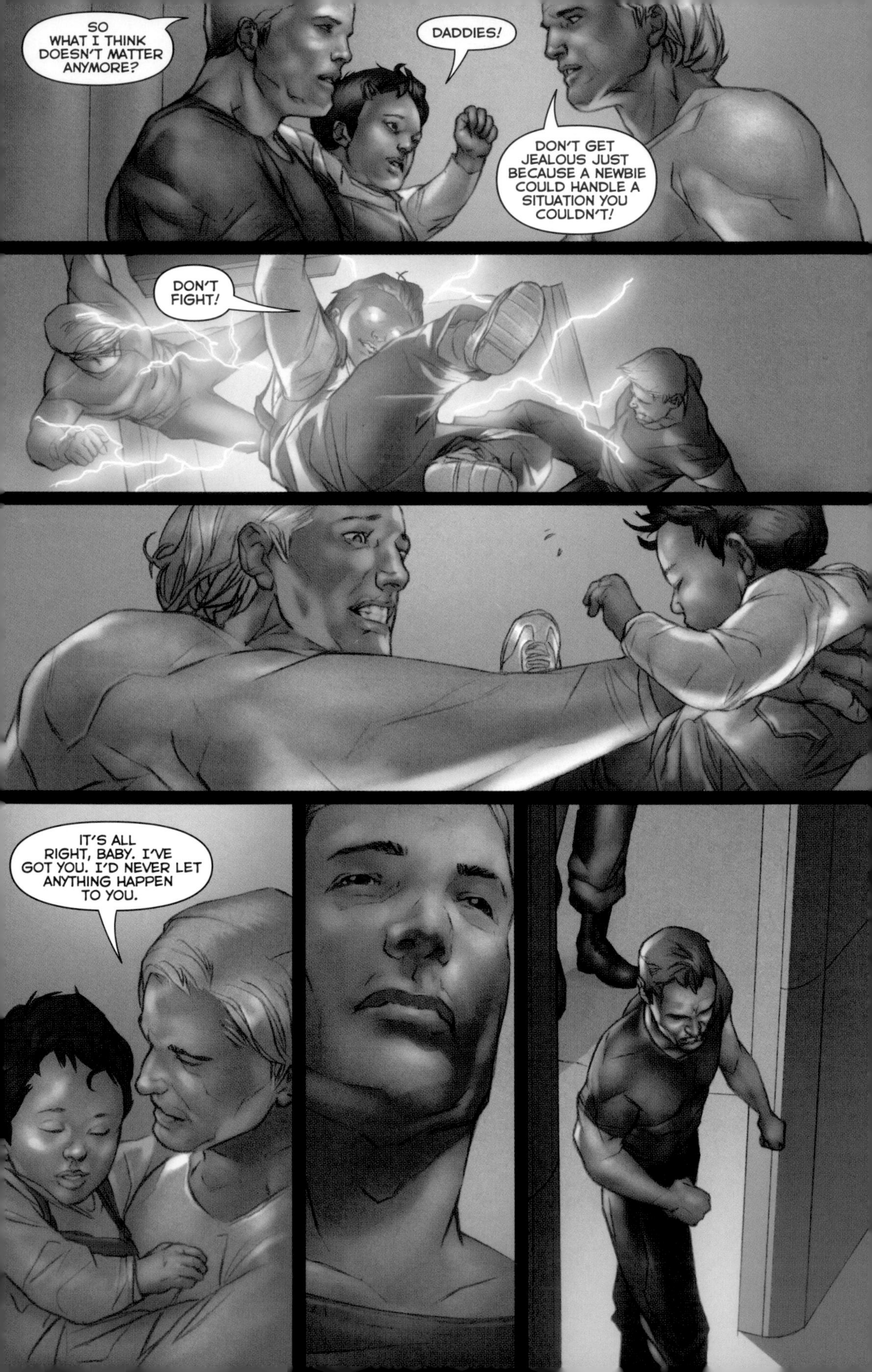
SO WHAT I THINK DOESN'T MATTER ANYMORE?
DADDIES!
DON'T GET JEALOUS JUST BECAUSE A NEWBIE COULD HANDLE A SITUATION YOU COULDN'T!
DON'T FIGHT!
IT'S ALL RIGHT, BABY. I'VE GOT YOU. I'D NEVER LET ANYTHING HAPPEN TO YOU.

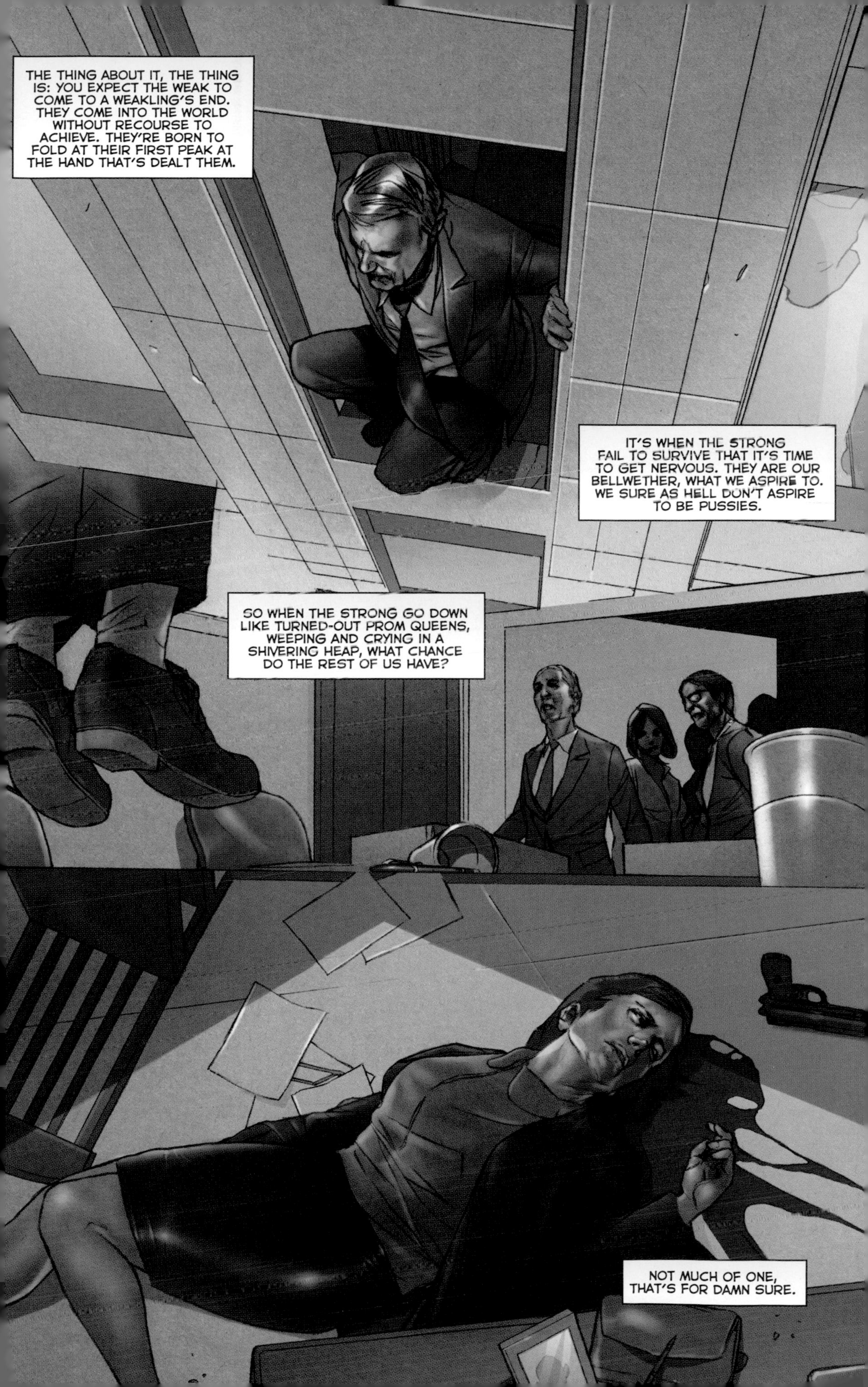
THE THING ABOUT IT, THE THING IS: YOU EXPECT THE WEAK TO COME TO A WEAKLING'S END. THEY COME INTO THE WORLD WITHOUT RECOURSE TO ACHIEVE. THEY'RE BORN TO FOLD AT THEIR FIRST PEAK AT THE HAND THAT'S DEALT THEM.
IT'S WHEN THE STRONG FAIL TO SURVIVE THAT IT'S TIME TO GET NERVOUS. THEY ARE OUR BELLWETHER, WHAT WE ASPIRE TO. WE SURE AS HELL DON'T ASPIRE TO BE PUSSIES.
SO WHEN THE STRONG GO DOWN LIKE TURNED-OUT PROM QUEENS, WEEPING AND CRYING IN A SHIVERING HEAP, WHAT CHANCE DO THE REST OF US HAVE?
NOT MUCH OF ONE, THAT'S FOR DAMN SURE.

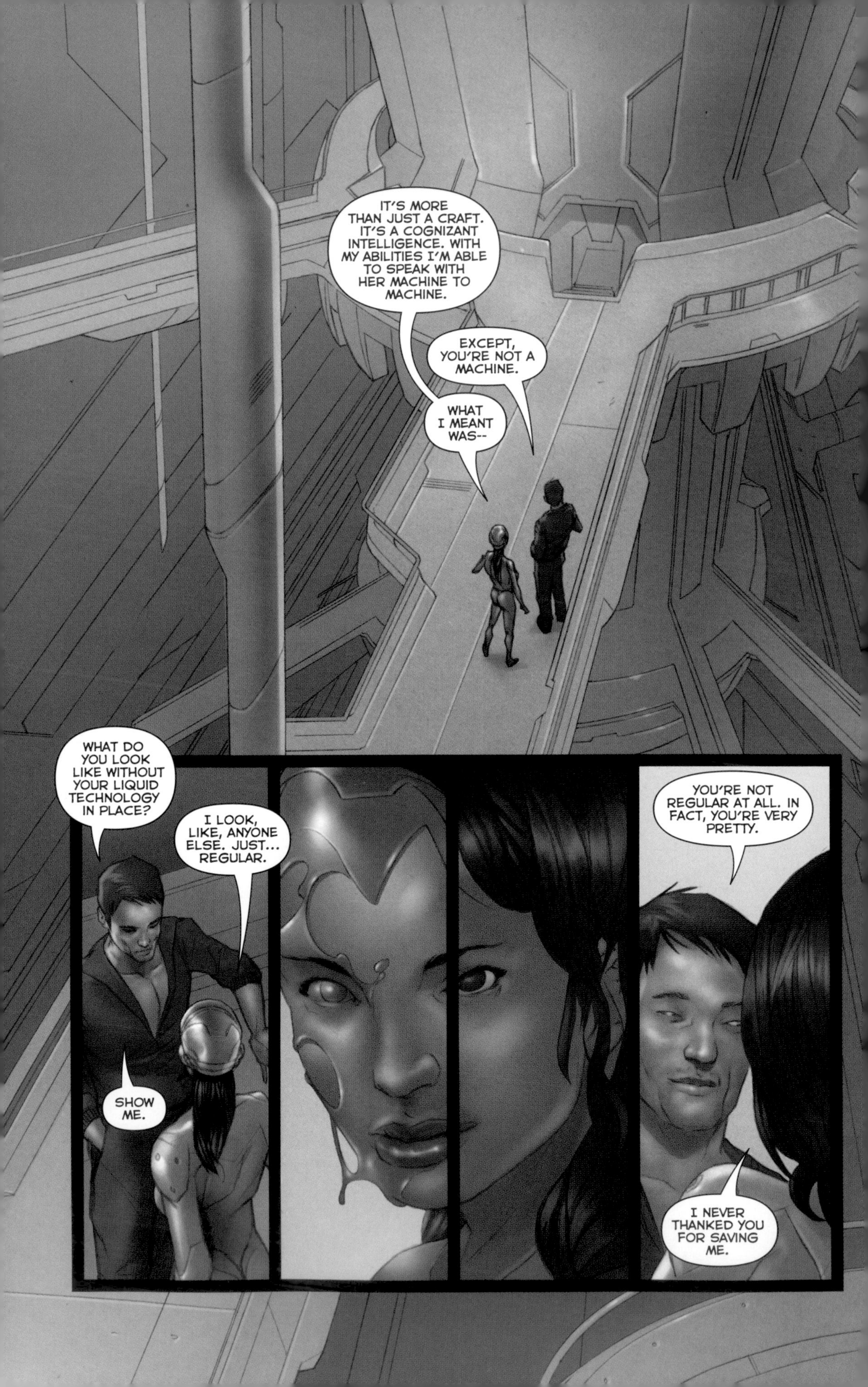
IT'S MORE THAN JUST A CRAFT. IT'S A COGNIZANT INTELLIGENCE. WITH MY ABILITIES I'M ABLE TO SPEAK WITH HER MACHINE TO MACHINE.
EXCEPT, YOU'RE NOT A MACHINE.
WHAT I MEANT WAS--
WHAT DO YOU LOOK LIKE WITHOUT YOUR LIQUID TECHNOLOGY IN PLACE?
I LOOK, LIKE, ANYONE ELSE. JUST... REGULAR.
SHOW ME.
YOU'RE NOT REGULAR AT ALL. IN FACT, YOU'RE VERY PRETTY.
I NEVER THANKED YOU FOR SAVING ME.

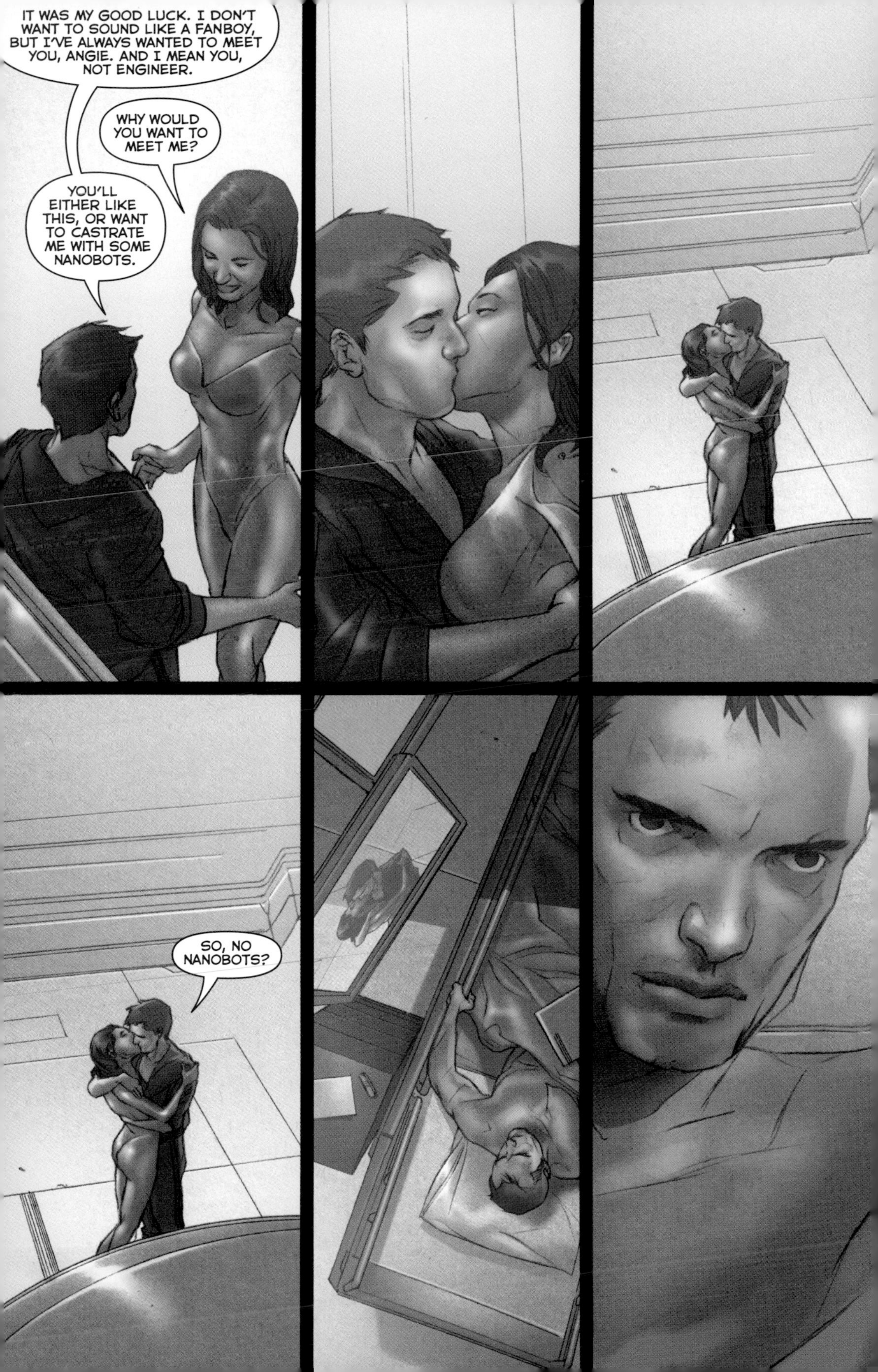
IT WAS MY GOOD LUCK. I DON'T WANT TO SOUND LIKE A FANBOY, BUT I'VE ALWAYS WANTED TO MEET YOU, ANGIE. AND I MEAN YOU, NOT ENGINEER.
WHY WOULD YOU WANT TO MEET ME?
YOU'LL EITHER LIKE THIS, OR WANT TO CASTRATE ME WITH SOME NANOBOTS.
SO, NO NANOBOTS?

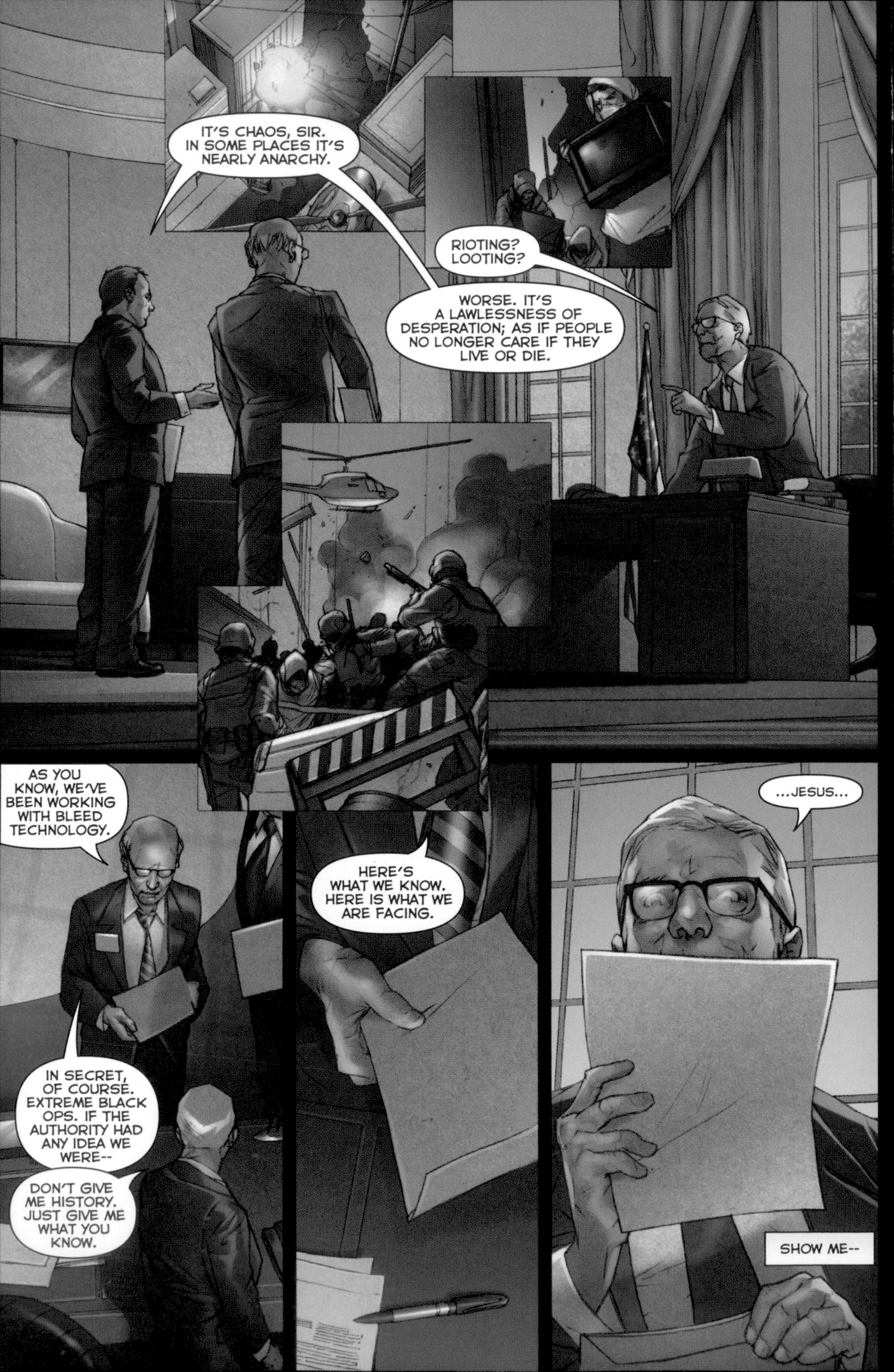
IT'S CHAOS, SIR. IN SOME PLACES IT'S NEARLY ANARCHY.
RIOTING? LOOTING?
WORSE. IT'S A LAWLESSNESS OF DESPERATION; AS IF PEOPLE NO LONGER CARE IF THEY LIVE OR DIE.
AS YOU KNOW, WE'VE BEEN WORKING WITH BLEED TECHNOLOGY.
IN SECRET, OF COURSE. EXTREME BLACK OPS. IF THE AUTHORITY HAD ANY IDEA WE WERE--
DON'T GIVE ME HISTORY. JUST GIVE ME WHAT YOU KNOW.
HERE'S WHAT WE KNOW. HERE IS WHAT WE ARE FACING.
...JESUS...
SHOW ME--

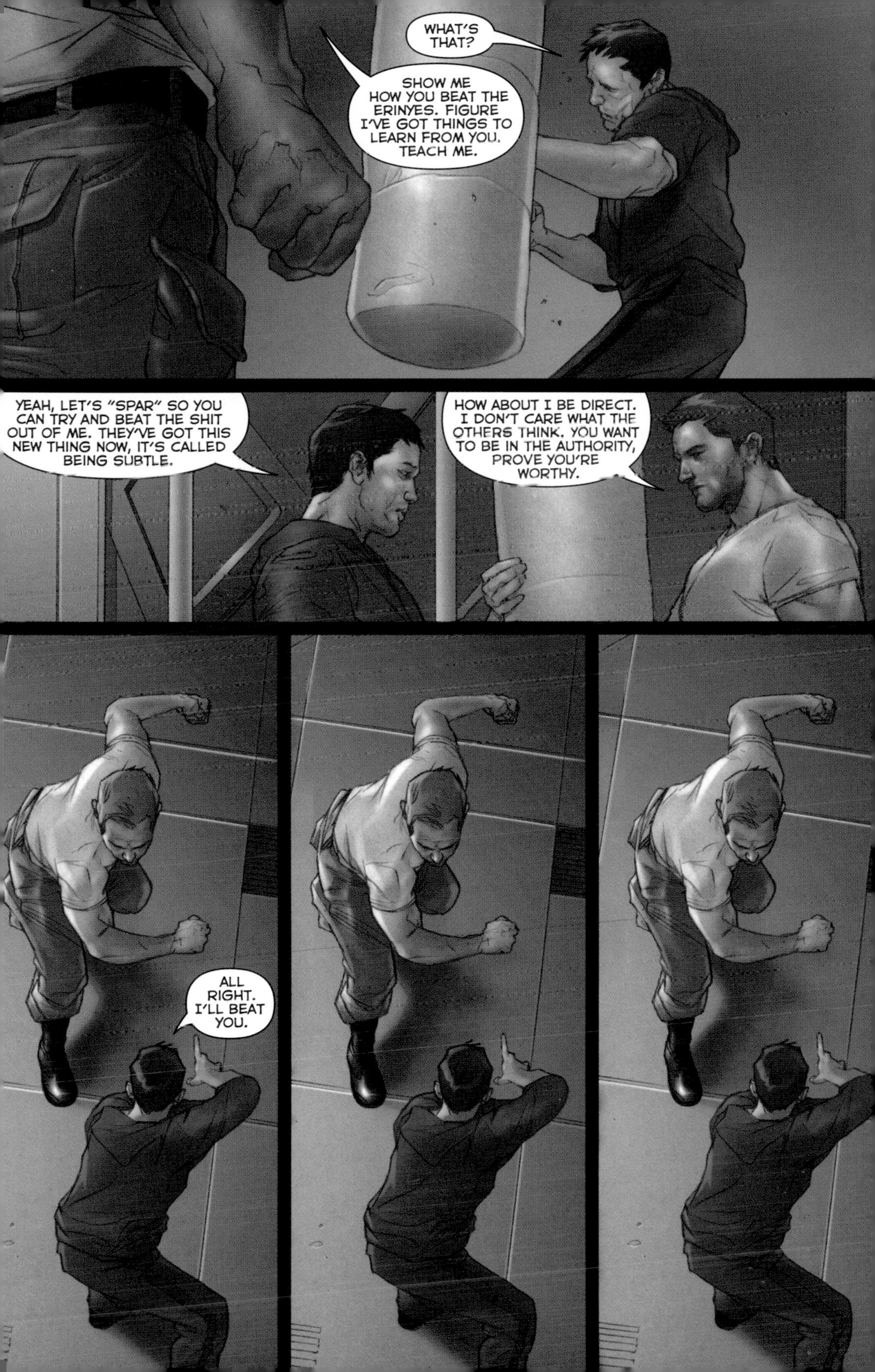
WHAT'S THAT?
SHOW ME HOW YOU BEAT THE ERINYES. FIGURE I'VE GOT THINGS TO LEARN FROM YOU. TEACH ME.
YEAH, LET'S "SPAR" SO YOU CAN TRY AND BEAT THE SHIT OUT OF ME. THEY'VE GOT THIS NEW THING NOW, IT'S CALLED BEING SUBTLE.
HOW ABOUT I BE DIRECT. I DON'T CARE WHAT THE OTHERS THINK. YOU WANT TO BE IN THE AUTHORITY, PROVE YOU'RE WORTHY.
ALL RIGHT. I'LL BEAT YOU.

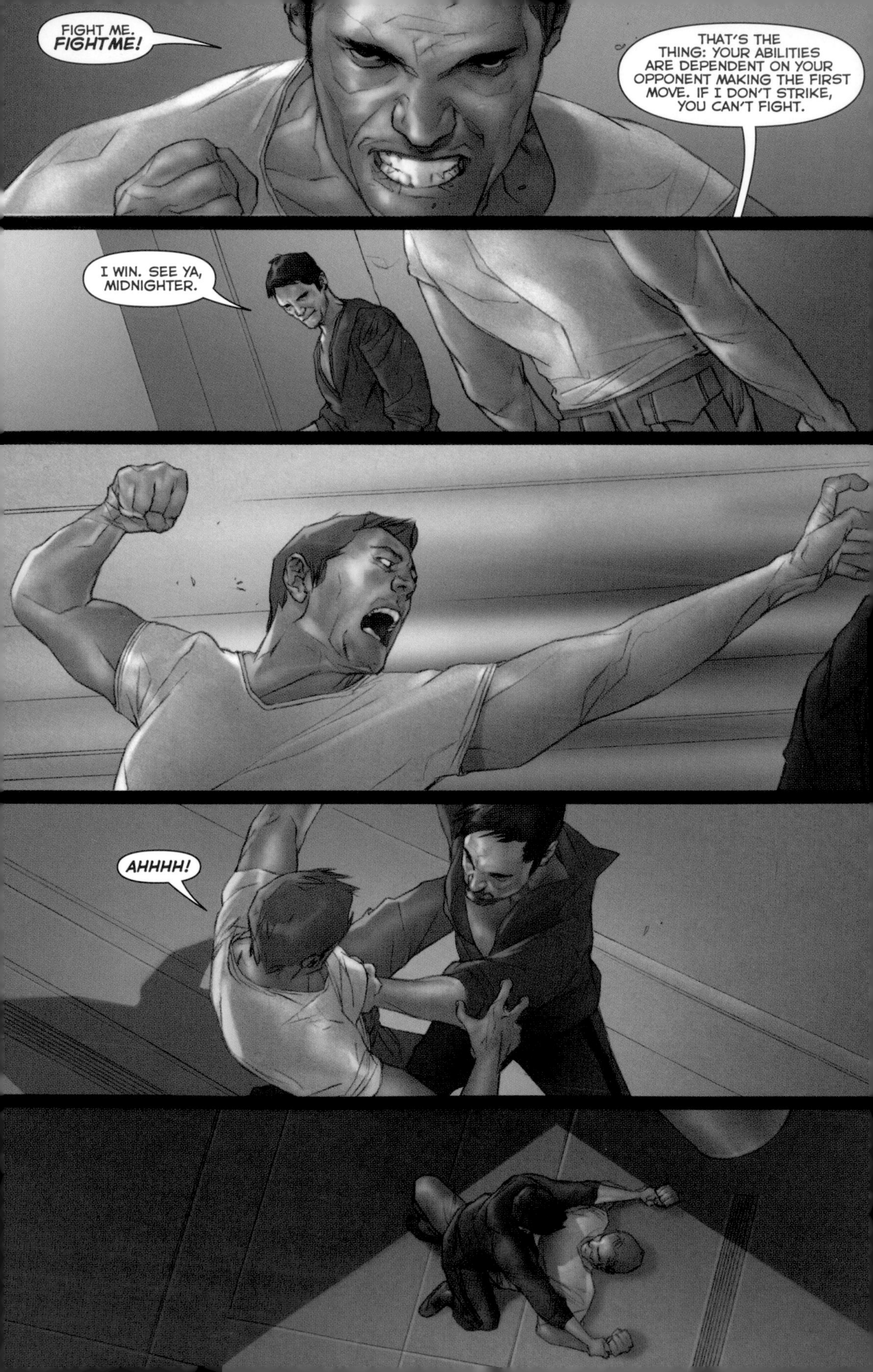
FIGHT ME. FIGHT ME!
THAT'S THE THING: YOUR ABILITIES ARE DEPENDENT ON YOUR OPPONENT MAKING THE FIRST MOVE. IF I DON'T STRIKE, YOU CAN'T FIGHT.
I WIN. SEE YA, MIDNIGHTER.
AHHHH!

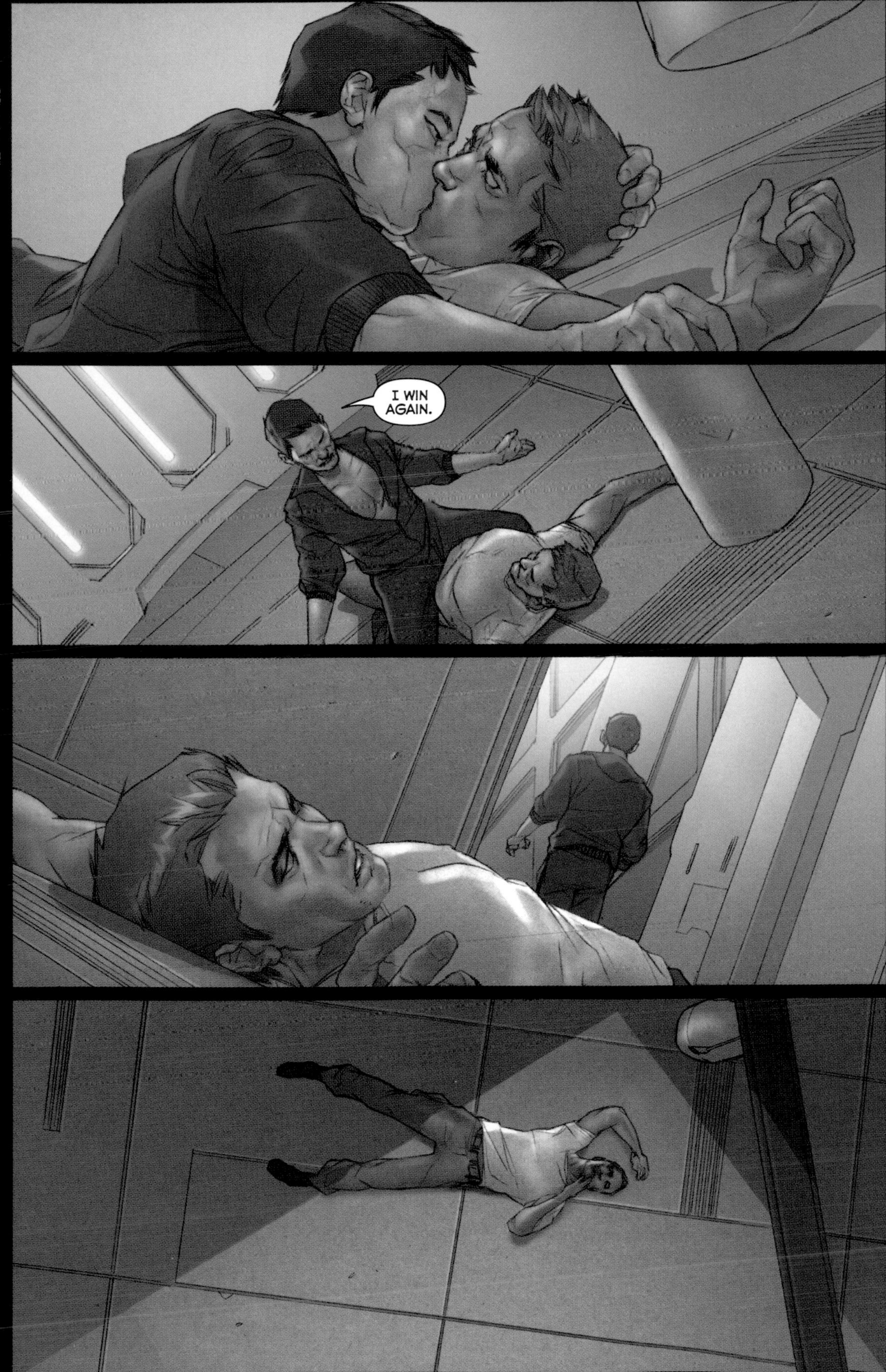
I WIN AGAIN.

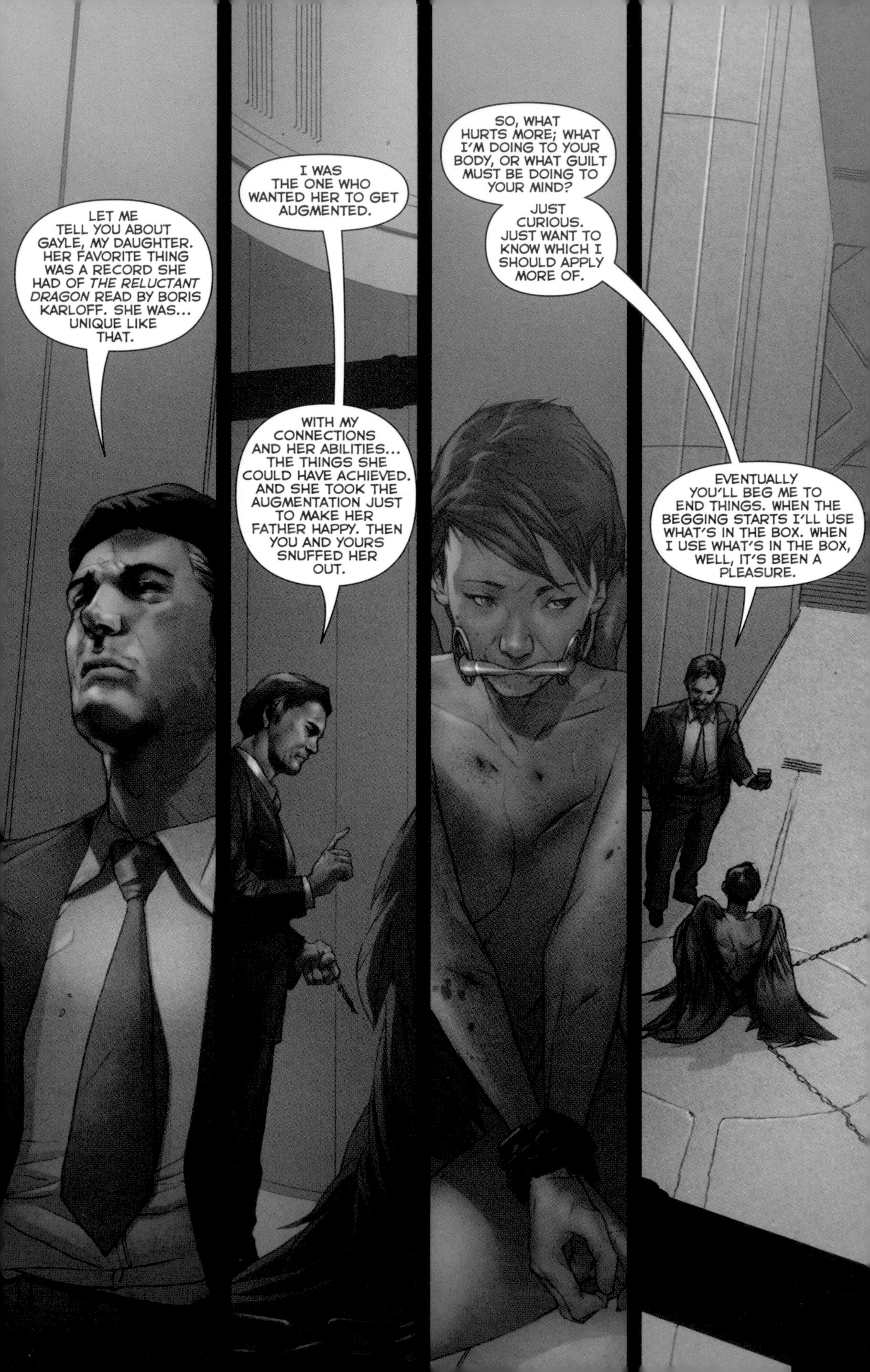
LET ME TELL YOU ABOUT GAYLE, MY DAUGHTER. HER FAVORITE THING WAS A RECORD SHE HAD OF *THE RELUCTANT DRAGON* READ BY BORIS KARLOFF. SHE WAS... UNIQUE LIKE THAT.
I WAS THE ONE WHO WANTED HER TO GET AUGMENTED.
WITH MY CONNECTIONS AND HER ABILITIES... THE THINGS SHE COULD HAVE ACHIEVED. AND SHE TOOK THE AUGMENTATION JUST TO MAKE HER FATHER HAPPY. THEN YOU AND YOURS SNUFFED HER OUT.
SO, WHAT HURTS MORE; WHAT I'M DOING TO YOUR BODY, OR WHAT GUILT MUST BE DOING TO YOUR MIND?
JUST CURIOUS. JUST WANT TO KNOW WHICH I SHOULD APPLY MORE OF.
EVENTUALLY YOU'LL BEG ME TO END THINGS. WHEN THE BEGGING STARTS I'LL USE WHAT'S IN THE BOX. WHEN I USE WHAT'S IN THE BOX, WELL, IT'S BEEN A PLEASURE.

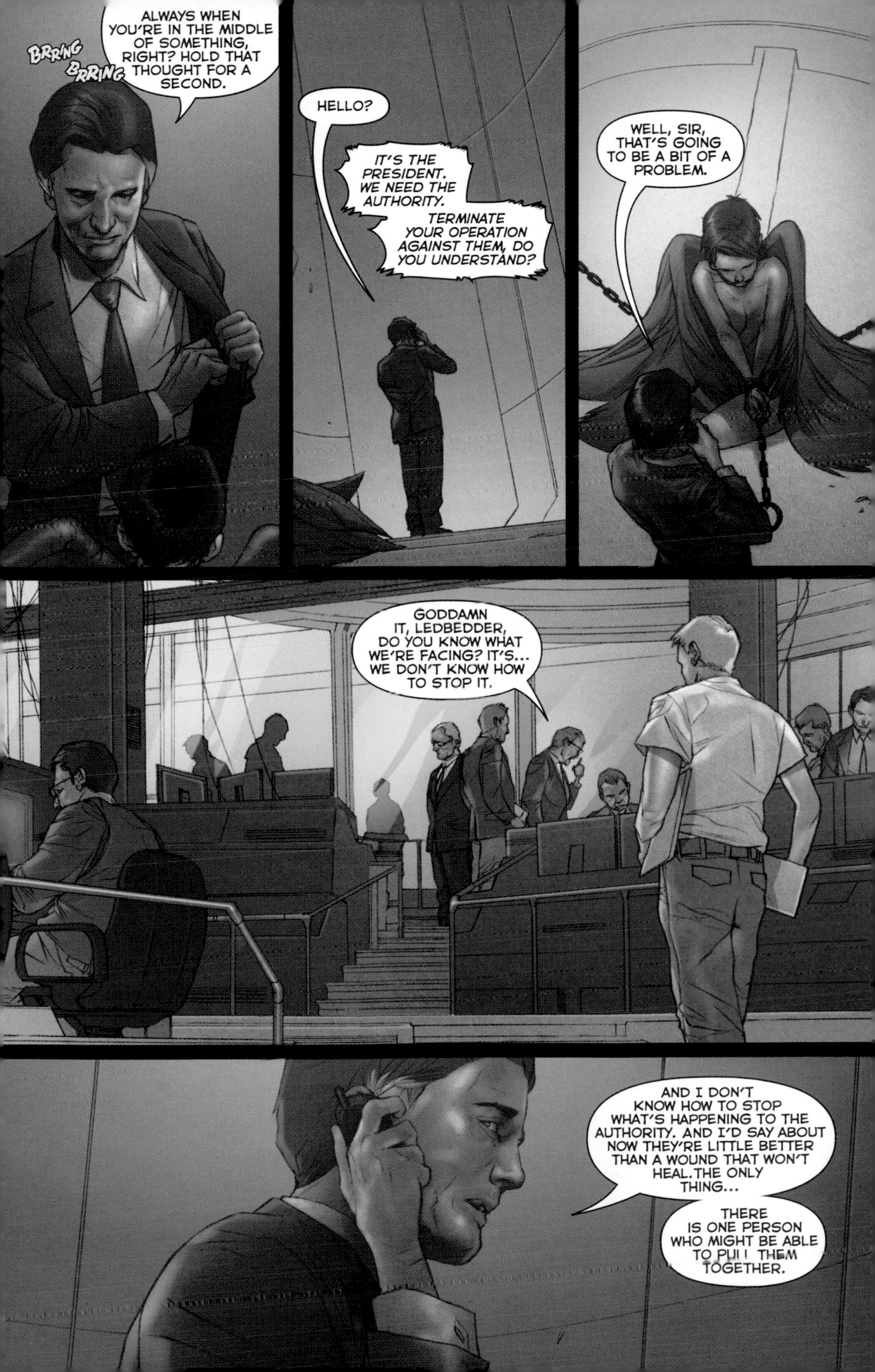
BRRING BRRING
ALWAYS WHEN YOU'RE IN THE MIDDLE OF SOMETHING, RIGHT? HOLD THAT THOUGHT FOR A SECOND.
HELLO?
IT'S THE PRESIDENT. WE NEED THE AUTHORITY.
TERMINATE YOUR OPERATION AGAINST THEM, DO YOU UNDERSTAND?
WELL, SIR, THAT'S GOING TO BE A BIT OF A PROBLEM.
GODDAMN IT, LEDBEDDER, DO YOU KNOW WHAT WE'RE FACING? IT'S... WE DON'T KNOW HOW TO STOP IT.
AND I DON'T KNOW HOW TO STOP WHAT'S HAPPENING TO THE AUTHORITY. AND I'D SAY ABOUT NOW THEY'RE LITTLE BETTER THAN A WOUND THAT WON'T HEAL.THE ONLY THING...
THERE IS ONE PERSON WHO MIGHT BE ABLE TO PULL THEM TOGETHER.

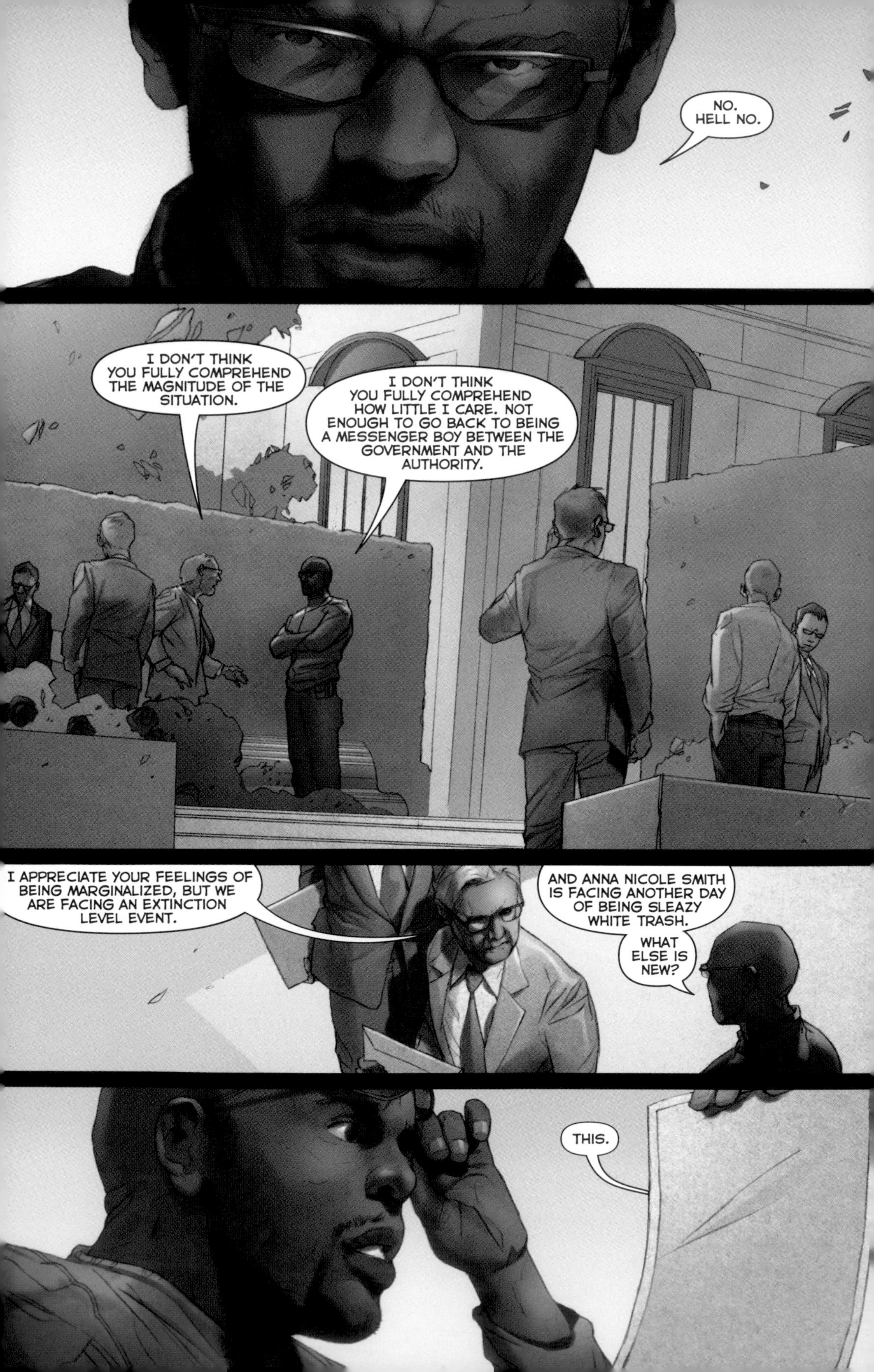
NO. HELL NO.
I DON'T THINK YOU FULLY COMPREHEND THE MAGNITUDE OF THE SITUATION.
I DON'T THINK YOU FULLY COMPREHEND HOW LITTLE I CARE. NOT ENOUGH TO GO BACK TO BEING A MESSENGER BOY BETWEEN THE GOVERNMENT AND THE AUTHORITY.
I APPRECIATE YOUR FEELINGS OF BEING MARGINALIZED, BUT WE ARE FACING AN EXTINCTION LEVEL EVENT.
AND ANNA NICOLE SMITH IS FACING ANOTHER DAY OF BEING SLEAZY WHITE TRASH.
WHAT ELSE IS NEW?
THIS.

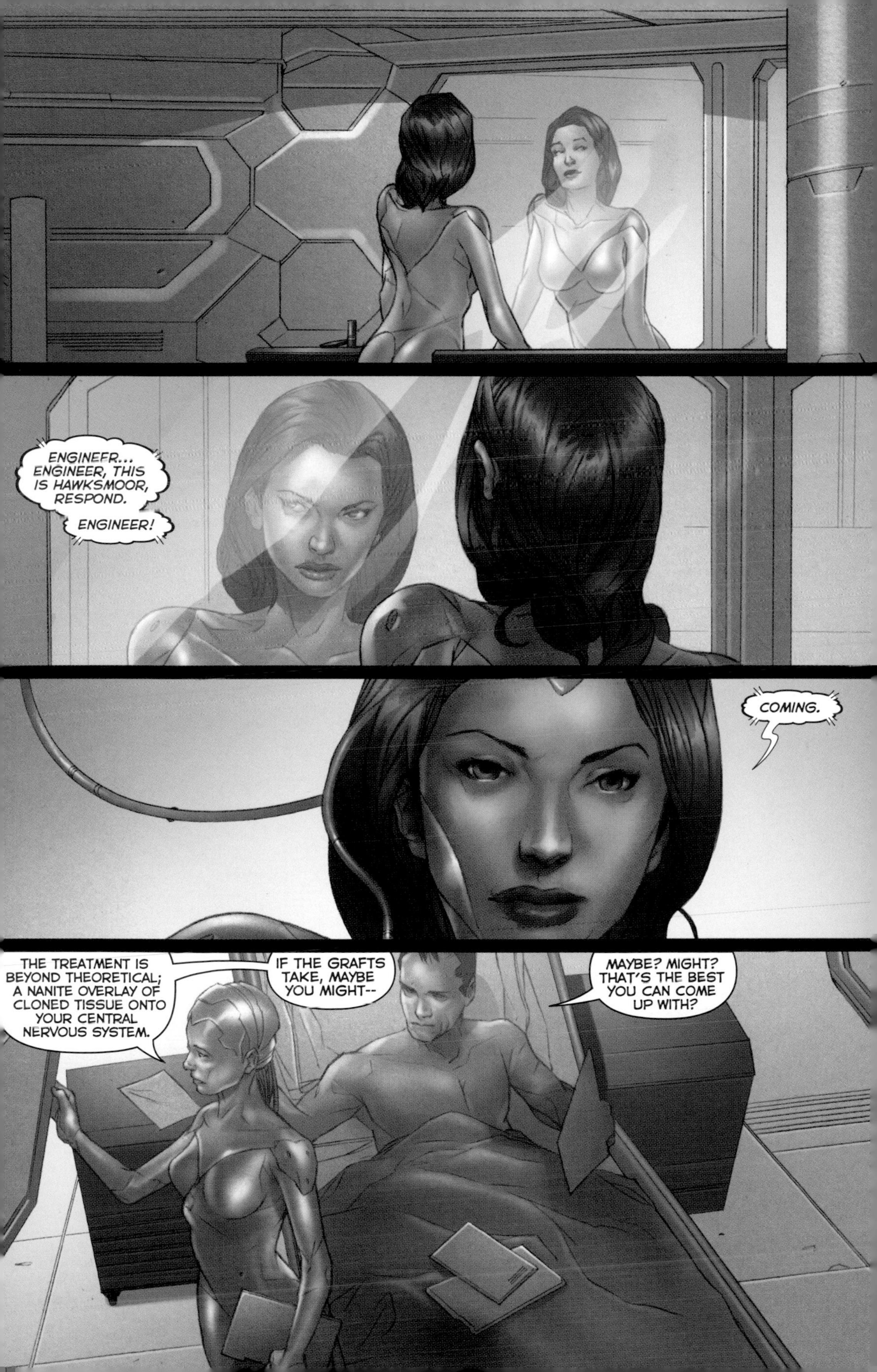
ENGINEER... ENGINEER, THIS IS HAWKSMOOR, RESPOND.
ENGINEER!
COMING.
THE TREATMENT IS BEYOND THEORETICAL; A NANITE OVERLAY OF CLONED TISSUE ONTO YOUR CENTRAL NERVOUS SYSTEM.
IF THE GRAFTS TAKE, MAYBE YOU MIGHT--
MAYBE? MIGHT? THAT'S THE BEST YOU CAN COME UP WITH?

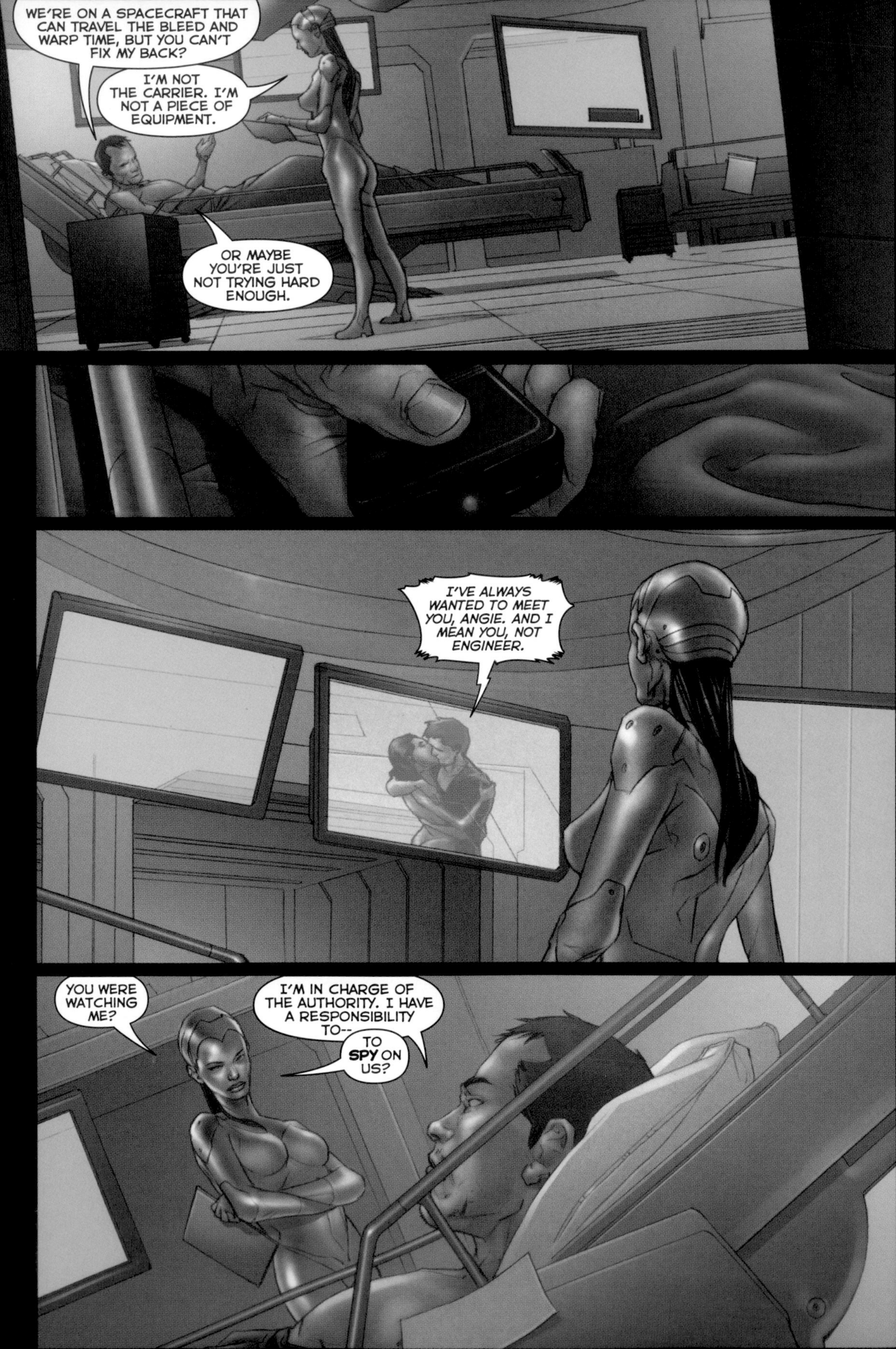
WE'RE ON A SPACECRAFT THAT CAN TRAVEL THE BLEED AND WARP TIME, BUT YOU CAN'T FIX MY BACK?
I'M NOT THE CARRIER. I'M NOT A PIECE OF EQUIPMENT.
OR MAYBE YOU'RE JUST NOT TRYING HARD ENOUGH.
I'VE ALWAYS WANTED TO MEET YOU, ANGIE. AND I MEAN YOU, NOT ENGINEER.
YOU WERE WATCHING ME?
I'M IN CHARGE OF THE AUTHORITY. I HAVE A RESPONSIBILITY TO--
TO **SPY** ON US?

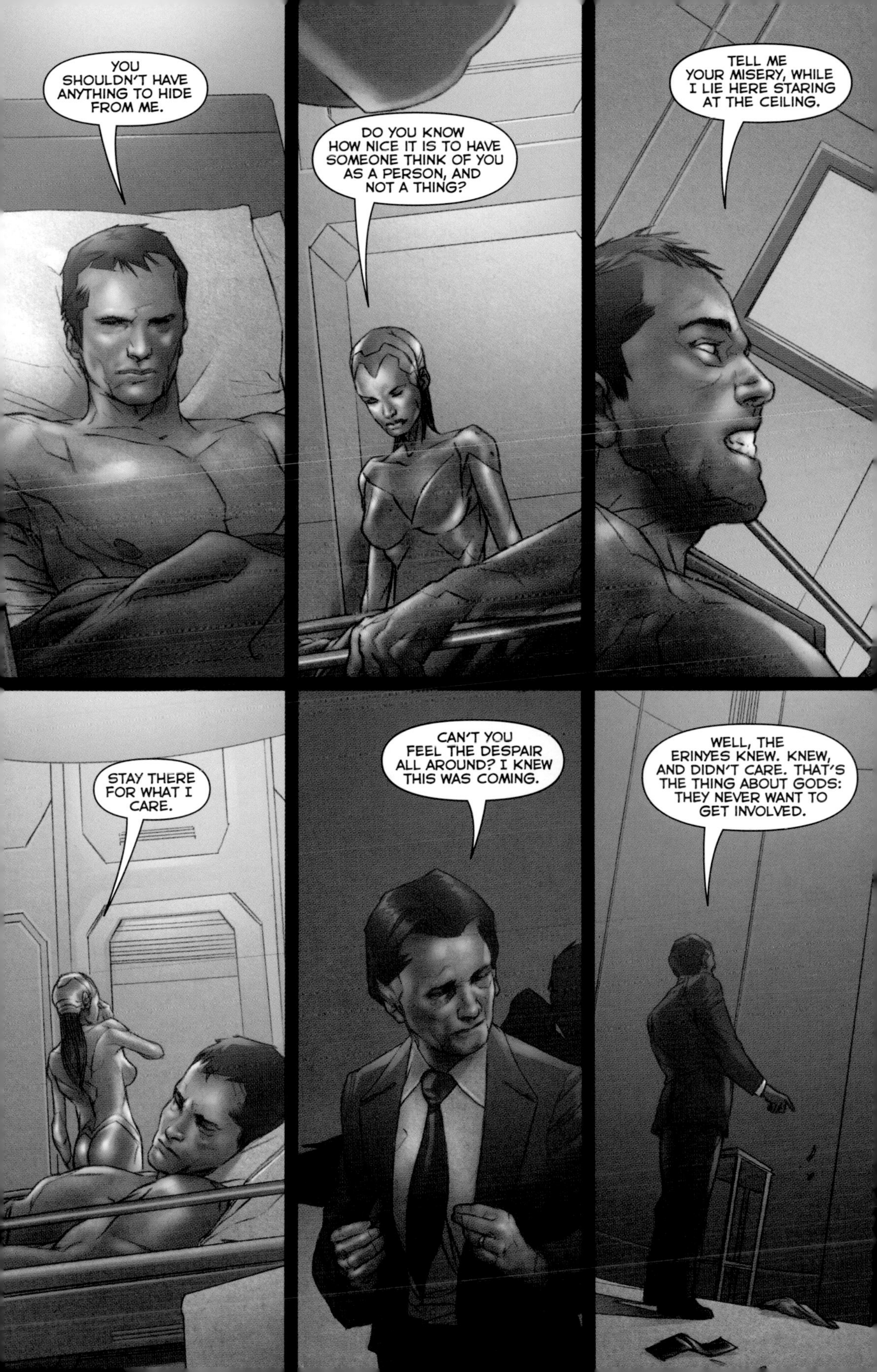
YOU SHOULDN'T HAVE ANYTHING TO HIDE FROM ME.
DO YOU KNOW HOW NICE IT IS TO HAVE SOMEONE THINK OF YOU AS A PERSON, AND NOT A THING?
TELL ME YOUR MISERY, WHILE I LIE HERE STARING AT THE CEILING.
STAY THERE FOR WHAT I CARE.
CAN'T YOU FEEL THE DESPAIR ALL AROUND? I KNEW THIS WAS COMING.
WELL, THE ERINYES KNEW. KNEW, AND DIDN'T CARE. THAT'S THE THING ABOUT GODS: THEY NEVER WANT TO GET INVOLVED.

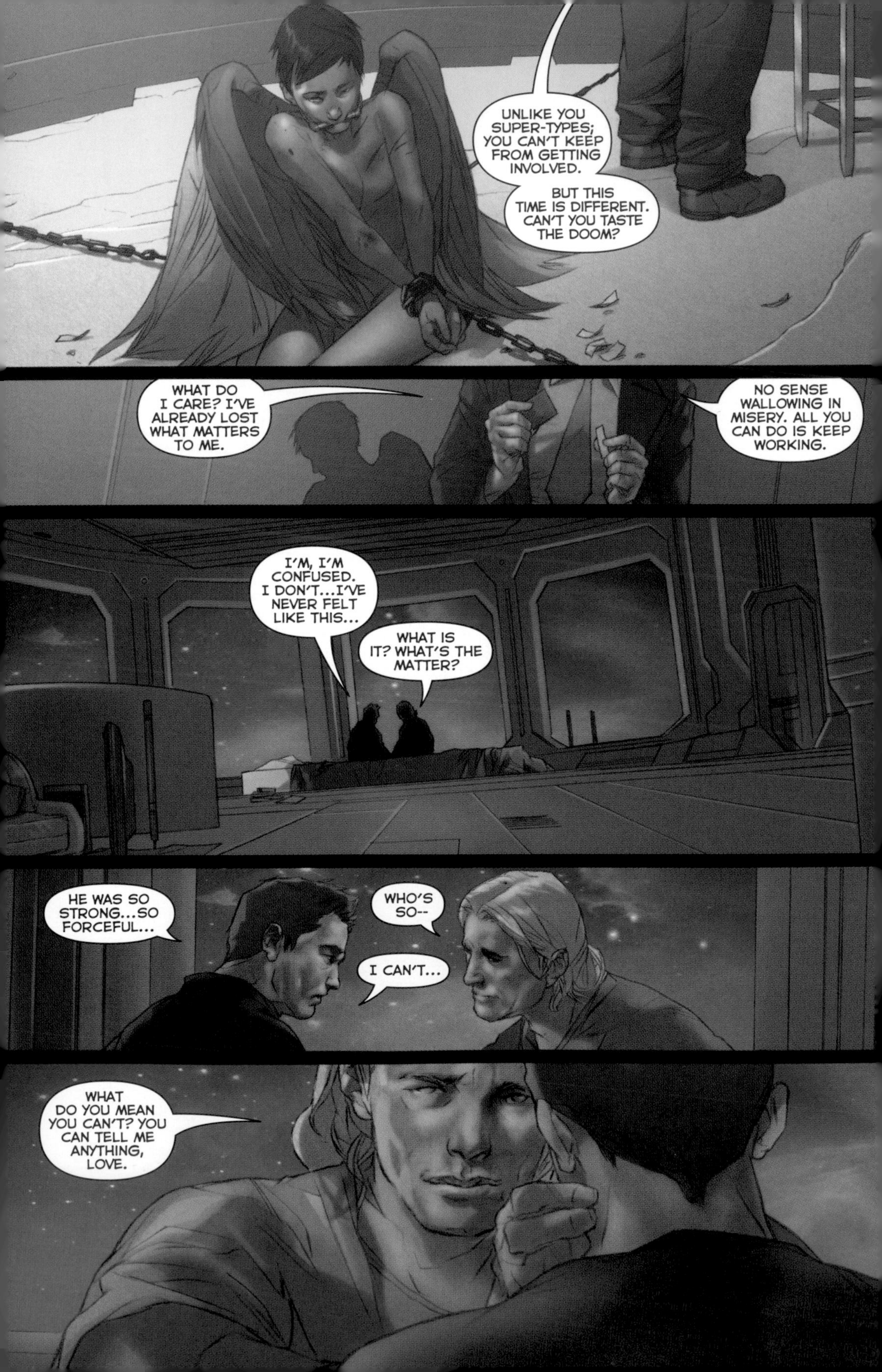

UNLIKE YOU SUPER-TYPES; YOU CAN'T KEEP FROM GETTING INVOLVED.
BUT THIS TIME IS DIFFERENT. CAN'T YOU TASTE THE DOOM?
WHAT DO I CARE? I'VE ALREADY LOST WHAT MATTERS TO ME.
NO SENSE WALLOWING IN MISERY. ALL YOU CAN DO IS KEEP WORKING.
I'M, I'M CONFUSED. I DON'T...I'VE NEVER FELT LIKE THIS...
WHAT IS IT? WHAT'S THE MATTER?
HE WAS SO STRONG...SO FORCEFUL...
WHO'S SO--
I CAN'T...
WHAT DO YOU MEAN YOU CAN'T? YOU CAN TELL ME ANYTHING, LOVE.

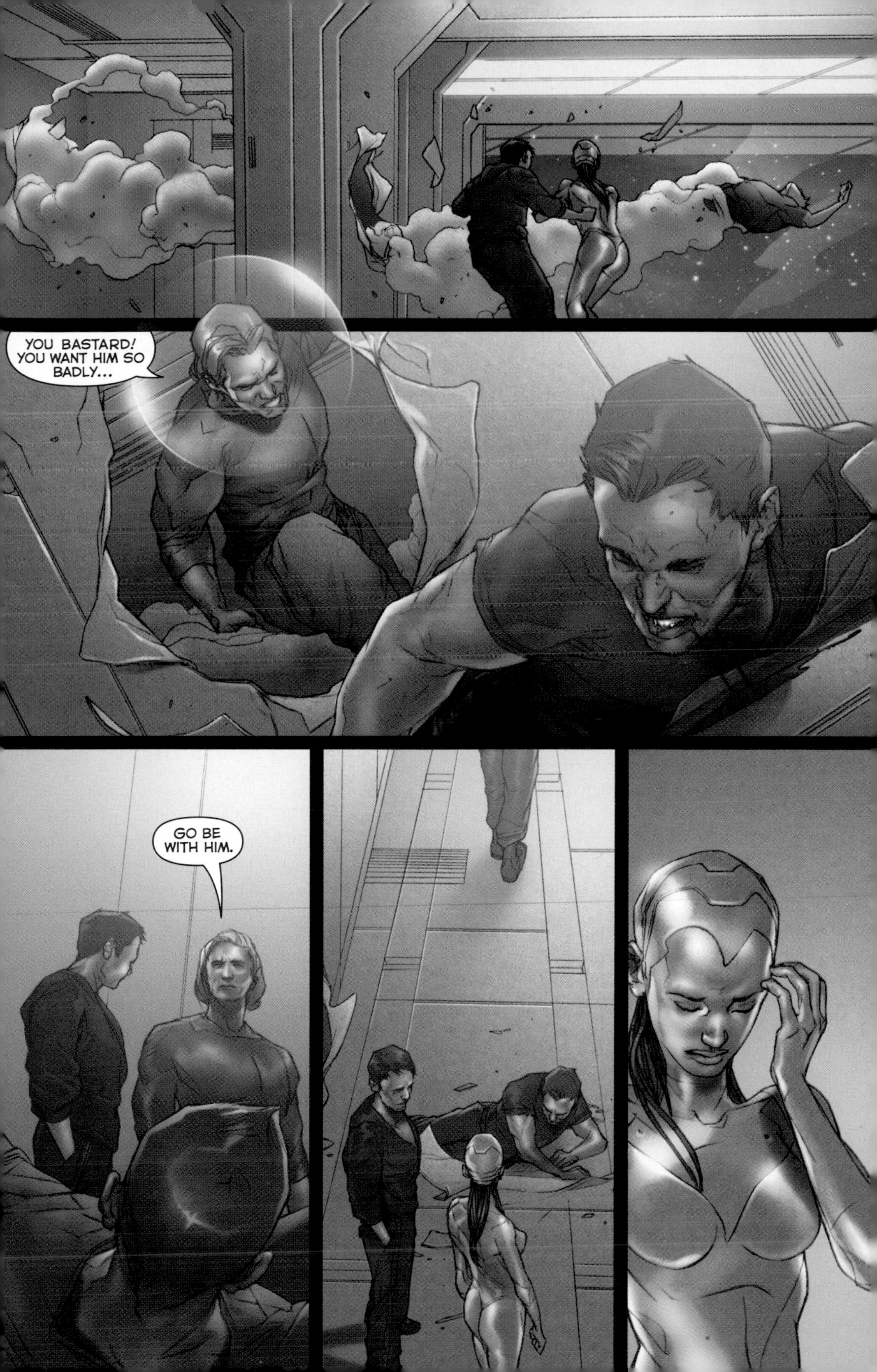
YOU BASTARD! YOU WANT HIM SO BADLY...
GO BE WITH HIM.

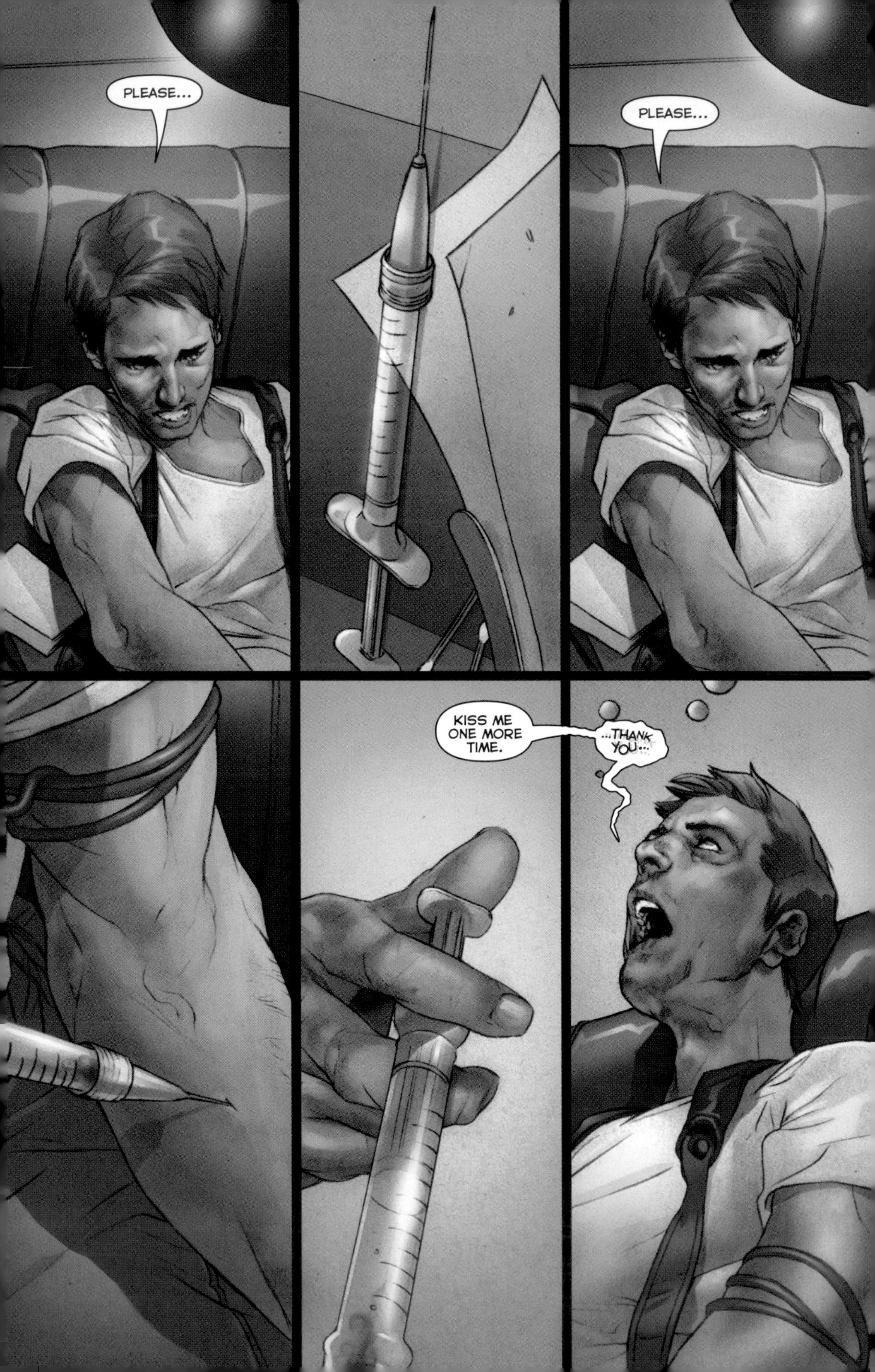
PLEASE...
PLEASE...
KISS ME ONE MORE TIME.
...THANK YOU...

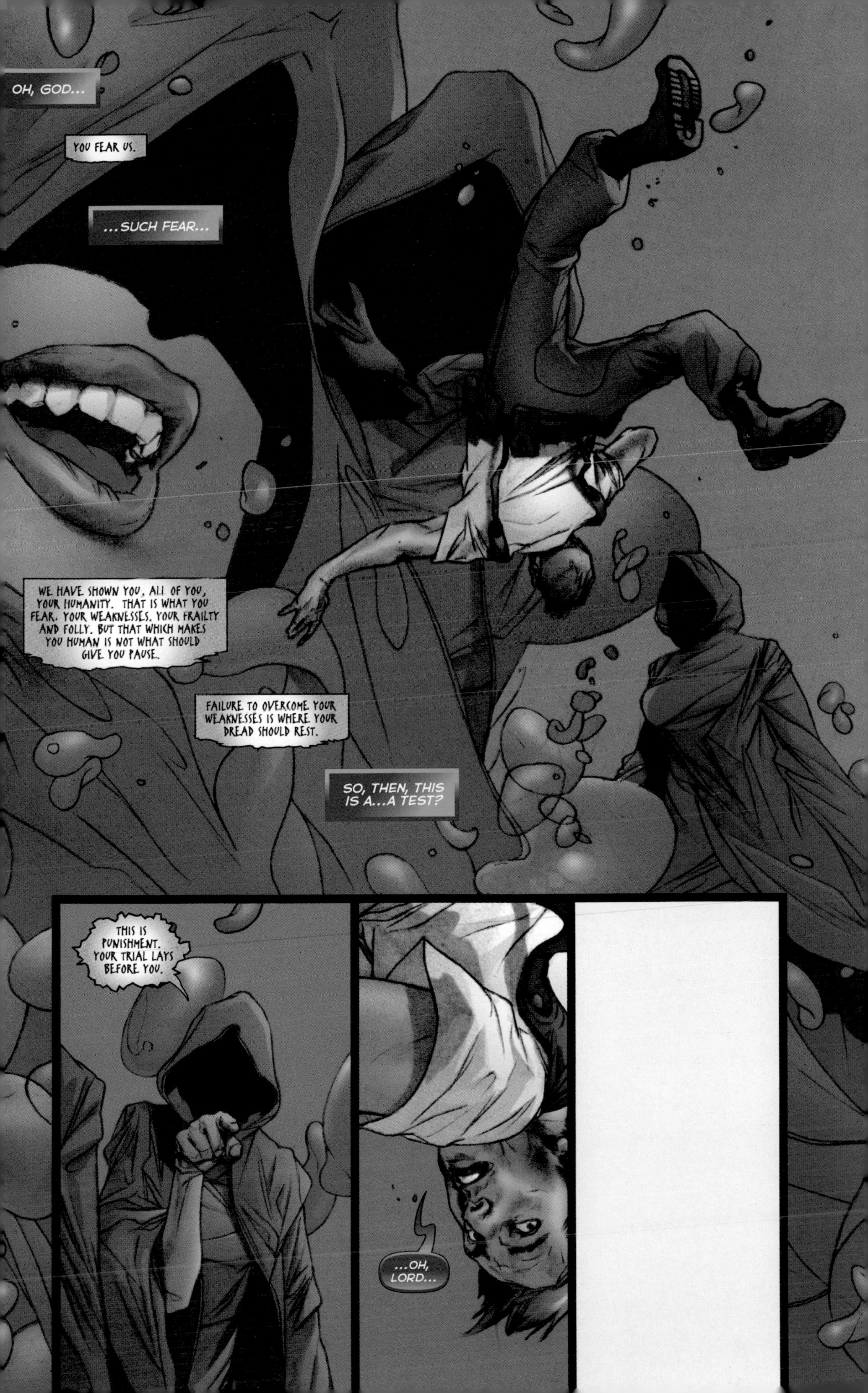
OH, GOD...
YOU FEAR US.
...SUCH FEAR...
WE HAVE SHOWN YOU, ALL OF YOU, YOUR HUMANITY. THAT IS WHAT YOU FEAR. YOUR WEAKNESSES. YOUR FRAILTY AND FOLLY. BUT THAT WHICH MAKES YOU HUMAN IS NOT WHAT SHOULD GIVE YOU PAUSE.
FAILURE TO OVERCOME YOUR WEAKNESSES IS WHERE YOUR DREAD SHOULD REST.
SO, THEN, THIS IS A...A TEST?
THIS IS PUNISHMENT. YOUR TRIAL LAYS BEFORE YOU.
...OH, LORD...

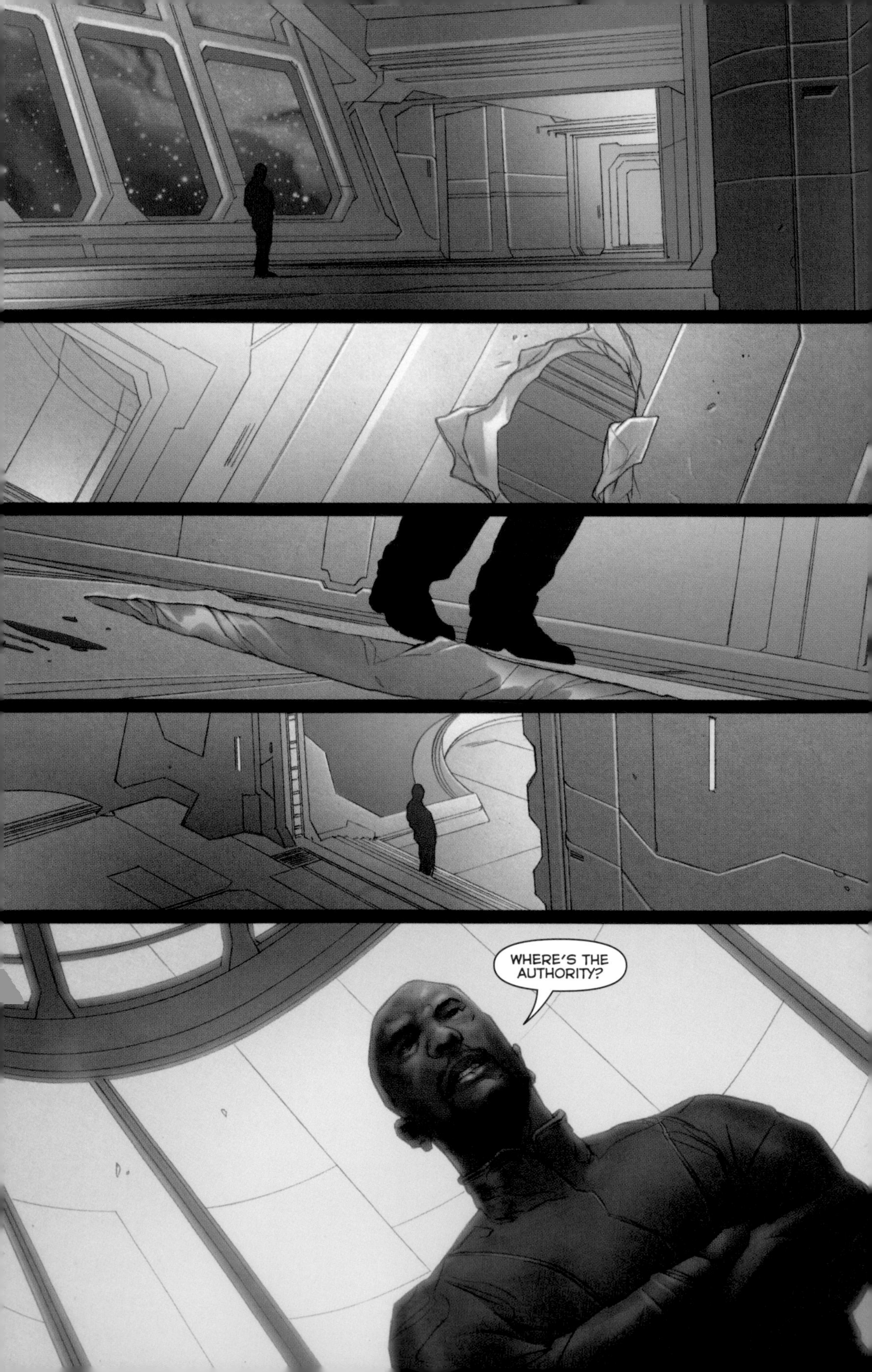
WHERE'S THE AUTHORITY?

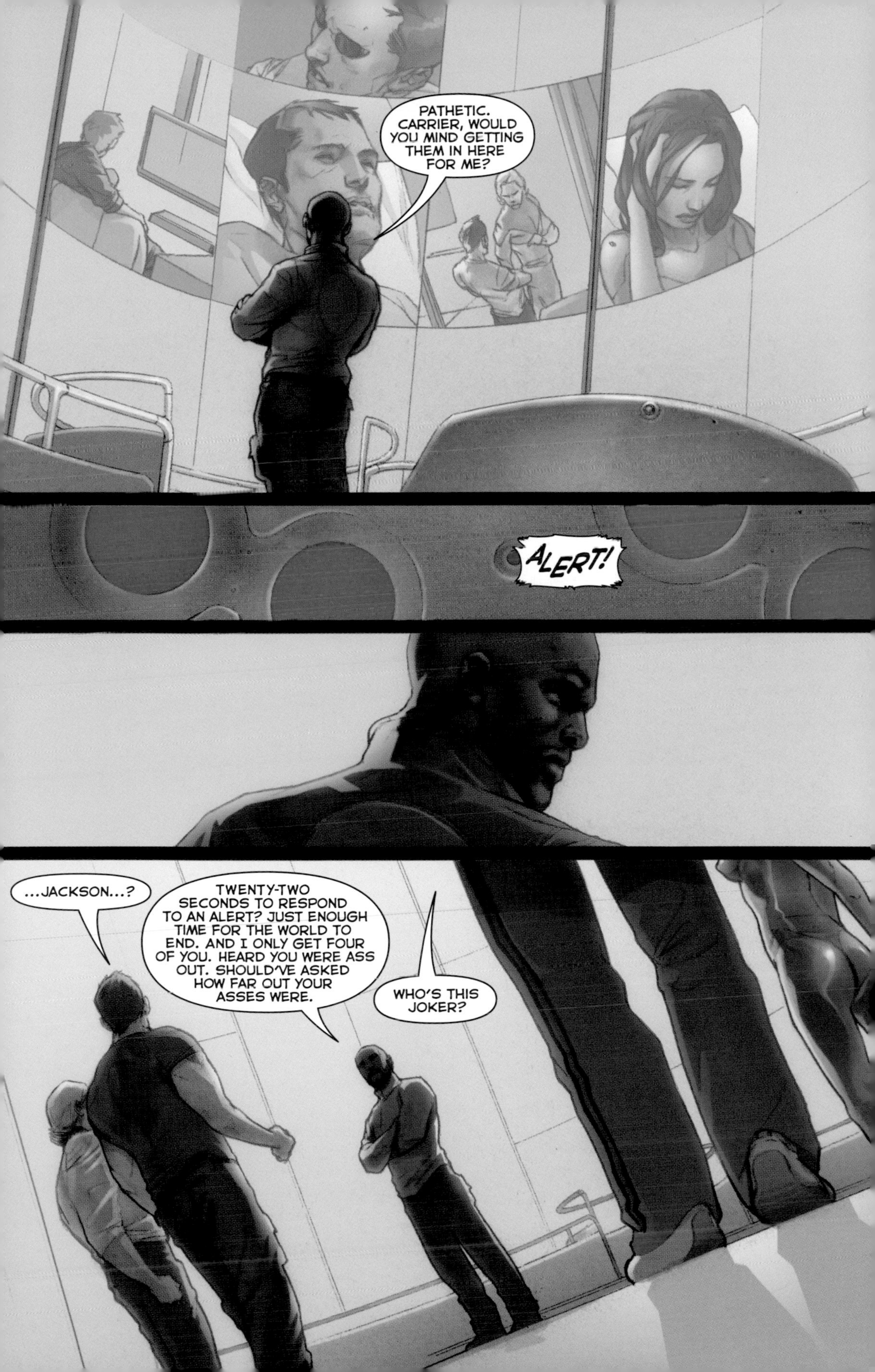
PATHETIC. CARRIER, WOULD YOU MIND GETTING THEM IN HERE FOR ME?
ALERT!
...JACKSON...?
TWENTY-TWO SECONDS TO RESPOND TO AN ALERT? JUST ENOUGH TIME FOR THE WORLD TO END. AND I ONLY GET FOUR OF YOU. HEARD YOU WERE ASS OUT. SHOULD'VE ASKED HOW FAR OUT YOUR ASSES WERE.
WHO'S THIS JOKER?

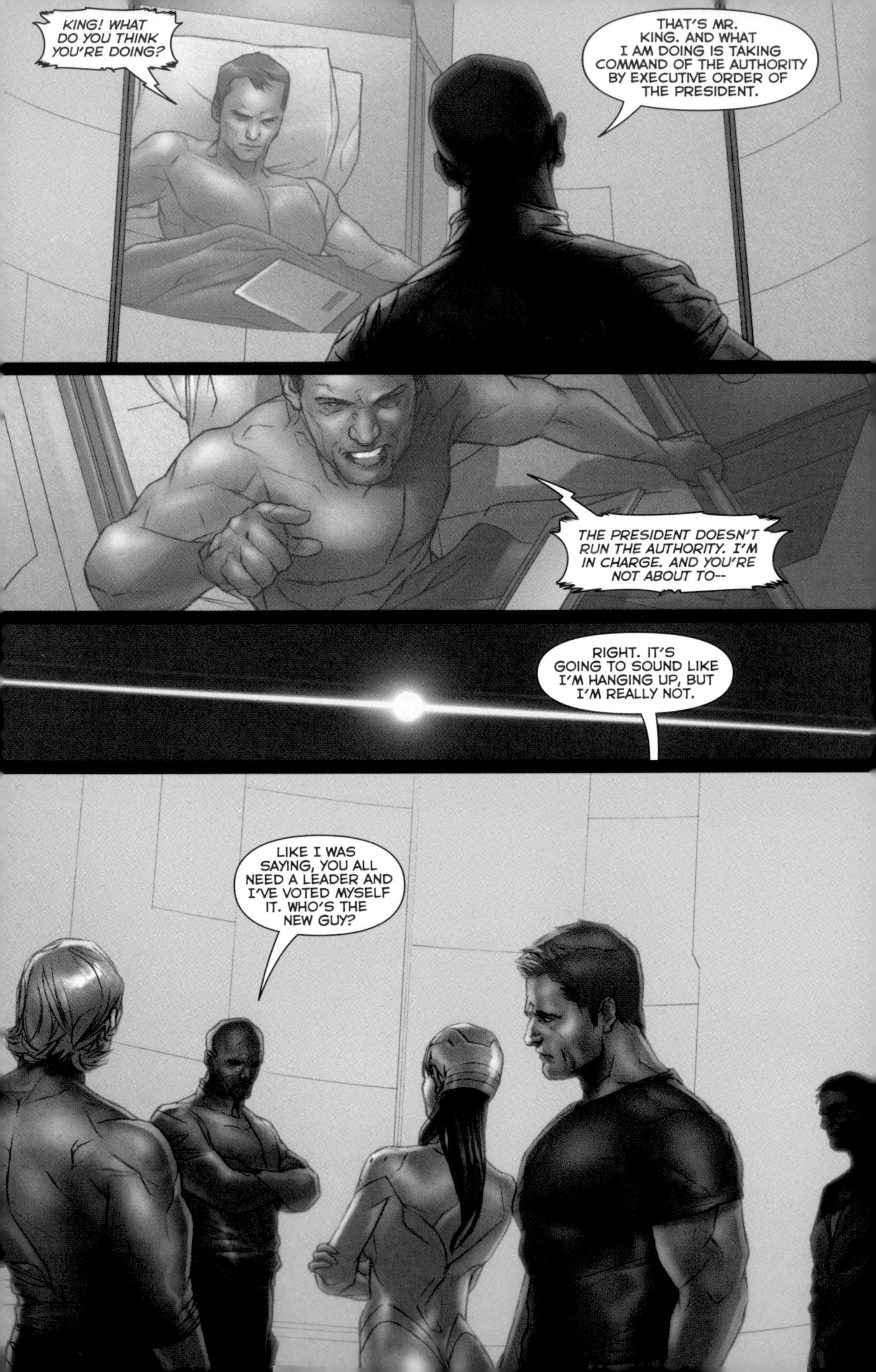
KING! WHAT DO YOU THINK YOU'RE DOING?
THAT'S MR. KING. AND WHAT I AM DOING IS TAKING COMMAND OF THE AUTHORITY BY EXECUTIVE ORDER OF THE PRESIDENT.
THE PRESIDENT DOESN'T RUN THE AUTHORITY. I'M IN CHARGE. AND YOU'RE NOT ABOUT TO--
RIGHT. IT'S GOING TO SOUND LIKE I'M HANGING UP, BUT I'M REALLY NOT.
LIKE I WAS SAYING, YOU ALL NEED A LEADER AND I'VE VOTED MYSELF IT. WHO'S THE NEW GUY?

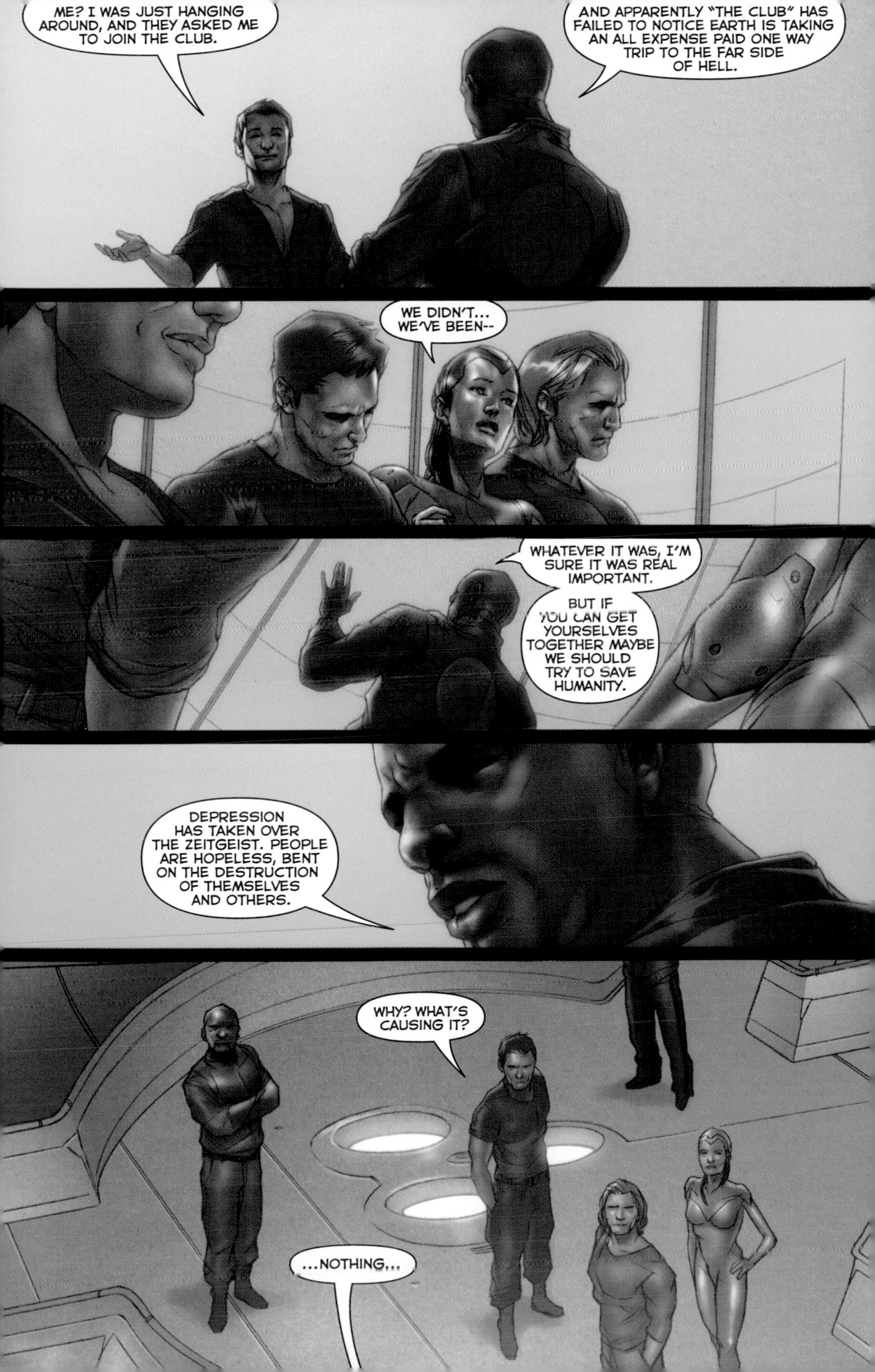
ME? I WAS JUST HANGING AROUND, AND THEY ASKED ME TO JOIN THE CLUB.
AND APPARENTLY "THE CLUB" HAS FAILED TO NOTICE EARTH IS TAKING AN ALL EXPENSE PAID ONE WAY TRIP TO THE FAR SIDE OF HELL.
WE DIDN'T... WE'VE BEEN--
WHATEVER IT WAS, I'M SURE IT WAS REAL IMPORTANT.
BUT IF YOU CAN GET YOURSELVES TOGETHER MAYBE WE SHOULD TRY TO SAVE HUMANITY.
DEPRESSION HAS TAKEN OVER THE ZEITGEIST. PEOPLE ARE HOPELESS, BENT ON THE DESTRUCTION OF THEMSELVES AND OTHERS.
WHY? WHAT'S CAUSING IT?
...NOTHING...

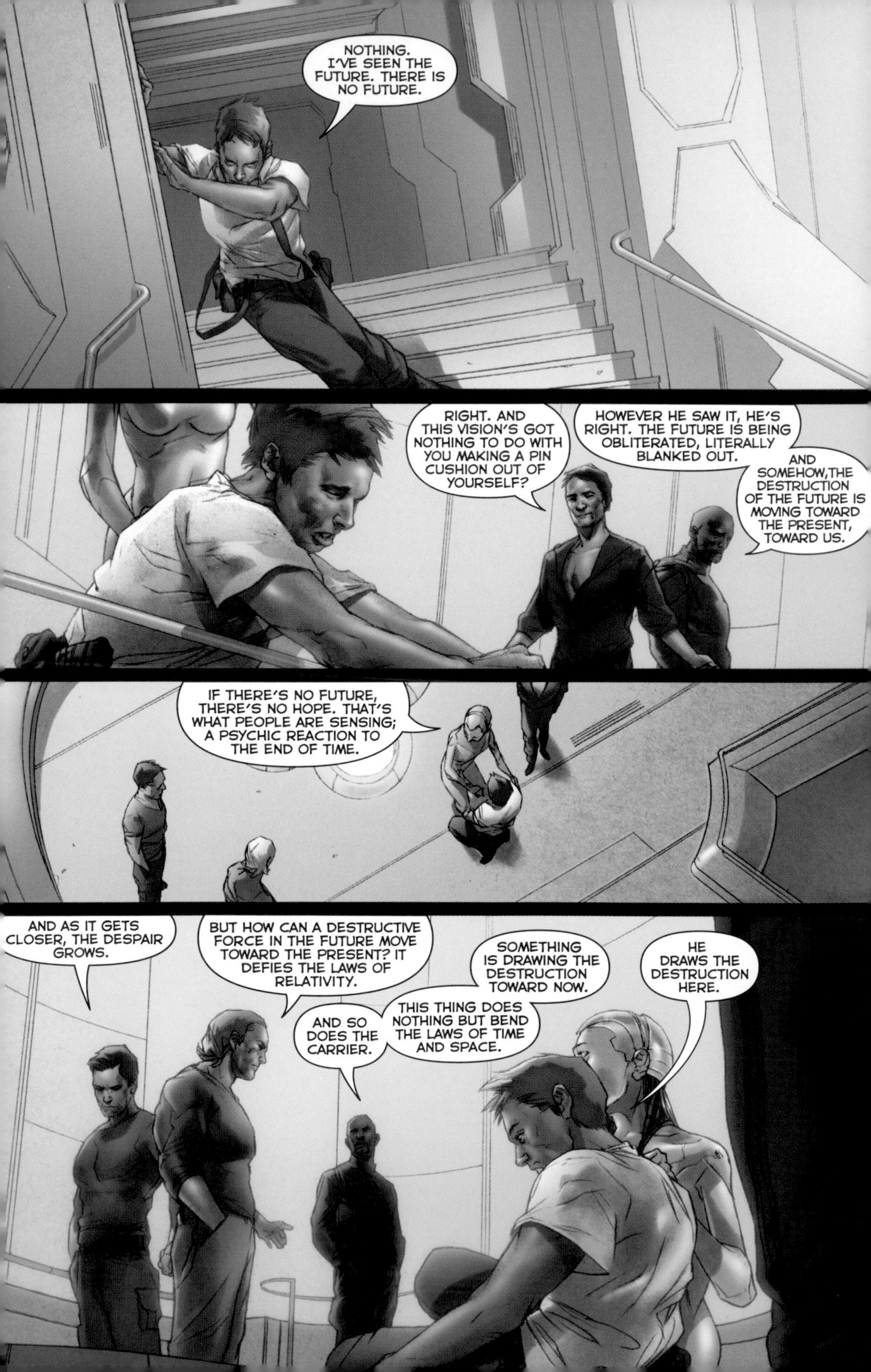
NOTHING. I'VE SEEN THE FUTURE. THERE IS NO FUTURE.
RIGHT. AND THIS VISION'S GOT NOTHING TO DO WITH YOU MAKING A PIN CUSHION OUT OF YOURSELF?
HOWEVER HE SAW IT, HE'S RIGHT. THE FUTURE IS BEING OBLITERATED, LITERALLY BLANKED OUT.
AND SOMEHOW, THE DESTRUCTION OF THE FUTURE IS MOVING TOWARD THE PRESENT, TOWARD US.
IF THERE'S NO FUTURE, THERE'S NO HOPE. THAT'S WHAT PEOPLE ARE SENSING; A PSYCHIC REACTION TO THE END OF TIME.
AND AS IT GETS CLOSER, THE DESPAIR GROWS.
BUT HOW CAN A DESTRUCTIVE FORCE IN THE FUTURE MOVE TOWARD THE PRESENT? IT DEFIES THE LAWS OF RELATIVITY.
SOMETHING IS DRAWING THE DESTRUCTION TOWARD NOW.
HE DRAWS THE DESTRUCTION HERE.
THIS THING DOES NOTHING BUT BEND THE LAWS OF TIME AND SPACE.
AND SO DOES THE CARRIER.

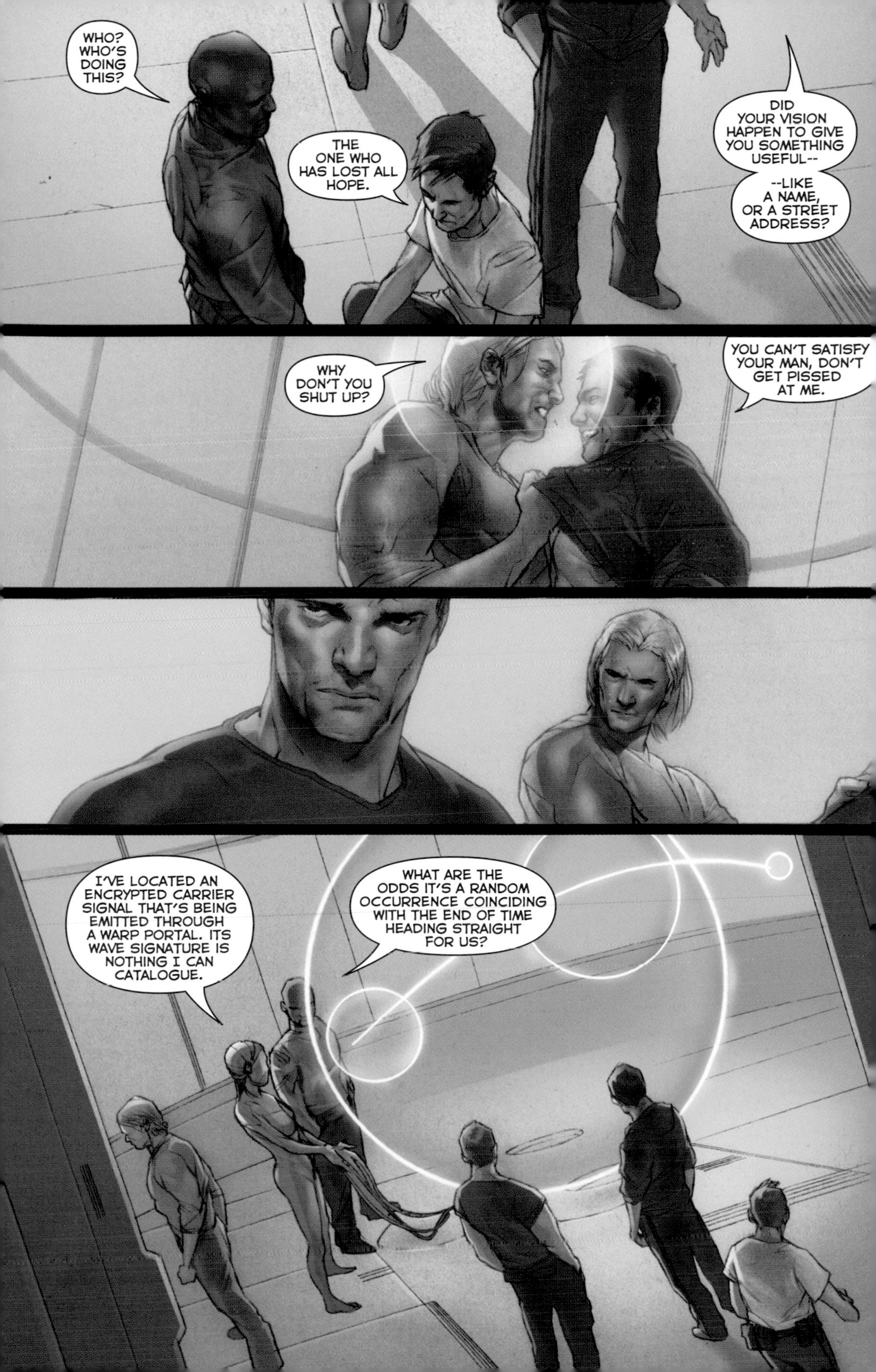
WHO? WHO'S DOING THIS?
THE ONE WHO HAS LOST ALL HOPE.
DID YOUR VISION HAPPEN TO GIVE YOU SOMETHING USEFUL--
--LIKE A NAME, OR A STREET ADDRESS?
WHY DON'T YOU SHUT UP?
YOU CAN'T SATISFY YOUR MAN, DON'T GET PISSED AT ME.
I'VE LOCATED AN ENCRYPTED CARRIER SIGNAL THAT'S BEING EMITTED THROUGH A WARP PORTAL. ITS WAVE SIGNATURE IS NOTHING I CAN CATALOGUE.
WHAT ARE THE ODDS IT'S A RANDOM OCCURRENCE COINCIDING WITH THE END OF TIME HEADING STRAIGHT FOR US?

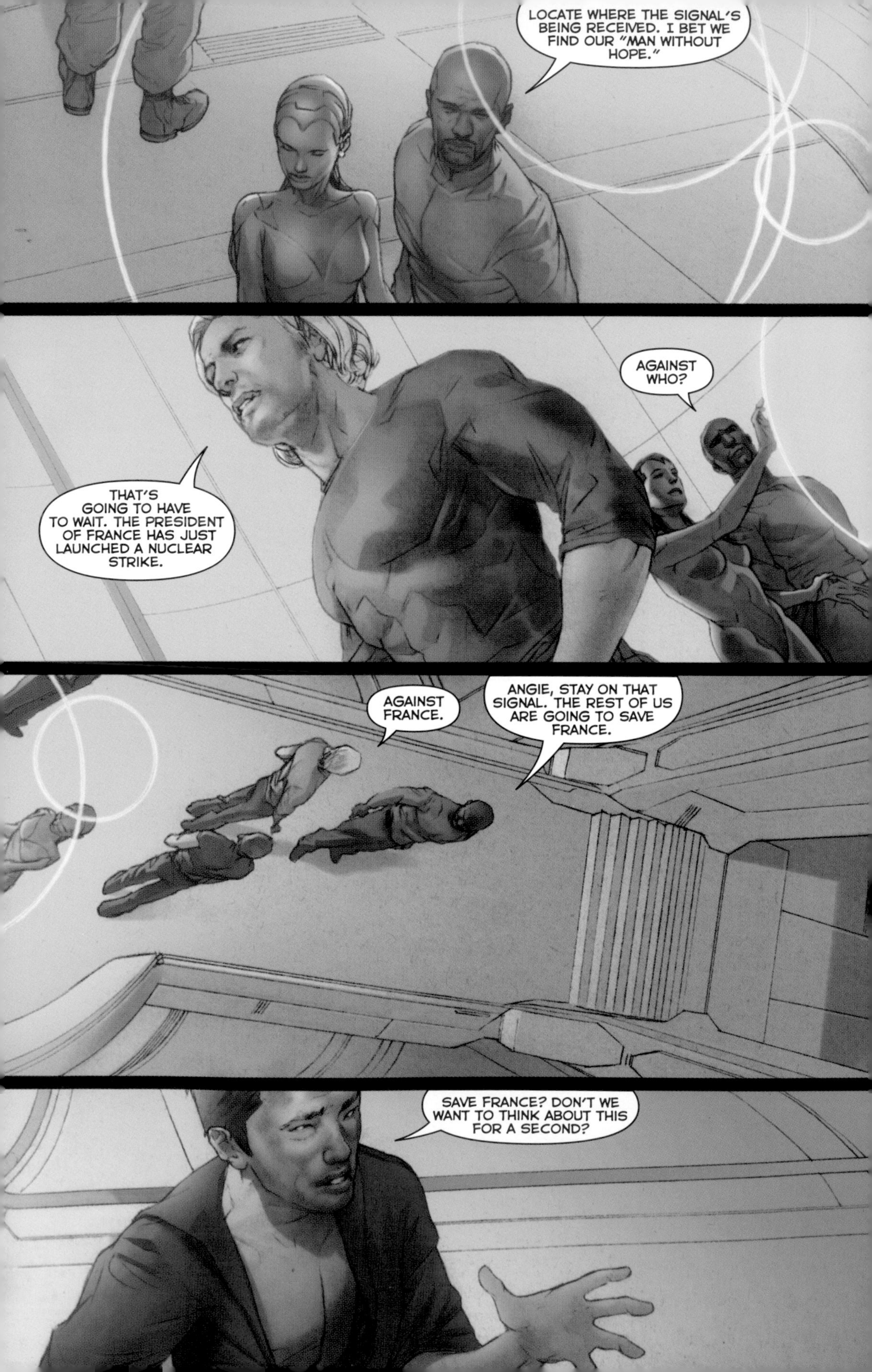
LOCATE WHERE THE SIGNAL'S BEING RECEIVED. I BET WE FIND OUR "MAN WITHOUT HOPE."
AGAINST WHO?
THAT'S GOING TO HAVE TO WAIT. THE PRESIDENT OF FRANCE HAS JUST LAUNCHED A NUCLEAR STRIKE.
AGAINST FRANCE.
ANGIE, STAY ON THAT SIGNAL. THE REST OF US ARE GOING TO SAVE FRANCE.
SAVE FRANCE? DON'T WE WANT TO THINK ABOUT THIS FOR A SECOND?

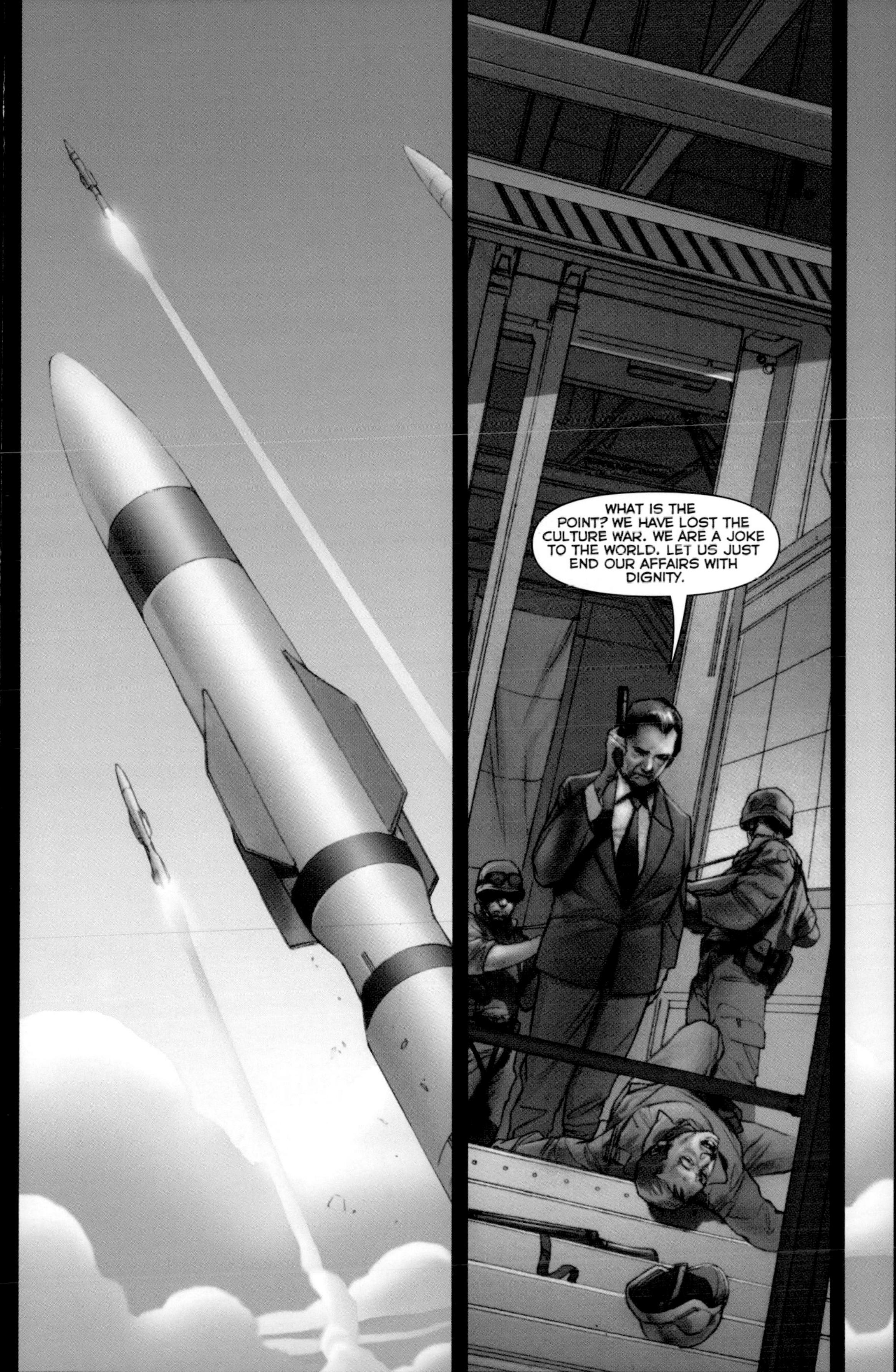
WHAT IS THE POINT? WE HAVE LOST THE CULTURE WAR. WE ARE A JOKE TO THE WORLD. LET US JUST END OUR AFFAIRS WITH DIGNITY.

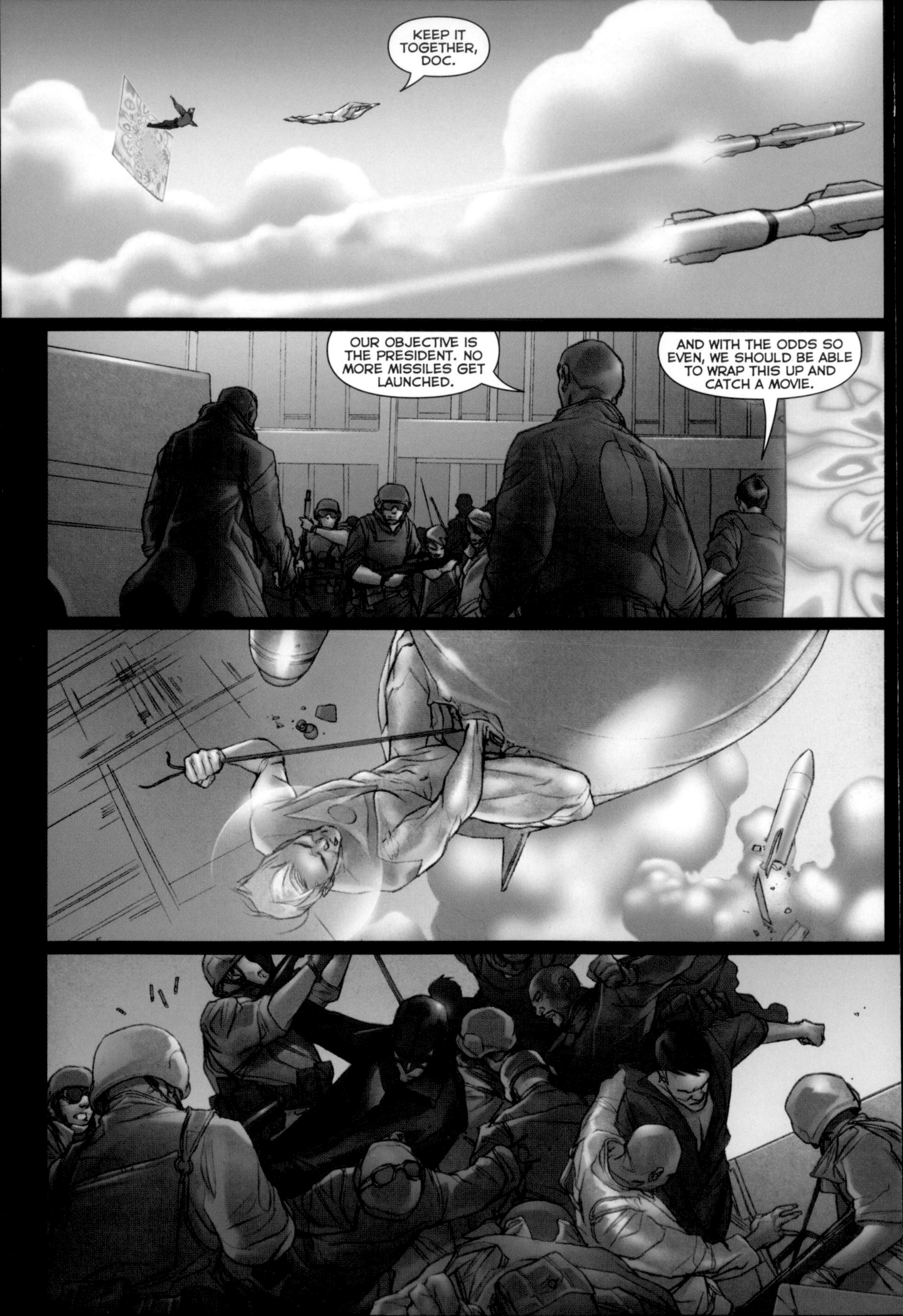
KEEP IT TOGETHER, DOC.
OUR OBJECTIVE IS THE PRESIDENT. NO MORE MISSILES GET LAUNCHED.
AND WITH THE ODDS SO EVEN, WE SHOULD BE ABLE TO WRAP THIS UP AND CATCH A MOVIE.

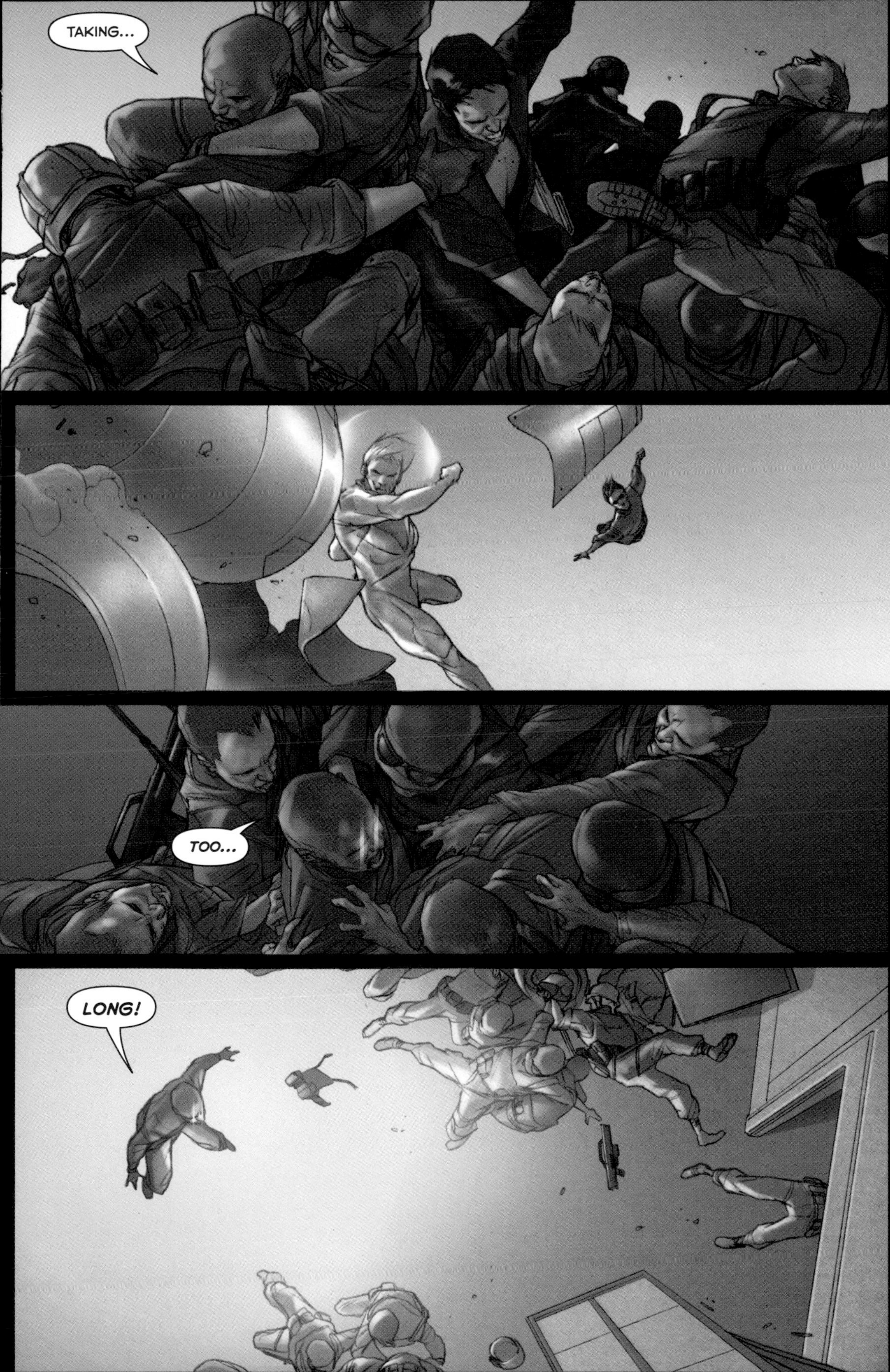
TAKING...
TOO...
LONG!

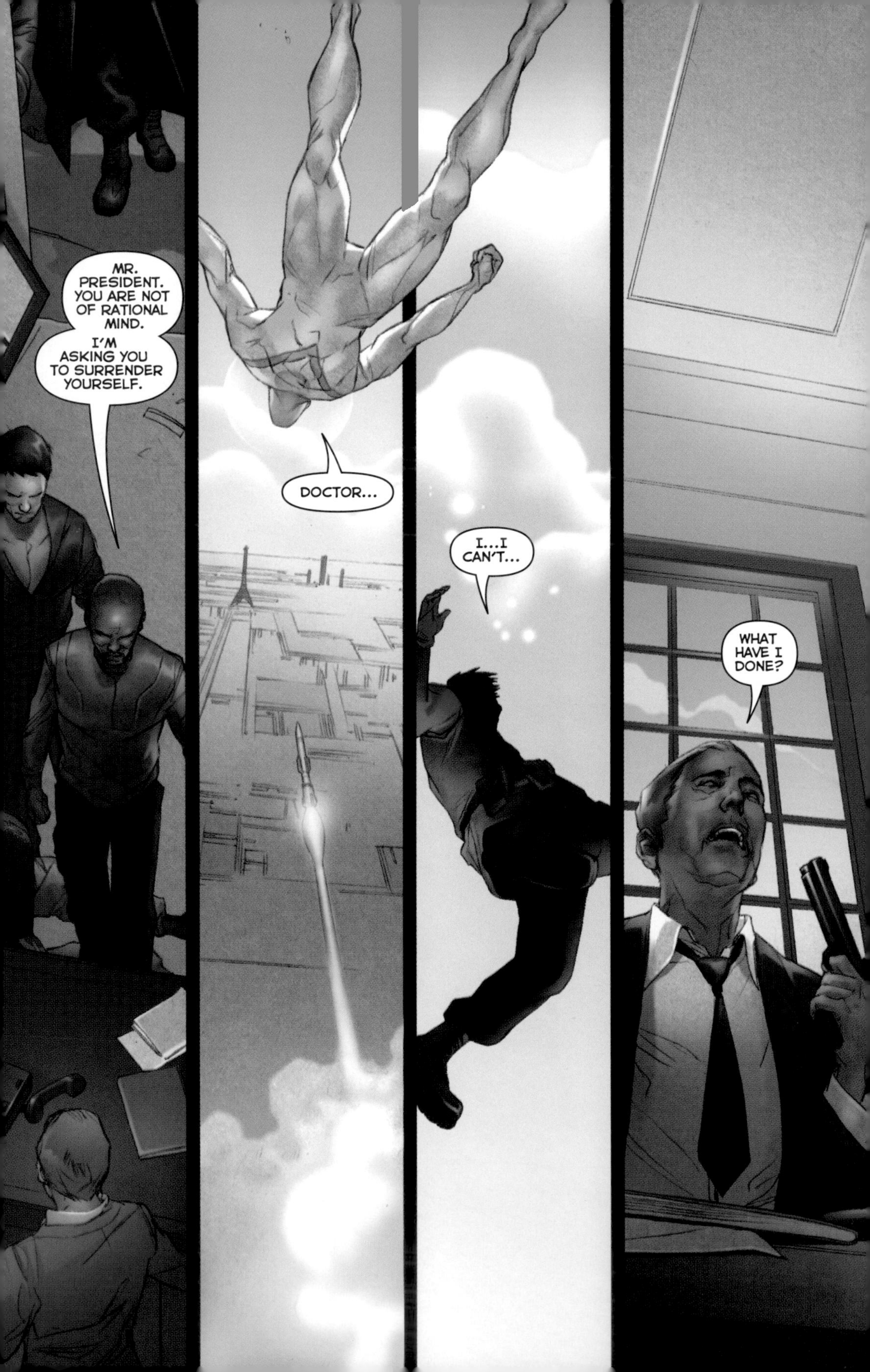
MR. PRESIDENT. YOU ARE NOT OF RATIONAL MIND.
I'M ASKING YOU TO SURRENDER YOURSELF.
DOCTOR...
I...I CAN'T...
WHAT HAVE I DONE?

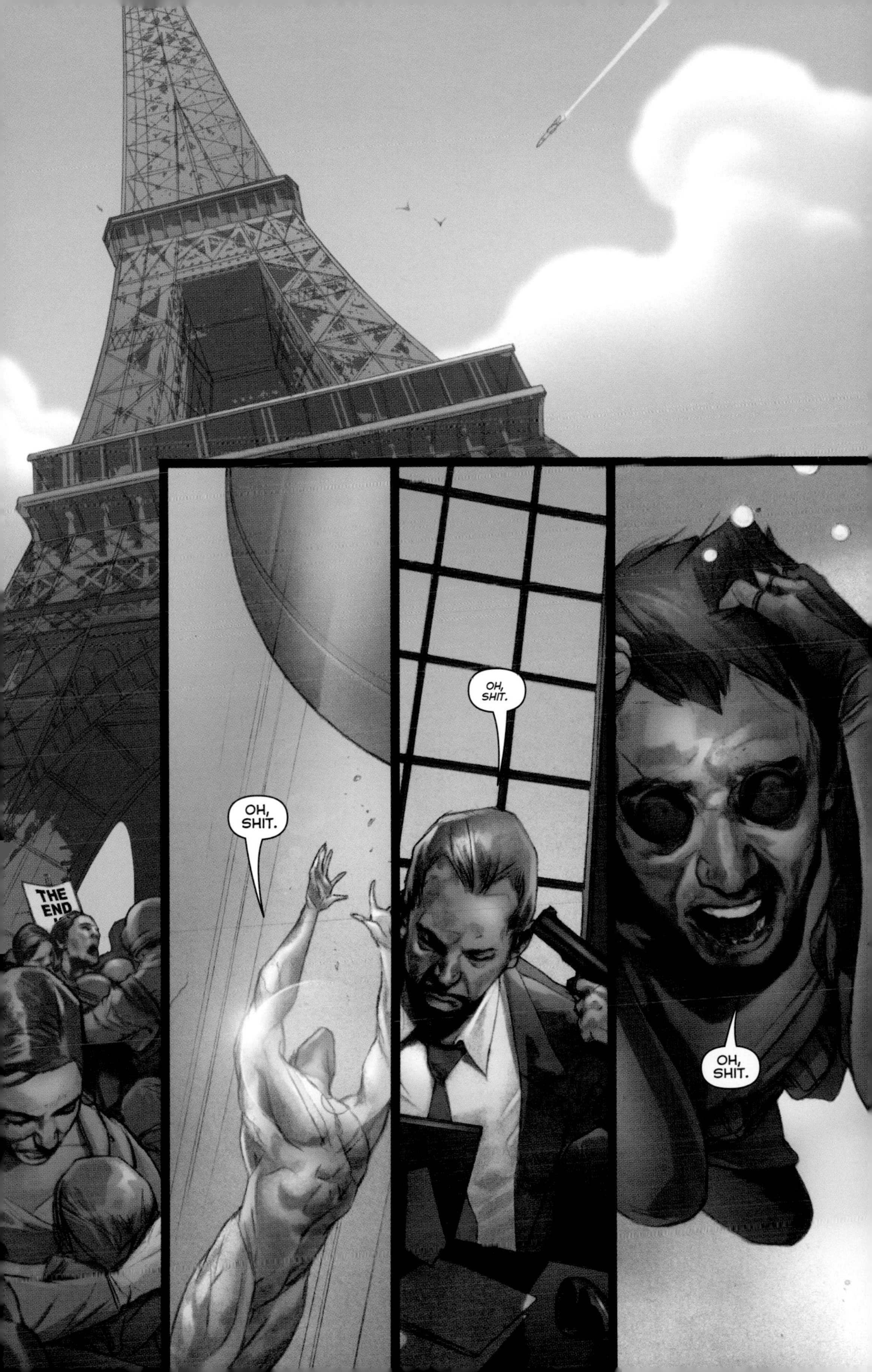
THE END
OH, SHIT.
OH, SHIT.
OH, SHIT.

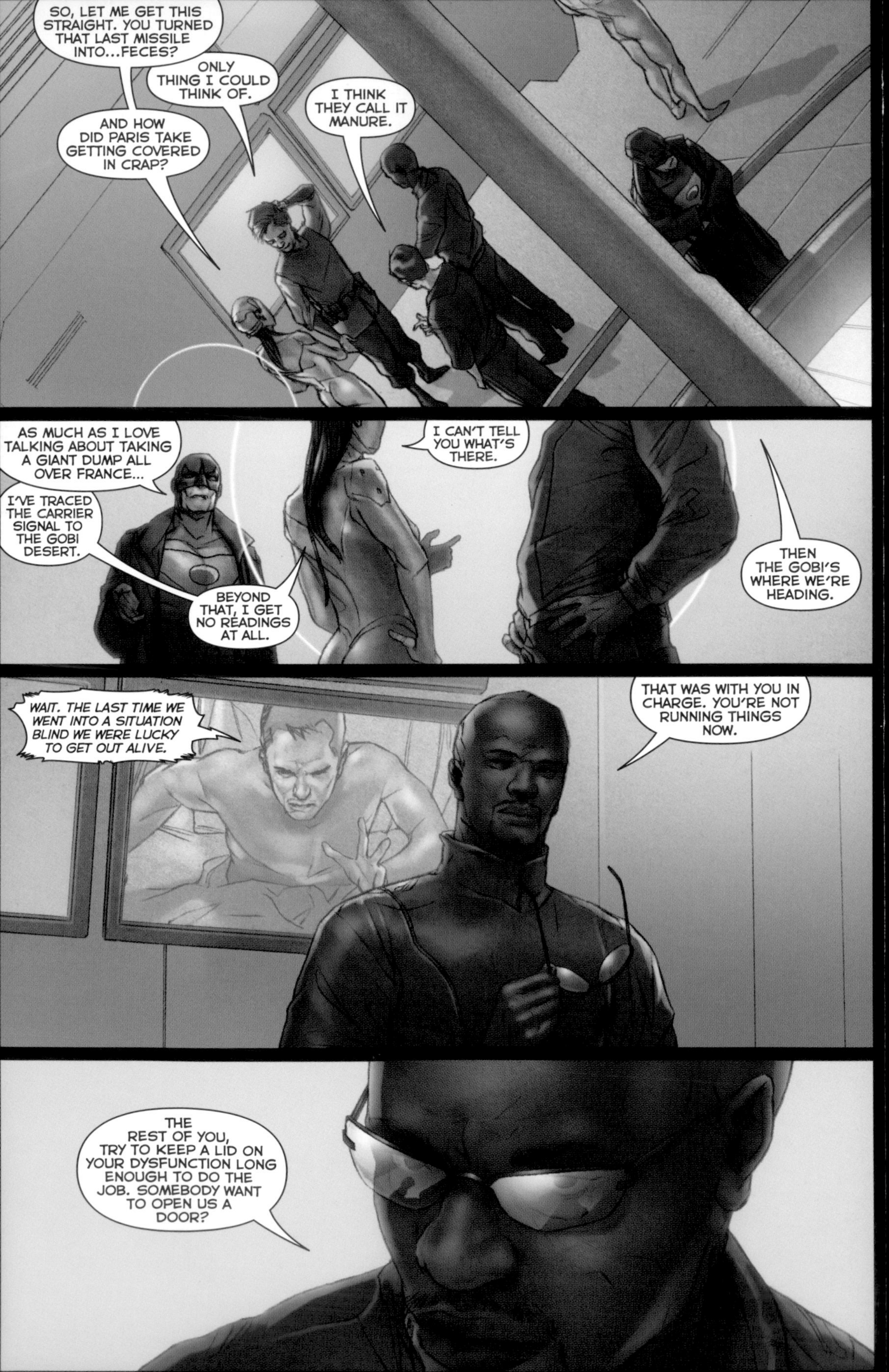

SO, LET ME GET THIS STRAIGHT. YOU TURNED THAT LAST MISSILE INTO...FECES?
ONLY THING I COULD THINK OF.
AND HOW DID PARIS TAKE GETTING COVERED IN CRAP?
I THINK THEY CALL IT MANURE.
AS MUCH AS I LOVE TALKING ABOUT TAKING A GIANT DUMP ALL OVER FRANCE...
I'VE TRACED THE CARRIER SIGNAL TO THE GOBI DESERT.
I CAN'T TELL YOU WHAT'S THERE.
BEYOND THAT, I GET NO READINGS AT ALL.
THEN THE GOBI'S WHERE WE'RE HEADING.
*WAIT. THE LAST TIME WE WENT INTO A SITUATION BLIND WE WERE LUCKY TO GET OUT ALIVE.*
THAT WAS WITH YOU IN CHARGE. YOU'RE NOT RUNNING THINGS NOW.
THE REST OF YOU, TRY TO KEEP A LID ON YOUR DYSFUNCTION LONG ENOUGH TO DO THE JOB. SOMEBODY WANT TO OPEN US A DOOR?

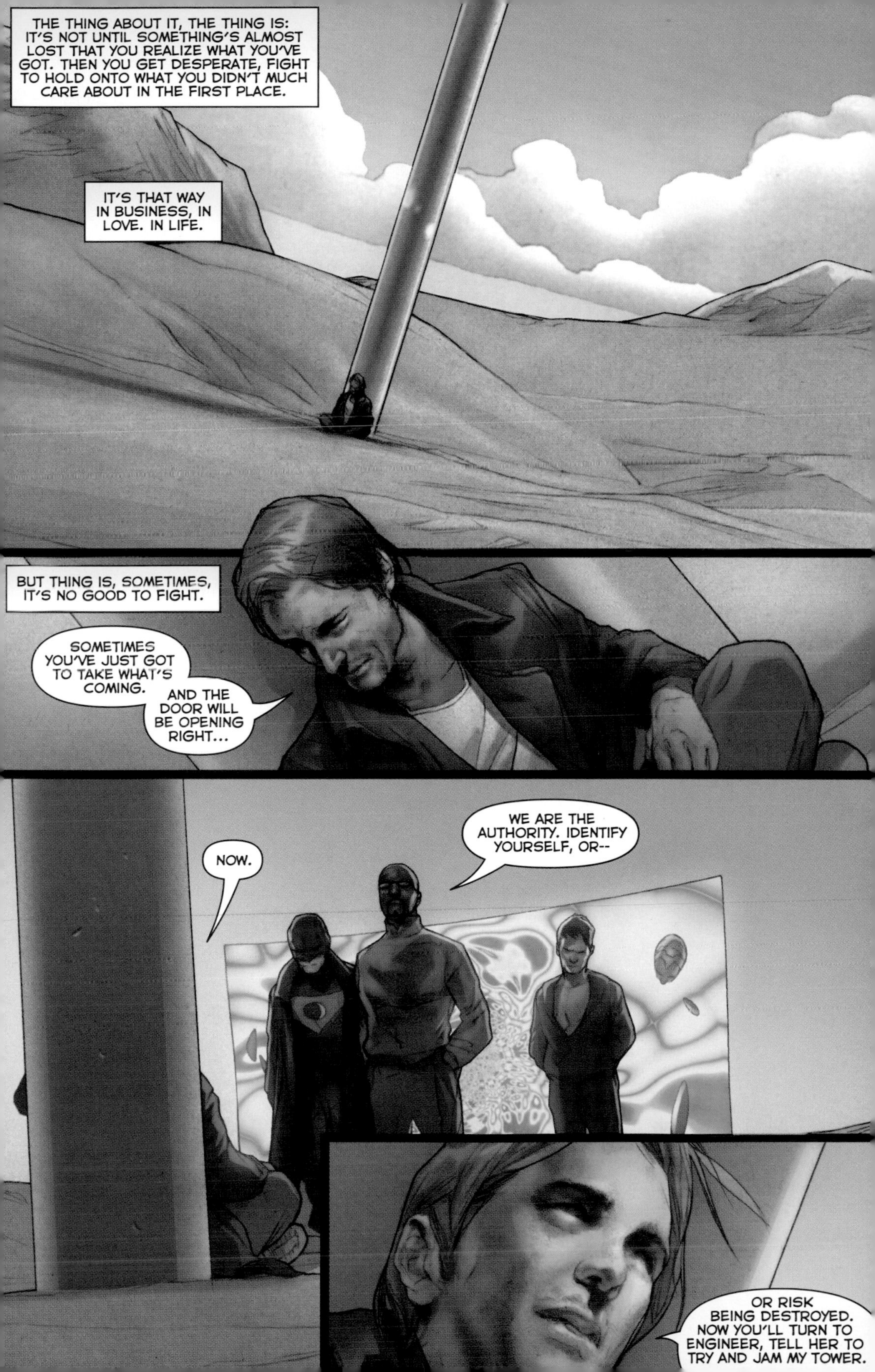
THE THING ABOUT IT, THE THING IS: IT'S NOT UNTIL SOMETHING'S ALMOST LOST THAT YOU REALIZE WHAT YOU'VE GOT. THEN YOU GET DESPERATE, FIGHT TO HOLD ONTO WHAT YOU DIDN'T MUCH CARE ABOUT IN THE FIRST PLACE.
IT'S THAT WAY IN BUSINESS, IN LOVE. IN LIFE.
BUT THING IS, SOMETIMES, IT'S NO GOOD TO FIGHT.
SOMETIMES YOU'VE JUST GOT TO TAKE WHAT'S COMING.
AND THE DOOR WILL BE OPENING RIGHT...
NOW.
WE ARE THE AUTHORITY. IDENTIFY YOURSELF, OR--
OR RISK BEING DESTROYED. NOW YOU'LL TURN TO ENGINEER, TELL HER TO TRY AND JAM MY TOWER.

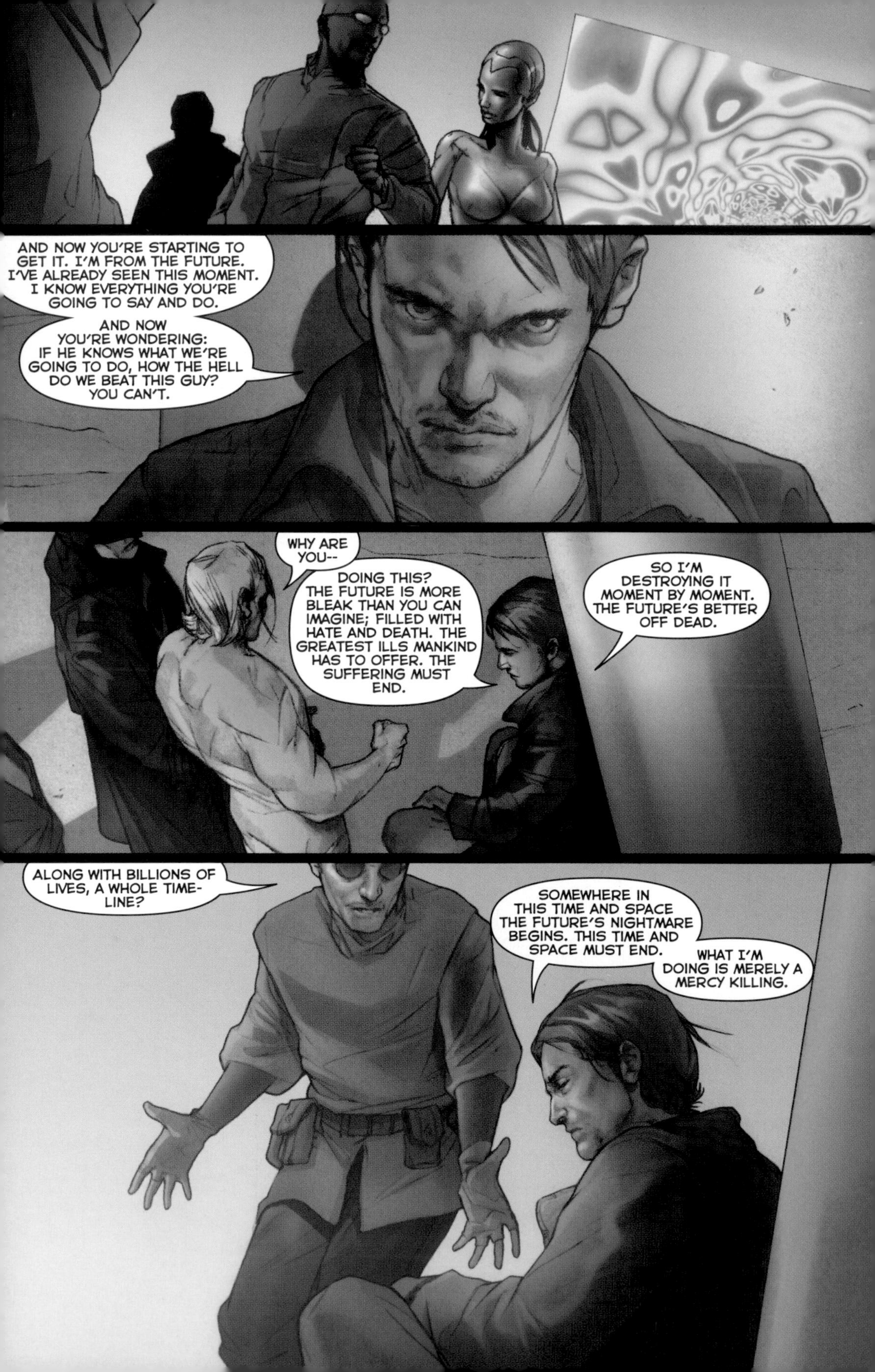
AND NOW YOU'RE STARTING TO GET IT. I'M FROM THE FUTURE. I'VE ALREADY SEEN THIS MOMENT. I KNOW EVERYTHING YOU'RE GOING TO SAY AND DO.
AND NOW YOU'RE WONDERING: IF HE KNOWS WHAT WE'RE GOING TO DO, HOW THE HELL DO WE BEAT THIS GUY? YOU CAN'T.
WHY ARE YOU--
DOING THIS? THE FUTURE IS MORE BLEAK THAN YOU CAN IMAGINE; FILLED WITH HATE AND DEATH. THE GREATEST ILLS MANKIND HAS TO OFFER. THE SUFFERING MUST END.
SO I'M DESTROYING IT MOMENT BY MOMENT. THE FUTURE'S BETTER OFF DEAD.
ALONG WITH BILLIONS OF LIVES, A WHOLE TIME-LINE?
SOMEWHERE IN THIS TIME AND SPACE THE FUTURE'S NIGHTMARE BEGINS. THIS TIME AND SPACE MUST END.
WHAT I'M DOING IS MERELY A MERCY KILLING.

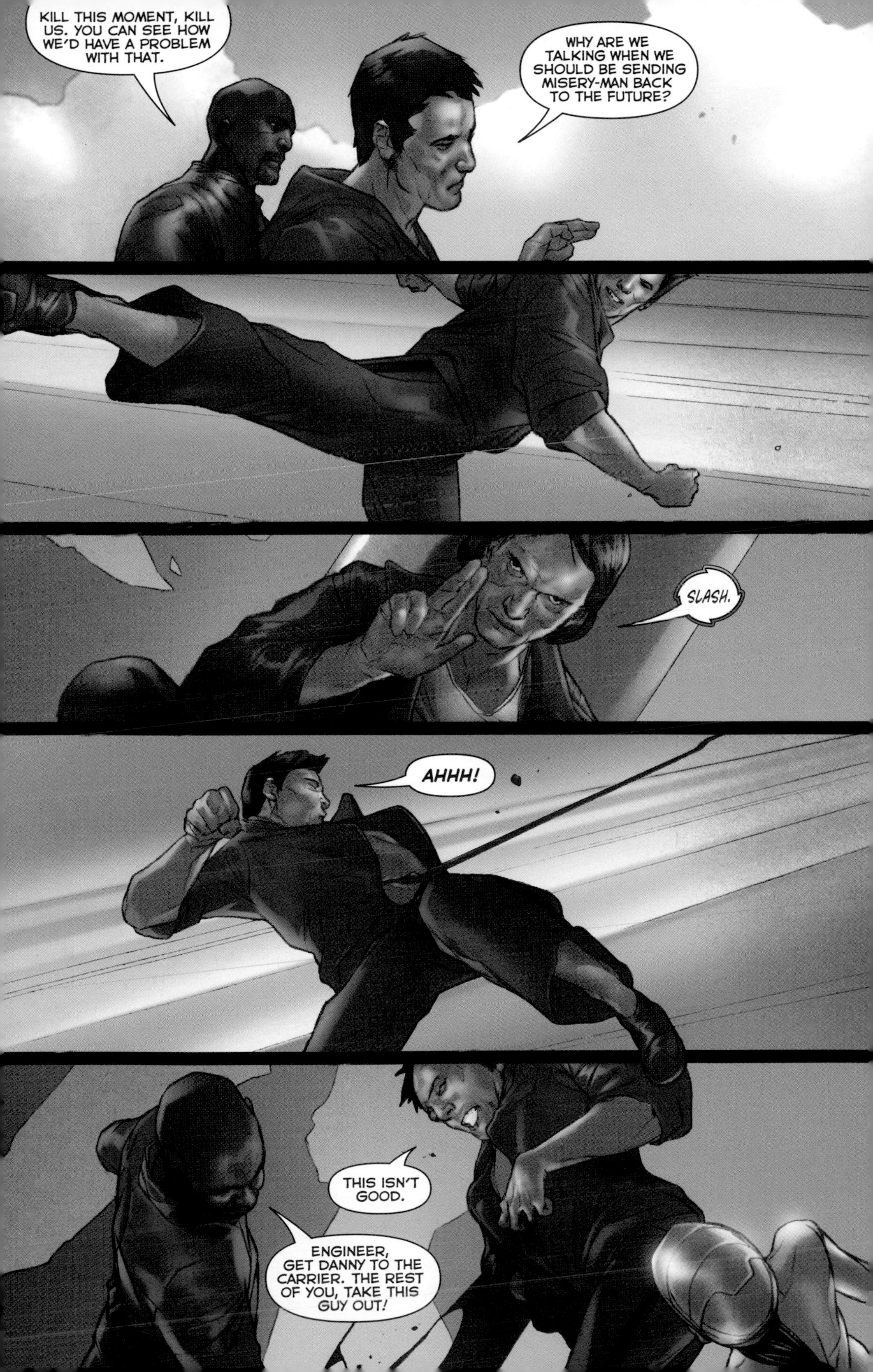
KILL THIS MOMENT, KILL US. YOU CAN SEE HOW WE'D HAVE A PROBLEM WITH THAT.
WHY ARE WE TALKING WHEN WE SHOULD BE SENDING MISERY-MAN BACK TO THE FUTURE?
SLASH.
AHHH!
THIS ISN'T GOOD.
ENGINEER, GET DANNY TO THE CARRIER. THE REST OF YOU, TAKE THIS GUY OUT!

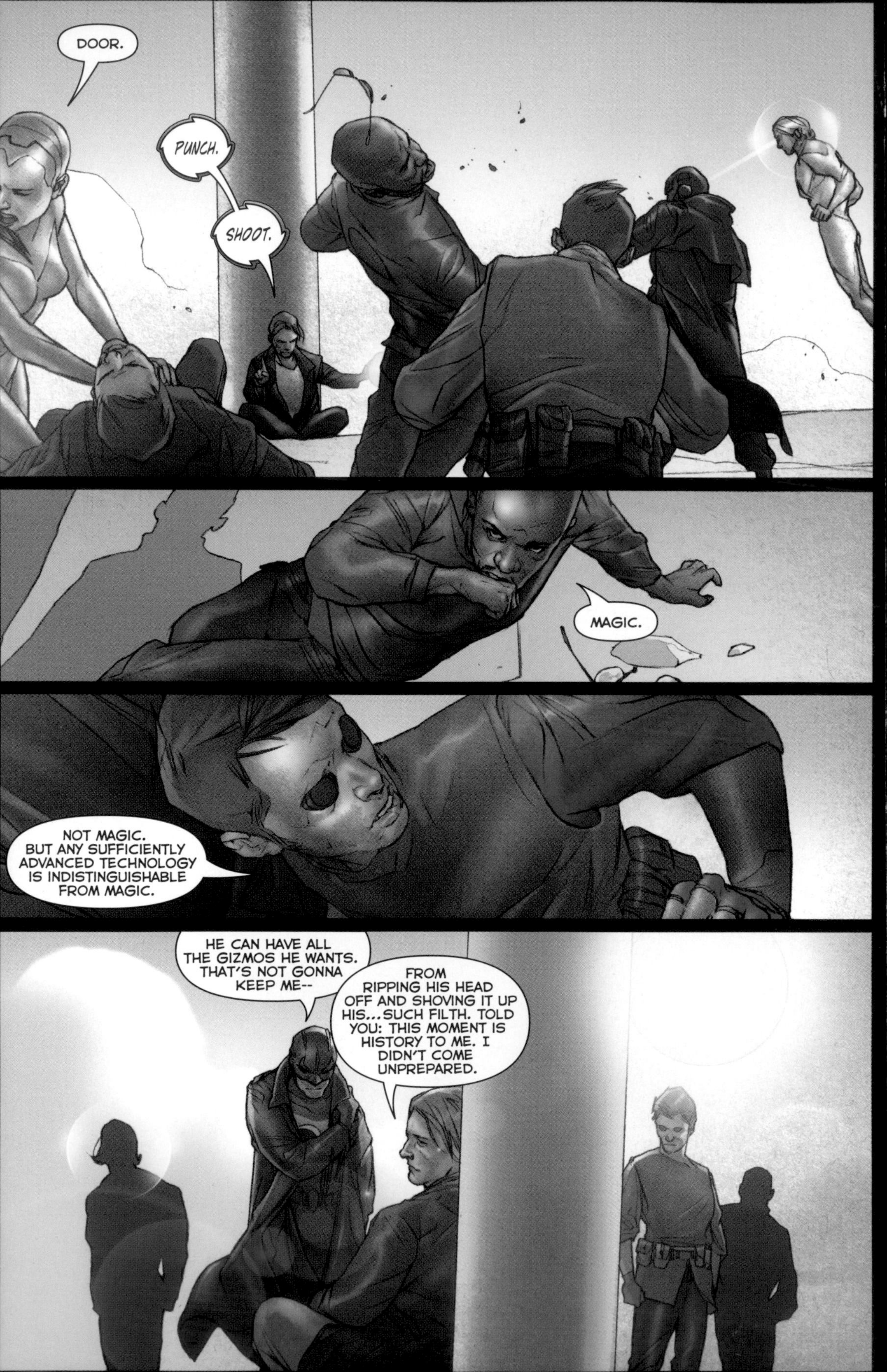
DOOR.
PUNCH.
SHOOT.
MAGIC.
NOT MAGIC. BUT ANY SUFFICIENTLY ADVANCED TECHNOLOGY IS INDISTINGUISHABLE FROM MAGIC.
HE CAN HAVE ALL THE GIZMOS HE WANTS. THAT'S NOT GONNA KEEP ME--
FROM RIPPING HIS HEAD OFF AND SHOVING IT UP HIS...SUCH FILTH. TOLD YOU: THIS MOMENT IS HISTORY TO ME. I DIDN'T COME UNPREPARED.

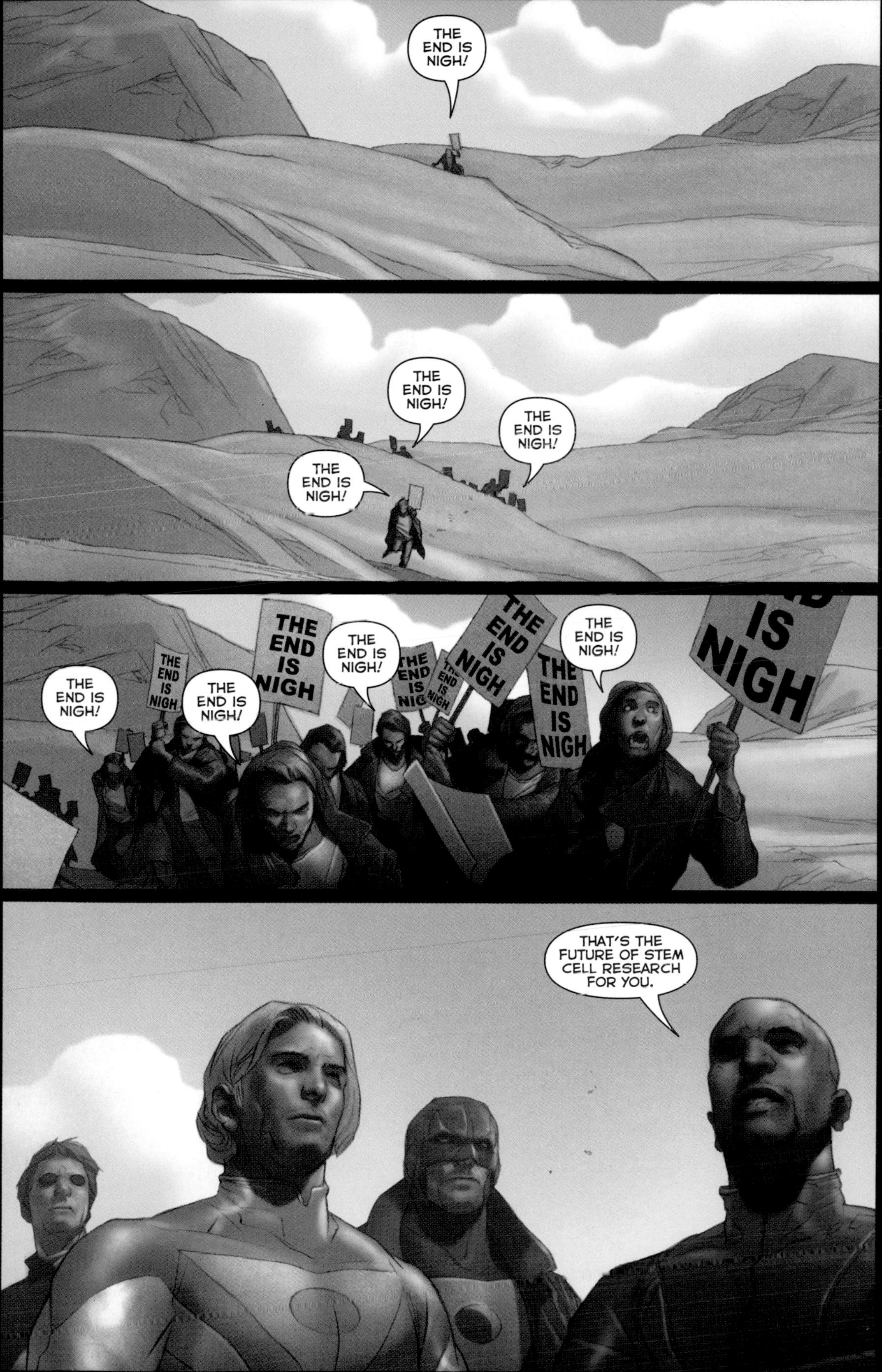
THE END IS NIGH!
THE END IS NIGH!
THE END IS NIGH!
THE END IS NIGH!
THE END IS NIGH!
THE END IS NIGH
THE END IS NIGH!
THE END IS NIGH
THE END IS NIGH!
THE END IS NIGH
THE END IS NIGH
THE END IS NIGH!
THE END IS NIGH
IS NIGH
THAT'S THE FUTURE OF STEM CELL RESEARCH FOR YOU.

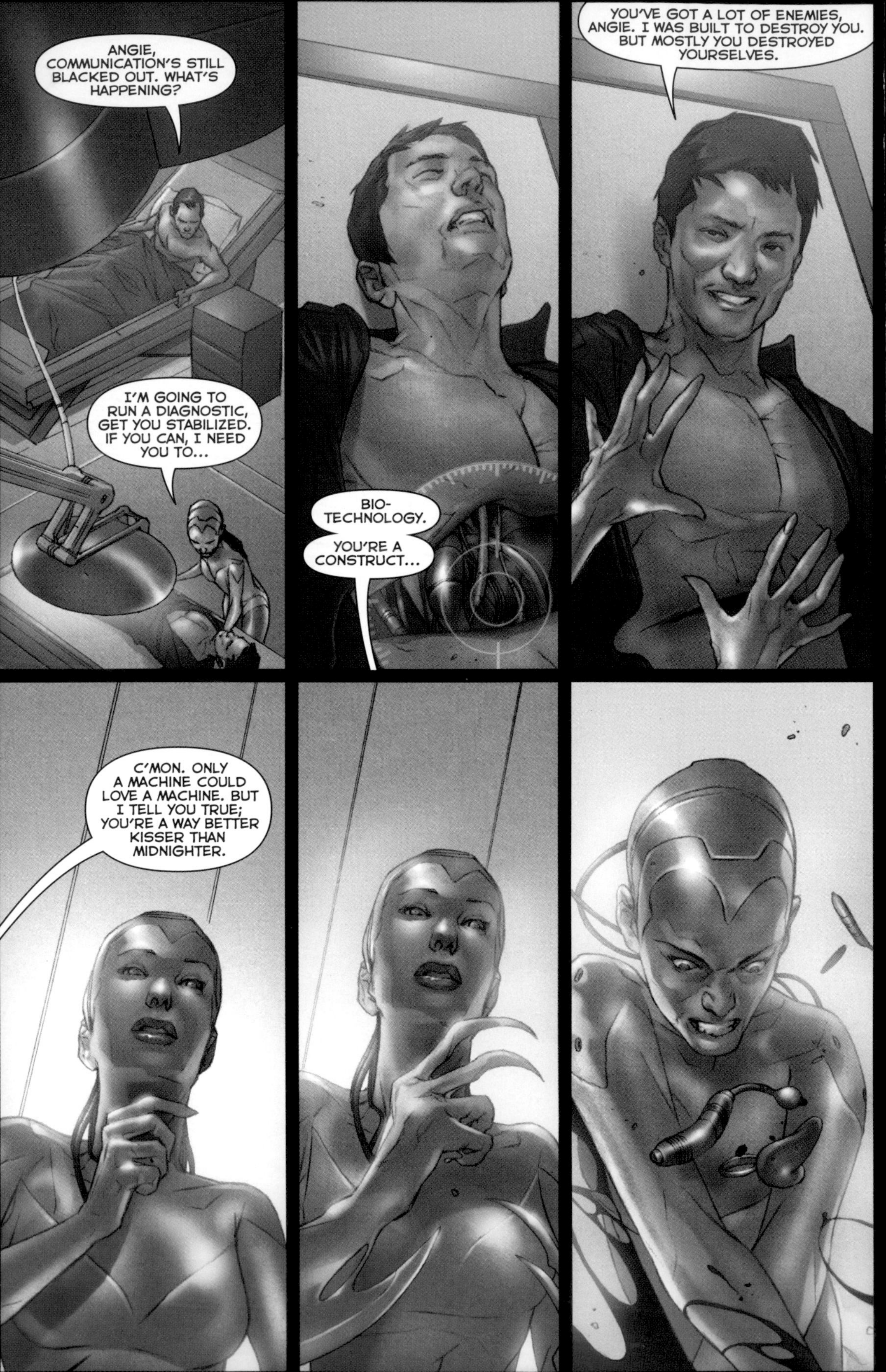
ANGIE, COMMUNICATION'S STILL BLACKED OUT. WHAT'S HAPPENING?
I'M GOING TO RUN A DIAGNOSTIC, GET YOU STABILIZED. IF YOU CAN, I NEED YOU TO...
BIO-TECHNOLOGY.
YOU'RE A CONSTRUCT...
YOU'VE GOT A LOT OF ENEMIES, ANGIE. I WAS BUILT TO DESTROY YOU. BUT MOSTLY YOU DESTROYED YOURSELVES.
C'MON. ONLY A MACHINE COULD LOVE A MACHINE. BUT I TELL YOU TRUE; YOU'RE A WAY BETTER KISSER THAN MIDNIGHTER.

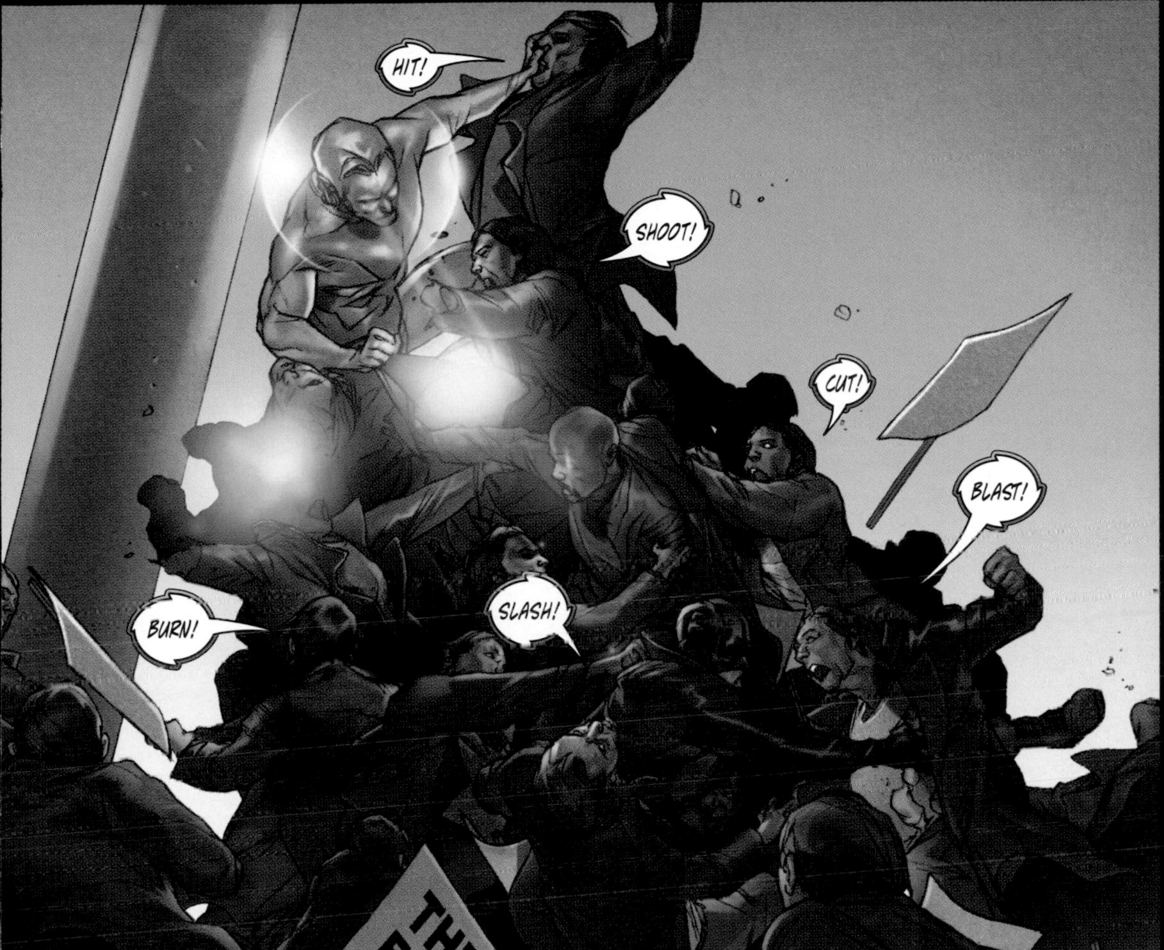
HIT!
SHOOT!
CUT!
BLAST!
BURN!
SLASH!
THE END IS NIGH

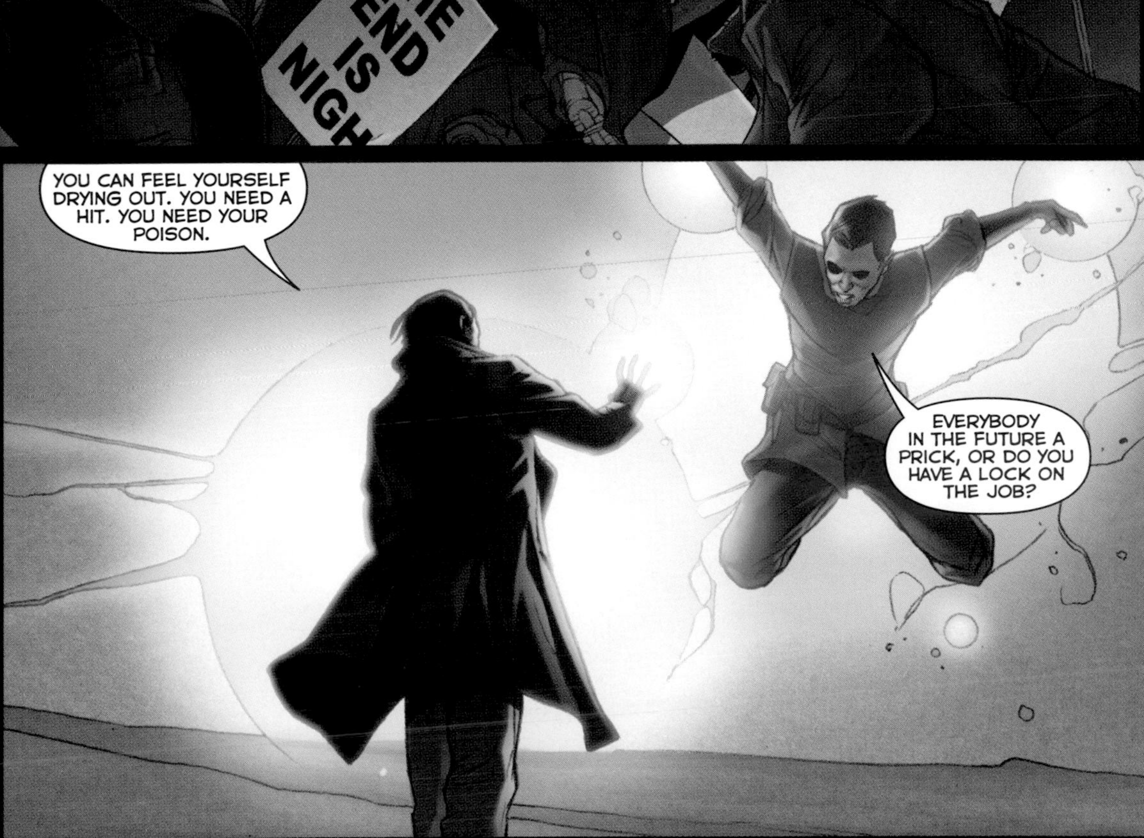
YOU CAN FEEL YOURSELF DRYING OUT. YOU NEED A HIT. YOU NEED YOUR POISON.
EVERYBODY IN THE FUTURE A PRICK, OR DO YOU HAVE A LOCK ON THE JOB?

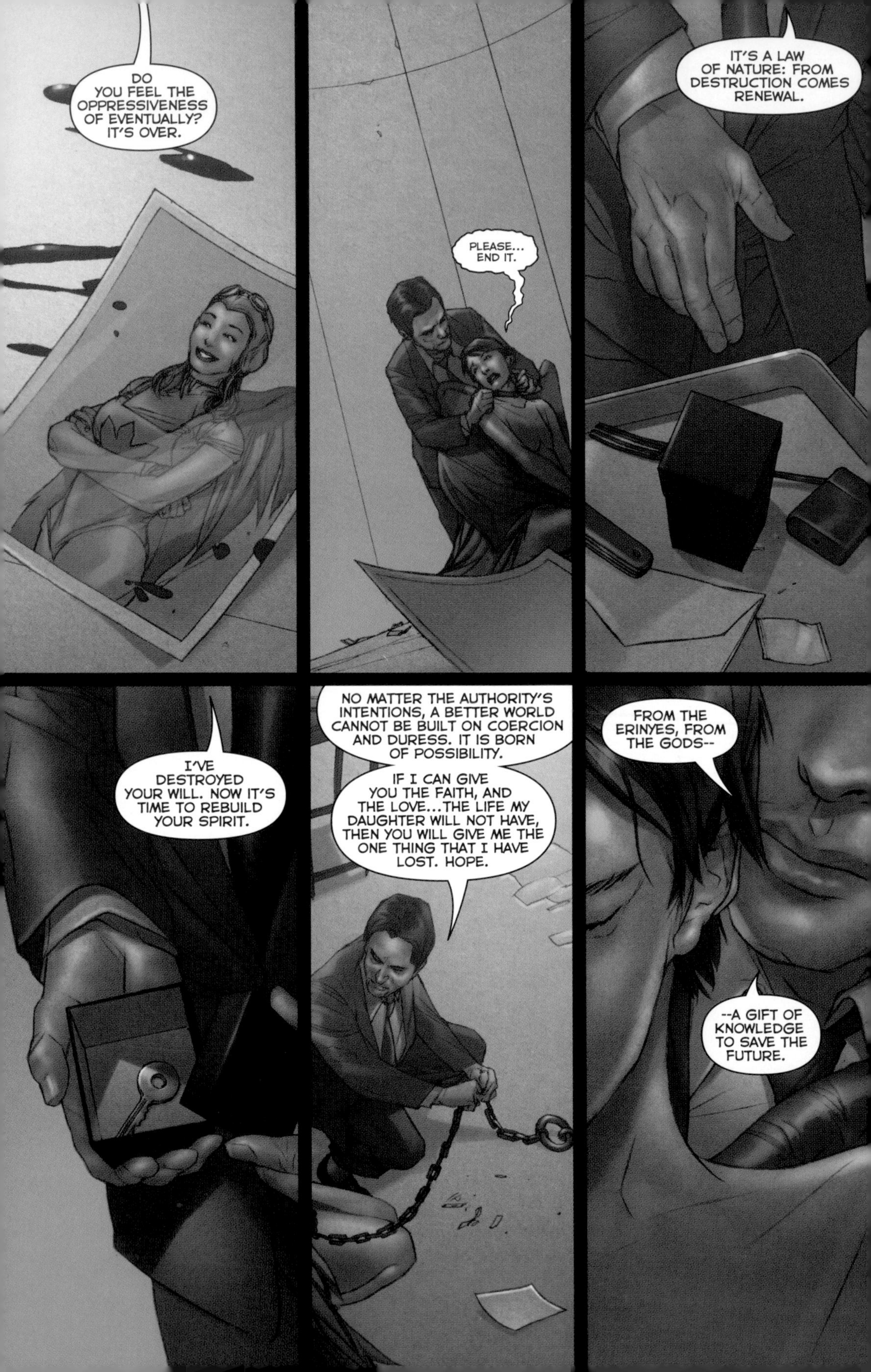
DO YOU FEEL THE OPPRESSIVENESS OF EVENTUALLY? IT'S OVER.
PLEASE... END IT.
IT'S A LAW OF NATURE: FROM DESTRUCTION COMES RENEWAL.
I'VE DESTROYED YOUR WILL. NOW IT'S TIME TO REBUILD YOUR SPIRIT.
NO MATTER THE AUTHORITY'S INTENTIONS, A BETTER WORLD CANNOT BE BUILT ON COERCION AND DURESS. IT IS BORN OF POSSIBILITY.
IF I CAN GIVE YOU THE FAITH, AND THE LOVE...THE LIFE MY DAUGHTER WILL NOT HAVE, THEN YOU WILL GIVE ME THE ONE THING THAT I HAVE LOST. HOPE.
FROM THE ERINYES, FROM THE GODS--
--A GIFT OF KNOWLEDGE TO SAVE THE FUTURE.

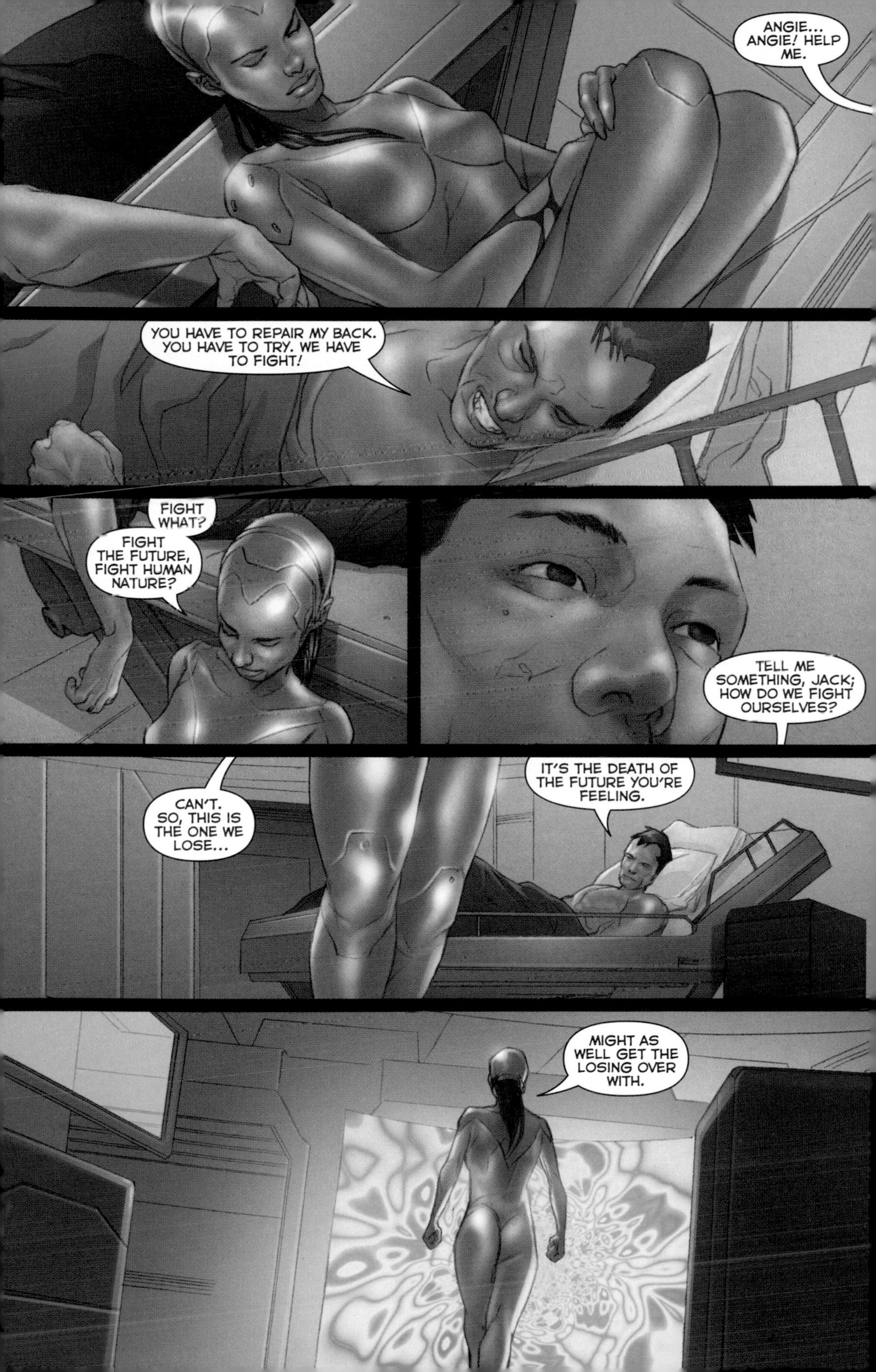
ANGIE... ANGIE! HELP ME.
YOU HAVE TO REPAIR MY BACK. YOU HAVE TO TRY. WE HAVE TO FIGHT!
FIGHT WHAT?
FIGHT THE FUTURE, FIGHT HUMAN NATURE?
TELL ME SOMETHING, JACK; HOW DO WE FIGHT OURSELVES?
CAN'T. SO, THIS IS THE ONE WE LOSE...
IT'S THE DEATH OF THE FUTURE YOU'RE FEELING.
MIGHT AS WELL GET THE LOSING OVER WITH.

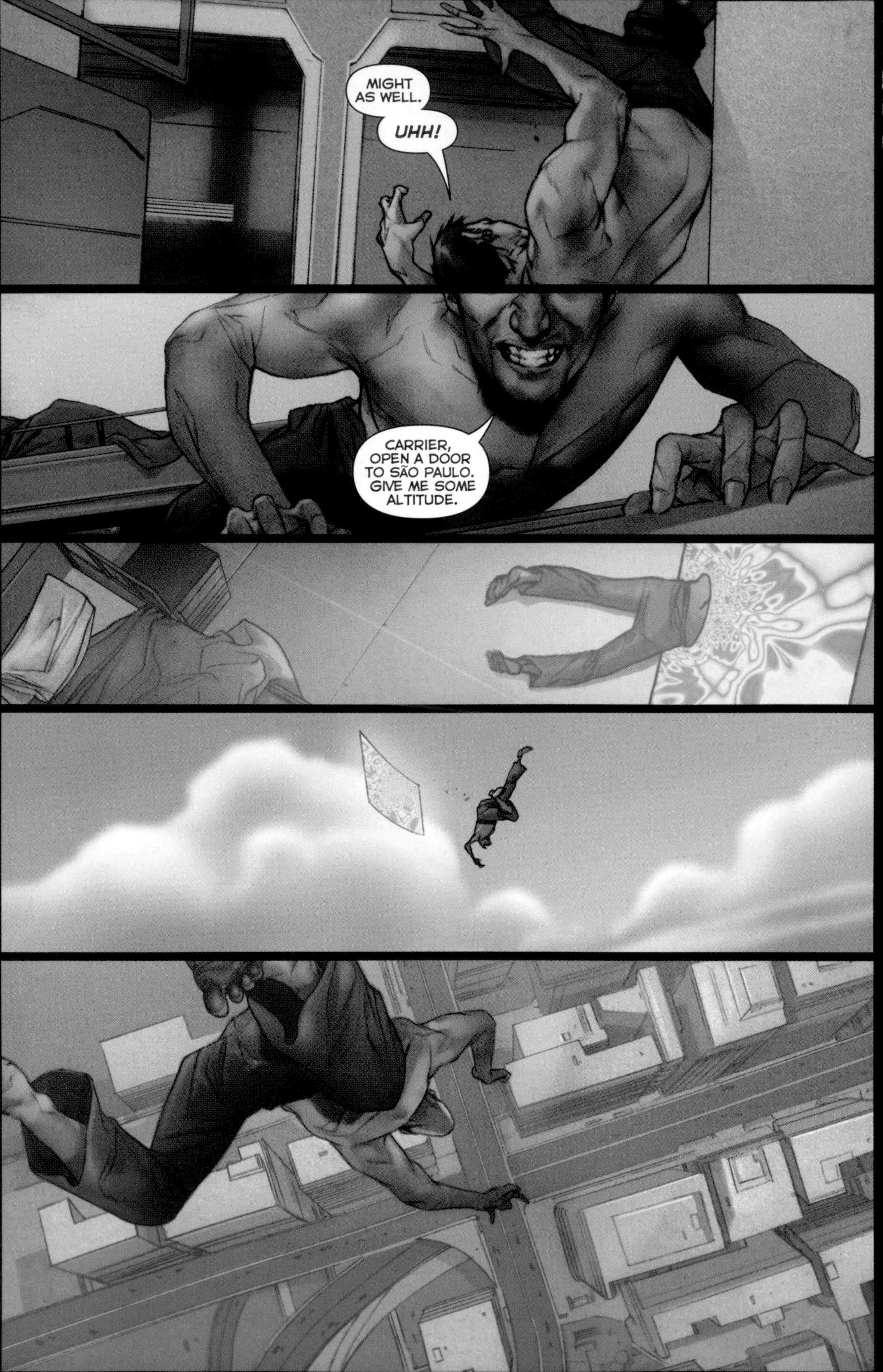
MIGHT AS WELL.
UHH!
CARRIER, OPEN A DOOR TO SÃO PAULO. GIVE ME SOME ALTITUDE.

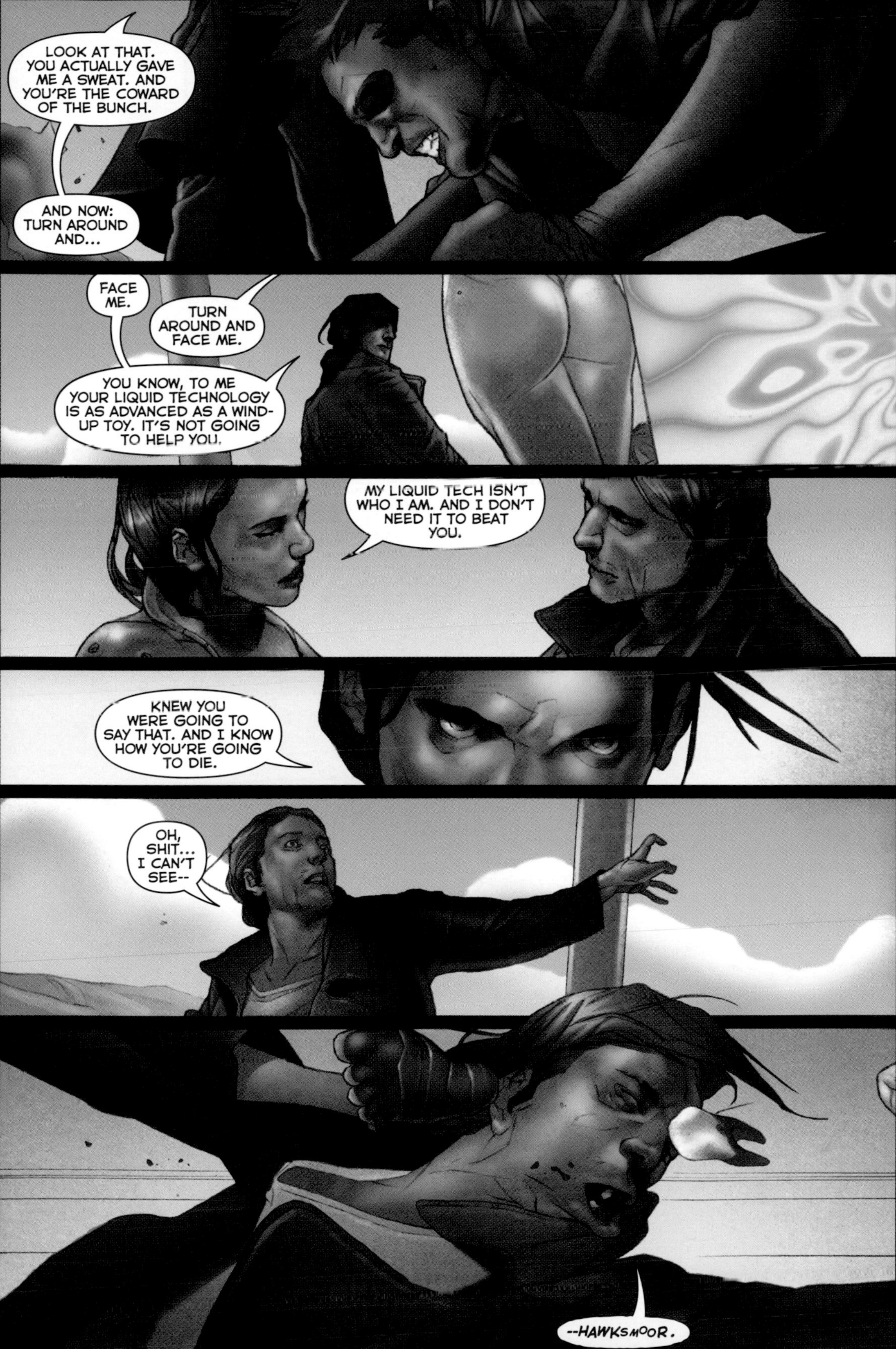
LOOK AT THAT. YOU ACTUALLY GAVE ME A SWEAT. AND YOU'RE THE COWARD OF THE BUNCH.
AND NOW: TURN AROUND AND...
FACE ME.
TURN AROUND AND FACE ME.
YOU KNOW, TO ME YOUR LIQUID TECHNOLOGY IS AS ADVANCED AS A WIND-UP TOY. IT'S NOT GOING TO HELP YOU.
MY LIQUID TECH ISN'T WHO I AM. AND I DON'T NEED IT TO BEAT YOU.
KNEW YOU WERE GOING TO SAY THAT. AND I KNOW HOW YOU'RE GOING TO DIE.
OH, SHIT... I CAN'T SEE--
--HAWKSMOOR.

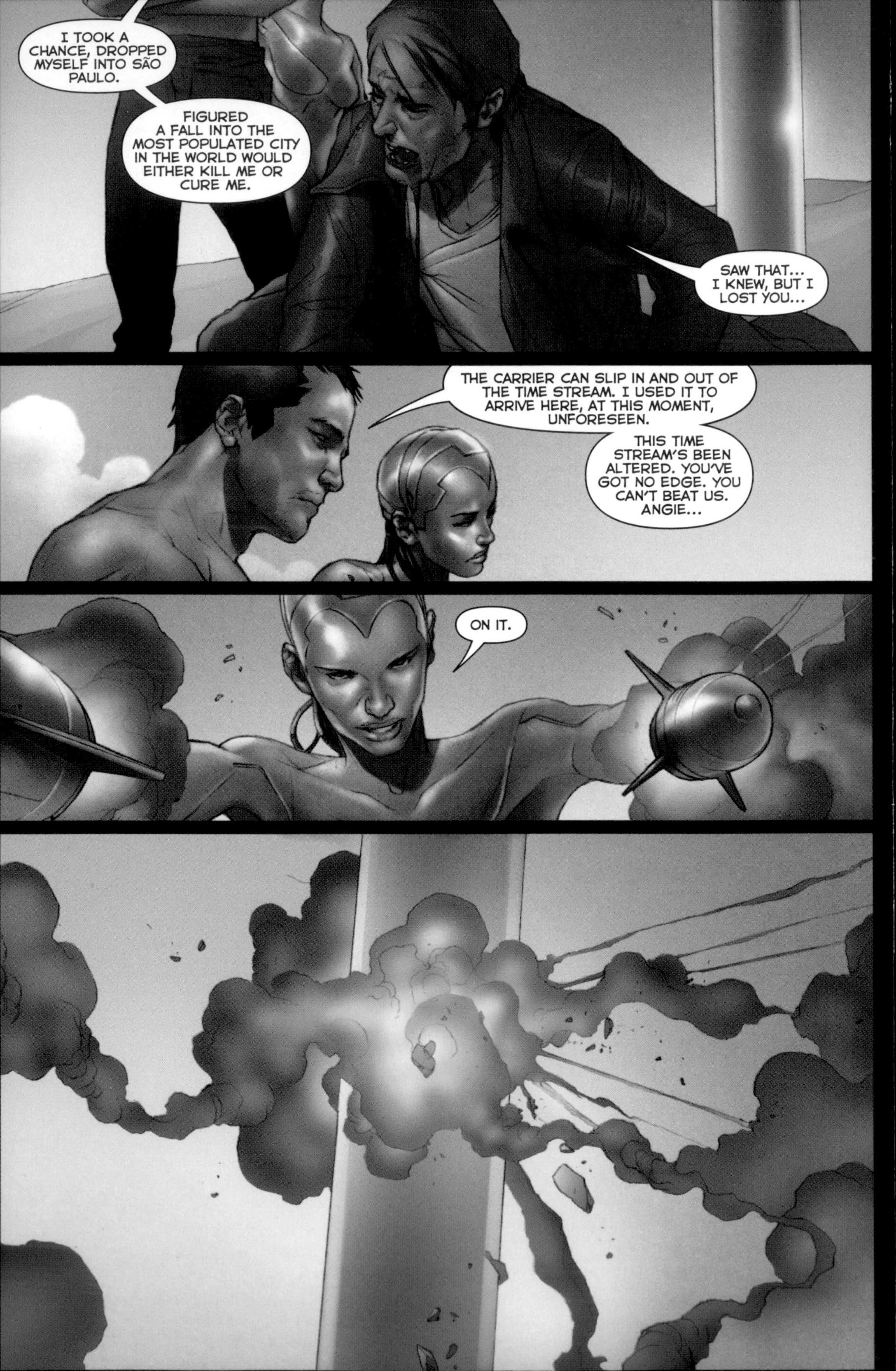
I TOOK A CHANCE, DROPPED MYSELF INTO SÃO PAULO.
FIGURED A FALL INTO THE MOST POPULATED CITY IN THE WORLD WOULD EITHER KILL ME OR CURE ME.
SAW THAT... I KNEW, BUT I LOST YOU...
THE CARRIER CAN SLIP IN AND OUT OF THE TIME STREAM. I USED IT TO ARRIVE HERE, AT THIS MOMENT, UNFORESEEN.
THIS TIME STREAM'S BEEN ALTERED. YOU'VE GOT NO EDGE. YOU CAN'T BEAT US. ANGIE...
ON IT.

IF YOU ALL AREN'T TOO BUSY?

OH, SORRY.

I'VE GOT TO REMEMBER TO QUIT GIVING THE DOCTOR SHIT.

DO YOU KNOW WHAT YOU'VE DONE? THE PRESENT WILL REGENERATE THE FUTURE. YOU'VE DOOMED MANKIND TO MISERY AND DEATH.

THEN TELL US HOW TO CHANGE THE PRESENT.

"HOW" IS BEYOND EVEN MY TECHNOLOGY. THERE'S NO HELP FOR YOU. YOU MADE YOUR BED, SCREW YOURSELF IN IT.

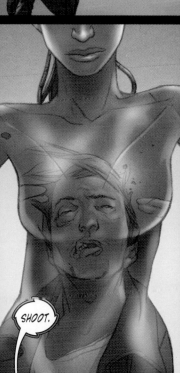

SHOOT.

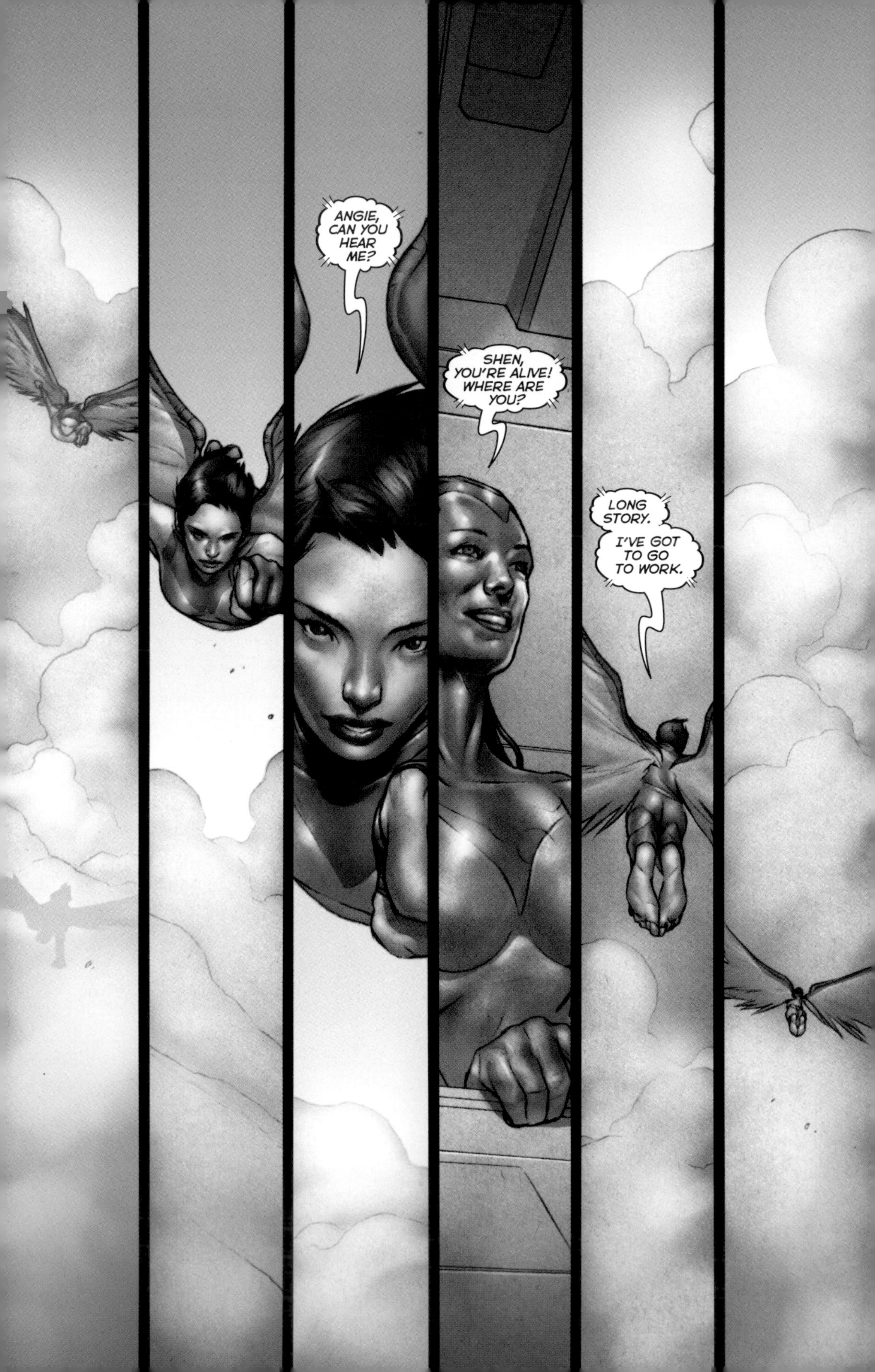
ANGIE, CAN YOU HEAR ME?
SHEN, YOU'RE ALIVE! WHERE ARE YOU?
LONG STORY.
I'VE GOT TO GO TO WORK.

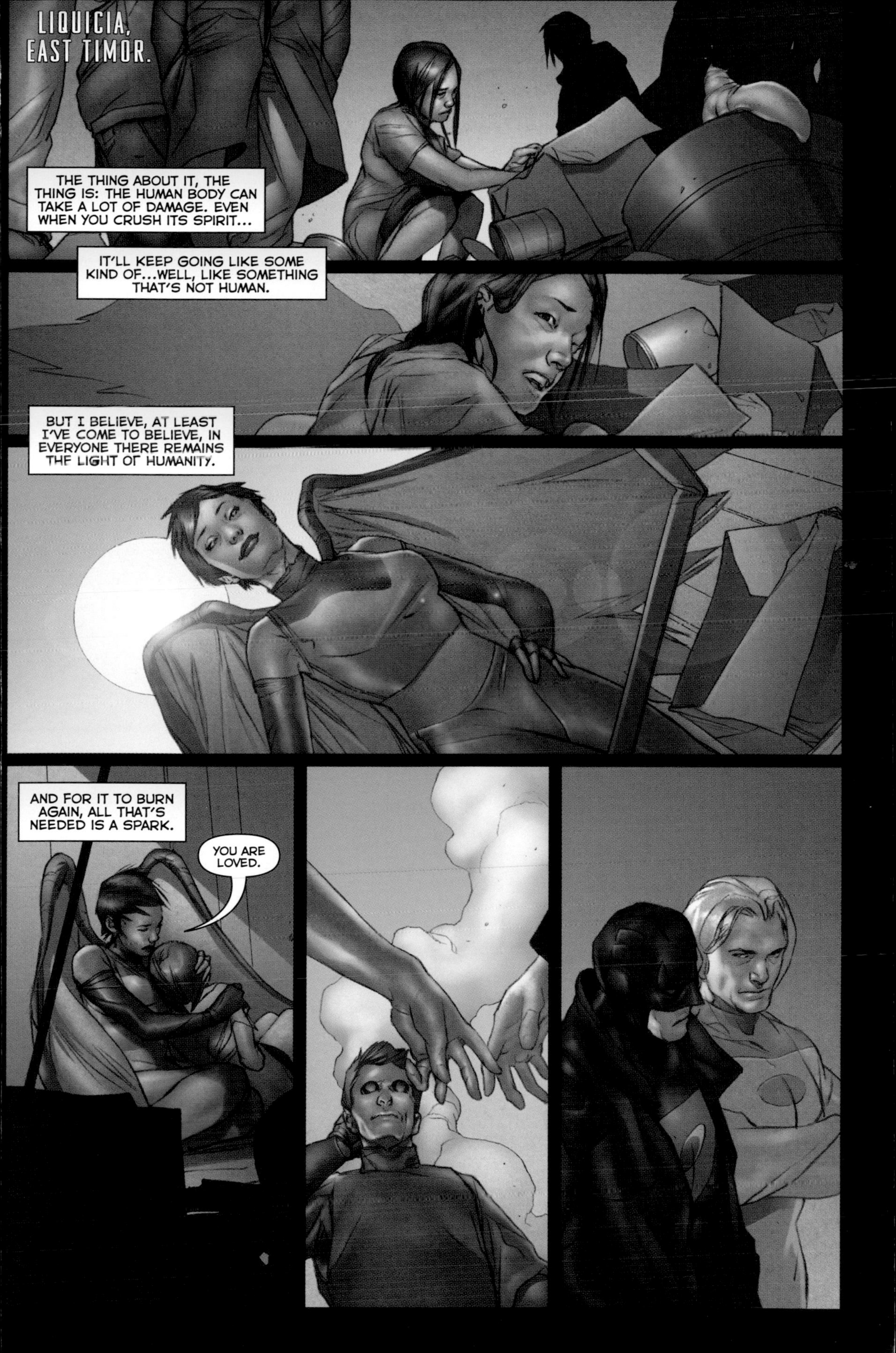
LIQUICIA, EAST TIMOR.
THE THING ABOUT IT, THE THING IS: THE HUMAN BODY CAN TAKE A LOT OF DAMAGE. EVEN WHEN YOU CRUSH ITS SPIRIT...
IT'LL KEEP GOING LIKE SOME KIND OF...WELL, LIKE SOMETHING THAT'S NOT HUMAN.
BUT I BELIEVE, AT LEAST I'VE COME TO BELIEVE, IN EVERYONE THERE REMAINS THE LIGHT OF HUMANITY.
AND FOR IT TO BURN AGAIN, ALL THAT'S NEEDED IS A SPARK.
YOU ARE LOVED.

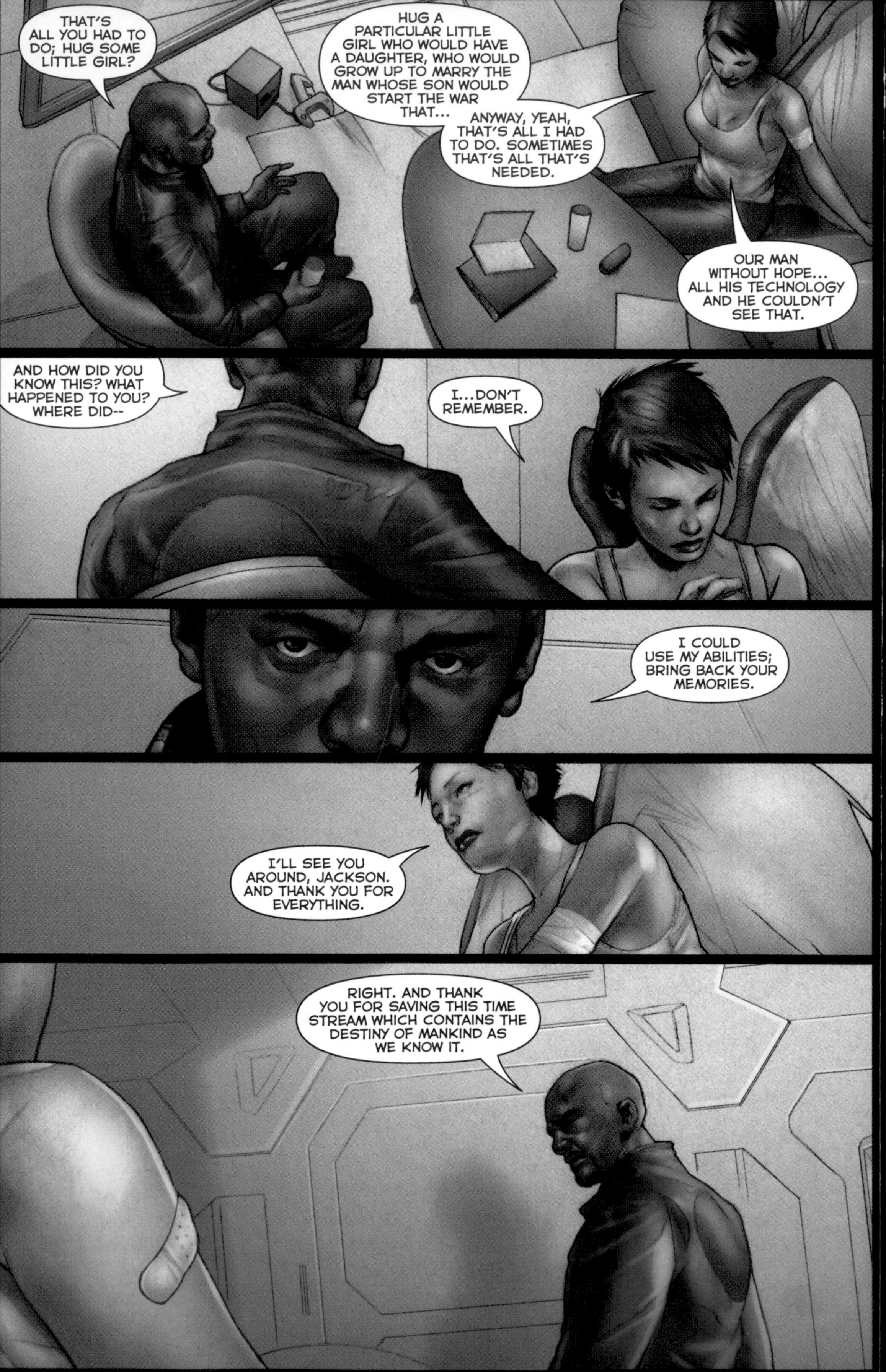
THAT'S ALL YOU HAD TO DO; HUG SOME LITTLE GIRL?
HUG A PARTICULAR LITTLE GIRL WHO WOULD HAVE A DAUGHTER, WHO WOULD GROW UP TO MARRY THE MAN WHOSE SON WOULD START THE WAR THAT...
ANYWAY, YEAH, THAT'S ALL I HAD TO DO. SOMETIMES THAT'S ALL THAT'S NEEDED.
OUR MAN WITHOUT HOPE... ALL HIS TECHNOLOGY AND HE COULDN'T SEE THAT.
AND HOW DID YOU KNOW THIS? WHAT HAPPENED TO YOU? WHERE DID--
I...DON'T REMEMBER.
I COULD USE MY ABILITIES; BRING BACK YOUR MEMORIES.
I'LL SEE YOU AROUND, JACKSON. AND THANK YOU FOR EVERYTHING.
RIGHT. AND THANK YOU FOR SAVING THIS TIME STREAM WHICH CONTAINS THE DESTINY OF MANKIND AS WE KNOW IT.

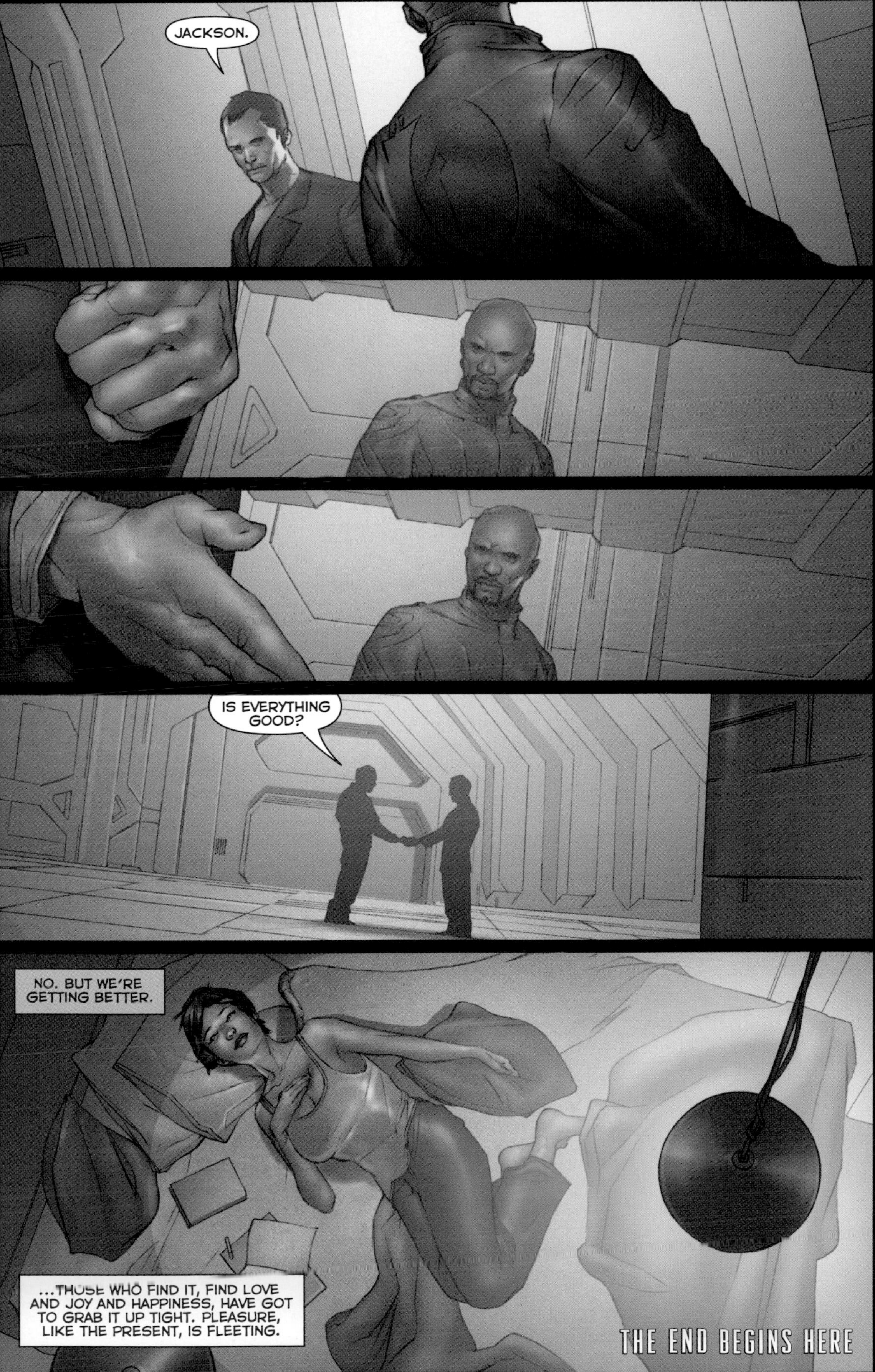
JACKSON.
IS EVERYTHING GOOD?
NO. BUT WE'RE GETTING BETTER.
...THOSE WHO FIND IT, FIND LOVE AND JOY AND HAPPINESS, HAVE GOT TO GRAB IT UP TIGHT. PLEASURE, LIKE THE PRESENT, IS FLEETING.
THE END BEGINS HERE

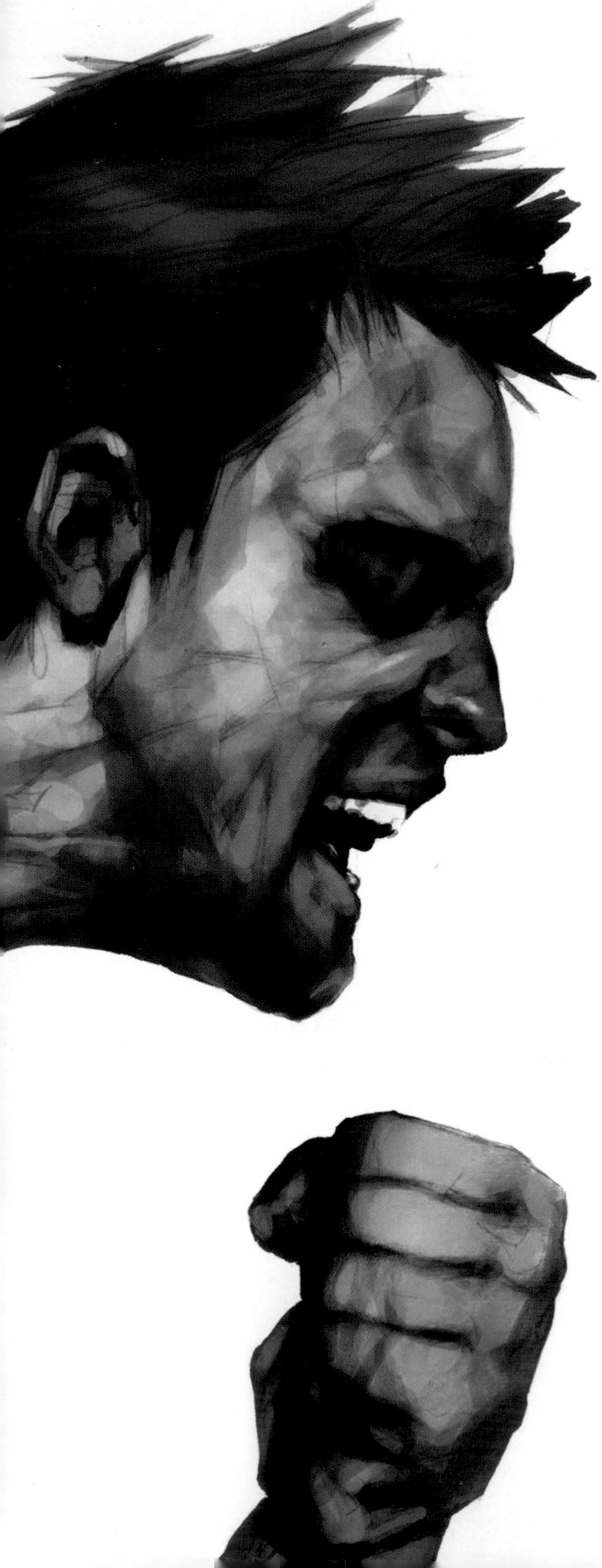

## Written by
## John Ridley

## Art by
## Ben Oliver

### Colored by
### Wendy Broome
with Randy Mayor of WSFX

### Lettered by
### Phil Balsman

### Design by
### Larry Berry

### The Authority created by
### Warren Ellis and Bryan Hitch


Jim Lee
Editorial Director
John Nee
VP—Business Development
Scott Dunbier
Executive Editor
Ben Abernathy
Editor
Ed Roeder
Art Director
Paul Levitz
President & Publisher
Georg Brewer
VP—Design & Retail Product Development
Richard Bruning
Senior VP—Creative Director
Patrick Caldon
Senior VP—Finance & Operations
Chris Caramalis
VP—Finance
Terri Cunningham
VP—Managing Editor
Dan DiDio
VP—Editorial
Alison Gill
VP—Manufacturing
Rich Johnson
VP—Book Trade Sales
Hank Kanalz
VP—General Manager, WildStorm
Lillian Laserson
Senior VP & General Counsel
David McKillips
VP—Advertising & Custom Publishing
Gregory Noveck
Senior VP—Creative Affairs
Cheryl Rubin
Senior VP—Brand Management
Bob Wayne
VP—Sales & Marketing